The Death of Human Capital?

T0323647

The Death of Human Capital?

Its Failed Promise and How to Renew It in an Age of Disruption

PHILLIP BROWN,
HUGH LAUDER, AND
SIN YI CHEUNG

OXFORD
UNIVERSITY PRESS

OXFORD
UNIVERSITY PRESS

Oxford University Press is a department of the University of Oxford. It furthers
the University's objective of excellence in research, scholarship, and education
by publishing worldwide. Oxford is a registered trade mark of Oxford University
Press in the UK and certain other countries.

Published in the United States of America by Oxford University Press
198 Madison Avenue, New York, NY 10016, United States of America.

Library of Congress Cataloging-in-Publication Data
Names: Brown, Phillip, 1957– author. | Lauder, Hugh, 1948– author. |
Cheung, Sin Yi, author.
Title: The death of human capital? | its failed promise and how to renew it in an age of disruption
/ Phillip Brown, Hugh Lauder and Sin Yi Cheung.
Description: New York : Oxford University Press, 2020. |
Includes bibliographical references and index.
Identifiers: LCCN 2019055840 (print) | LCCN 2019055841 (ebook) |
ISBN 9780190644307 (hardback) | ISBN 9780190644314 (paperback) |
ISBN 9780190644321 | ISBN 9780190644338 (epub)
Subjects: LCSH: Human capital. | Labor market. | Competition.
Classification: LCC HD4904.7 .B74 2020 (print) | LCC HD4904.7 (ebook) |
DDC 331—dc23
LC record available at https://lccn.loc.gov/2019055840
LC ebook record available at https://lccn.loc.gov/2019055841

1 3 5 7 9 8 6 4 2

Paperback printed by LSC Communications, United States of America
Hardback printed by Bridgeport National Bindery, Inc., United States of America

Contents

Acknowledgements

WE WOULD LIKE to thank James Cook, from OUP, who has shared a vision of our intellectual aspirations for over ten years. We first talked about this book with him after *The Global Auction* (2011), and he has continued to offer invaluable support. Our thinking has also been informed by friends and colleagues across the globe, including Tien-Hui Chiang, Greg J. Duncan, Brian Easton, Soon Joo Gog, Craig Holmes, Ewart Keep, Antonia Kupfer, Henry (Hank) Levin, Caroline Lloyd, Ken Mayhew, Richard J. Murnane, Chris Martin, Nick Pearce, Robert B. Schwartz, Ivan Snook, Heike Solga, Manuel Souto-Otero, Johnny Sung, and Gerbrand Tholen.

I

Introduction

IN THEODORE W. SCHULTZ's presidential address to the American Economic Association in 1960, he proclaimed that human capital would revolutionize Western capitalism and the fate of developing nations. He told his audience that labor should no longer be treated as a factor of production like land, machines, or factories. Investment in education was the key to improving productivity and economic growth. He also told them that treating humans as capital was not economic slavery but an extension of individual freedom and human possibility. Everyone was to be given the chance to live a prosperous life by getting an education in a world hungry for skilled and talented people rather than through the redistribution of ownership and wealth.[1]

Such views sat comfortably with the idea of the American Dream, whereby individual rewards should reflect differences in ability, skills, and economic contribution. It was an open invitation for all those with ability and desire to succeed—regardless of social background, gender, or race—by investing in their human capital. An invitation that governments around the world have accepted: schools, colleges, and universities have been transformed into the drivers of capital accumulation in a new form of exchange where learning equals earning. It is estimated that close to a third of Americans are involved in education as students, teachers, college professors, or trainers. Globally, trillions of dollars are spent by governments, companies, families, and students in the hope that these investments will deliver economic growth, higher productivity, or a larger paycheck.

But as more people are encouraged to get a bachelor's degree, the competition for credentials and the scramble for decent jobs have intensified.

The Death of Human Capital? Phillip Brown, Hugh Lauder, and Sin Yi Cheung, Oxford University Press (2020).
© Oxford University Press. DOI: 10.1093/oso/9780190644307.001.0001

Many college-educated students have discovered that learning doesn't equal earning. It is estimated that student loan debt in the United States is over $1.3 trillion, exacerbated by a lack of well-paid jobs. Opting out of college is not much of an alternative, as some four-year college students now do the jobs once marked out for high school graduates, pushing those without a college education into precarious (un)employment. The individual costs are not only financial. Rather than education being a source of individual and economic freedom, there is increasing psychological pressure on students, resulting in rising numbers suffering from mental health problems.[2]

Young people in many countries have protested in the streets or on campuses against economic austerity and broken promises as national governments struggle to fund increasing student numbers and provide decent job opportunities. A report on intergenerational trends found that pessimism about the living standards of younger generations is common across high-income countries. In Belgium, France, Spain, South Korea, and the United Kingdom, under 25 percent of those surveyed in 2018 thought that young people will have a better life than their parents; the figure for the United States was 39 percent.[3]

Paradoxically, orthodox human capital theory has become a victim of its own success in getting individuals, families, and governments to believe that investments in education and training remain the route to better jobs, higher incomes, and economic growth. The massive growth in college diplomas and degrees that national governments believed were needed to meet the rising demand for high skills has instead resulted in credential hyperinflation.

The Death of Human Capital?

It may seem surprising to talk about the death of human capital at a time when record numbers of people are in higher education and employers continue to complain about a shortage of skilled workers. This book does not argue that skilled labor is becoming less important or that we are approaching the end of work in a world in which robots will take over. But we are arguing that the orthodox theory of human capital, which has guided public and economic policy, is no longer fit for purpose in the twenty-first century.

Our argument is that a *new* theory of human capital is required to address today's challenges presented by global competition, new technologies, and economic inequalities.[4] To develop an alternative theory, we reexamine the role of human beings and their relationship to capital. We argue that the story of human capital represents a conflict at the very heart of capitalism, where the outcome is yet to be decided. It has the potential to change how people think about education, jobs, and the contributions of others. It has the potential to transform capitalism and confront powerful vested interests, the beneficiaries of orthodox ideas, which justify inequalities in opportunity, power, and wealth. The *new* human capital involves rethinking supply, demand, and return, and in doing so highlights a fundamental change in the relationship between them. This book will describe our new approach and its wider implications, focusing on the lack of good-quality jobs that provide workers with a living wage. At the same time there is talent and work that is unrewarded, some of which lies outside the labor market, so we need to have a much wider understanding of contributions to society than is assumed by orthodox economics.

The *new* human capital is based on the idea of *job scarcity* as distinct from *labor scarcity*. Despite various attempts to update orthodox theory in light of the growing evidence calling into question the efficacy of educational investment to deliver economic growth and higher wages, many economists and policy advisors still believe the fundamental economic problem is labor scarcity.[5] They take this view because orthodox theory assumes that the more skilled a worker becomes, the greater their individual productivity and the more they will be paid.

David Autor, an MIT economist, writes, "The primary system of income distribution in market economies is rooted in labor scarcity; citizens possess (or acquire) a bundle of valuable 'human capital' that, due to its scarcity, generates a flow of income over the career path."[6] This is to envisage an economy in which there is a shortage (or scarcity) of people with higher-level skills. Education can then be thought of as an economic investment, as it enables people to acquire marketable skills to be traded for a higher income given its scarcity value, as people will be paid what they are worth, reflected in differences in individual productivity.

Our alternative theory is premised on job scarcity due to a capacity problem at the heart of market economies. We reject the view that new technologies invariably increase the demand for higher-level skills, or that the supply of more educated workers will energize employers to invest in new ways of exploiting their talents. There are not enough of the jobs that people want, especially at a wage their education and training were supposed to offer.[7] The scarcity of decent jobs has resulted in increasing social congestion, forcing students to compete with those already in the job market. At the same time there is intense competition to enter the best schools, colleges, and universities to win a competitive advantage.

Redefining human capital in the context of job scarcity leads to the study of how people seek to capitalize on their knowledge and skills in fundamentally different economic and social contexts. It rejects the idea of humans as capital because people can't be reduced to what they earn from learning or from the stock of their knowledge. It recognizes differences in how people understand, utilize, and seek to make a life from their knowledge and skills. It also recognizes differences in social and historical contexts, rejecting claims to a universal relationship between learning and earning.

Human societies are the foundations for capital accumulation (and translation) that have never been flattened in the shape of perfect competition or stable preferences. We cannot deduce from first principles the processes by which people capitalize and translate their resources into productive contributions. This requires a contextual understanding of how processes of capitalization and translation are turned into human capital.

This highlights the translation work required of individuals, employers, and nations typically ignored by orthodox theorists. When and how individuals try to translate their education into a productive contribution that extends beyond the confines of the labor market; how employers try to translate employee knowledge and skills into productive contribution; and how nations attempt to translate their investments in a productive workforce, require a new theory of human capital.[8]

We do not underestimate the scale of our task as orthodox human capital theory is so deeply ingrained in our societies and the way people have come to think about education, work, contribution, and income inequalities. There is a major challenge in showing how the economy does not start and finish with what commands a wage or that education is little more than an economic investment.

Given the uncertainties of investing in education, seeing human capital as a private good is flawed and cannot address the acute problems that most students and workers now face. It is predicted that widespread machine intelligence will become a reality, soon enough to have an impact on the lives of many already in the labor market. Equally, as we move into a new era, we need people to have the capabilities to deal with an increasingly complex world, not only in terms of getting a job. Given the rise of authoritarian populism, other aims, such as an education for democracy, should also be considered. From this standpoint, state(s) should invest in education, including higher and vocational education, making it low cost if not free and widely available.

This book offers a different account of labor supply and the role of education in a context of rapid technological advance. Technical skills are already subject to rapid obsolescence, and many of the tasks defining middle-class occupations are being disrupted by digital innovation and automation. People will need to develop the wherewithal to change jobs throughout their careers, to reinvent themselves occupationally and socially by creating a meaningful life no longer structured by full-time, regular employment. Such a view challenges today's high-stakes education system that stifles innovation. We can no longer think of the purpose of education as being limited to what is required to earn a living rather than as a more widely conceived contribution to the quality of individual and social life.

This book also rejects the idea that individuals are rewarded according to their market contribution because today's labor market is characterized by elites, typically educated at the most prestigious colleges and universities, who are able to leverage their individual market power to negotiate incomes that bear little relationship to their actual contribution. In rethinking economic returns we outline an alternative approach to the relationship between efficiency and inequality. Orthodox theorists, including Theodore Schultz and Gary Becker, have spent much time and energy seeking to distinguish between private returns to education and skill from social returns. However, this ignores the simple fact that all labor is a product of the society in which it has been developed. Wage inequalities not only reflect differences in the value of individual skills, knowledge, or credentials but also the structure of labor market opportunities and differences in market power. How individuals and companies capitalize on human labor rests on a social relationship in a permanent power struggle, often involving a conflict of interest between individuals seeking to increase the value of their labors and companies seeking to restrict, if not reduce, labor costs. Who has the upper hand in this relationship at any particular time depends on the balance of market and political power.

This is why we reject Gary Becker's assertion that there is no place for government involvement in industrial policy, along with the idea that market competition will ultimately resolve issues of demand as well as supply. This view has been largely discredited along with the neoliberal opposition of state versus market. Given the lack of good-quality jobs, we argue that there is an important place for industrial policy. Shaping markets to sustain economic growth and improve the quality of life for all may be difficult to achieve, but it is a major part of rebuilding productive, sustainable and inclusive economies, especially following the 2020 global pandemic. Here we need to recognize that national interests must redefine working relationships given that business interests may diverge in important ways. For example, Apple had record profits locked away in international tax havens to avoid paying tax on corporate profits in America. A key argument therefore must address how profits are redistributed.

Our view is that inequalities in income and wealth can be addressed by moving toward an active basic income as a form of social investment. And because paid employment has become highly insecure for many, a basic income will help to mitigate the absence of good-quality jobs.[9] It can be designed to help meet the needs of those who have been excluded from the labor market and those who need to reskill through a process of lifelong learning. And it can facilitate street-level innovation while providing a form of social investment for those who need time to match their skills to the available job opportunities. Many will need the security of a basic income, or some form of what in Scandinavian countries is called "flexicurity," whatever form this may ultimately take.

The criteria by which we judge worth and define contribution need to change from strictly wages earned in the labor market to include the widespread unpaid contributions people make to society. This means that we need to step outside the confines of the labor market as it is theorized by orthodox accounts to acknowledge the productive contribution that goes unrecognized, like domestic labor and caring, as feminist economists have long argued. We also need to consider the forms of social investment that give people the space and time to make considered choices in the productive contributions they can make.

Given today's inequalities and underutilization of human capabilities, the race between education and technology will not be won by training people for high-tech jobs but by reimagining education, work, and the labor market in a fundamentally different economic and social world. Issues of redistribution are unavoidable, leading us to conclude the book with the key message that we are in a race against time to reimagine human capital for the wider benefit of present and future generations.[10]

Structure of the Book

The book is divided into three parts, and although some readers may be more interested in some chapters than in others, it has a logical progression. In part I, we look at the history of orthodox human capital theory, describing the key ideas and assumptions and the social context in which they came to prominence. An account of the intellectual background of the theory is placed within the social and economic context leading to its emergence in the 1950s and 1960s. We show how, in policy terms, orthodox theories fundamentally altered perceptions of the role of education and the skills of the workforce as a source of individual prosperity, social mobility, and economic growth. These theories not only presented investments in education and training as the key driver of national development but also presented a policy response to long-standing problems of gender, ethnic, and racial inequalities. Consequently orthodox theories transformed the way private interests and the public good were represented in public policy.

In their original formulation human capital ideas coexisted with a Keynesian welfare state. It was Gary Becker who stripped away any doubts about the market's ability to deliver national prosperity, social welfare, and individual prosperity, by reframing human capital within an orthodox neoliberal theory. In the hands of Becker human capital was no longer a theory of how investments in individual skills contribute to rising national productivity and economic growth but was transformed into a universal theory of economic behavior. It was now about the essence of humanity (self-interest) and why market competition was an expression of our nature and therefore indispensable in delivering economic growth and an equitable society. Becker therefore offered a naked human capital that has exposed people to the full force of market competition.

Human capital ideas were taken up around the world, with particular interest in how investment in education could be used to reform less-developed nations in the erstwhile third world. We explain why orthodox theory and its progeny, skill-biased technological change (SBTC), have enjoyed continued support due to perceived changes in the market value of human capital closely aligned to the advent of the so-called knowledge economy in the 1980s, fueled by high-tech innovation.

Part II presents a systematic account of the failed promise of orthodox theory. At the turn of the twenty-first century Becker claimed that we had entered an age of human capital, but in reality the new century marked its demise. We draw on statistical evidence to show that the promise of human capital has not lived up to its billing. Our new analysis of rates of return to education in America and Britain over a forty-year period challenges the central claims that learning equals earning and that technological change has led to a rise in the wages of highly skilled workers. We examine the massive inequalities between winners and losers in returns to human capital, by social class, gender, and ethnicity. We also highlight how much of the benefit of productivity gains have been captured by supermanagers and business elites.[11]

As a result, governments are struggling to maintain any semblance of the opportunity bargain whereby the state offers an education to all those who have the motivation to study, assuming that this will lead to good-quality jobs.

We also examine orthodox theory's currency crisis and consider what it tells us about the changing role of credentials within the labor market. We reveal a precipitous decline in the exchange rate of credentials. Here the focus is not limited to wage data but points to high rates of underemployment (and unemployment), even for those who successfully complete a bachelor's degree. The competition for credentials has resulted in greater acquisitive rather than inquisitive learning that will have little impact on individual chances of getting ahead. Similar problems are evident in emerging as well as developed economies. We examine the failed promise of orthodox theory adopted by the World Bank as central to its development strategy. Notwithstanding the rapid economic advances made by some emerging economies, most notably China, the experience of development has left many people within these countries stranded in the rubble of modernization, while others, including those with a tertiary education, struggle to find meaningful employment. Here we describe some of the ways economic development in emerging economies is fueled by rising inequalities in opportunities, employment, and income.

In part III we begin the task of rethinking human capital in the twenty-first century. This includes chapters outlining different views of labor supply, demand, and returns through which we develop our new theory of human capital. We suggest ways to restructure the foundations of education, work, and the labor market to achieve what Amartya Sen describes as the "expansion of human freedom to live the kind of lives that people have reason to value."[12] In conclusion, we examine the prospects for a new human capital in a race against time to build a new opportunity bargain that can unite societies and improve the quality of life for everyone.

PART I

The Rise of Human Capital Theory

2

Origins

Intellectual Roots

Economics describes how people have found new ways of organizing themselves by harnessing land, technology, and labor to move from a perennial struggle for survival to deliver the wealth of nations witnessed today.[1] The changing nature and role of human capital, especially its relationship to individual freedom, capital accumulation, and the wealth of nations, represents a key part of this story.

Before the mid-twentieth century the idea of human capital had a checkered history. Ideas linking the role of human labor to wealth creation can be traced to the works of Aristotle, Ibn Khaldun, and Thomas Aquinas. But Sir William Petty, writing in 1662, is credited as one of first political economists to estimate the monetary value of human beings.[2] Expounding the idea that "Labour is the Father and active principle of Wealth, as Lands are the Mother," he viewed labor as a sacrifice that should be reflected in prices as a just reward for such sacrifice.[3] He also wrote that "half the People by very gentle labour, might much enrich the Kingdom," which led him to formulate the monetary value of laborers and the loss of revenue resulting from wars or plagues.[4]

In a similar vein, in 1853 William Farr proposed a distinction between property "inherent in a man" and "external property" made up of all other property "of which he has possession" to propose a statistical model of individual wealth and taxation: "The income of a lawyer, a doctor, a clergyman, a merchant, or a tradesman, is . . . as much produce as the proceeds of a farm. . . . All the free labourers, artizans, professional men, of the United Kingdom, having within them . . . power of production, are an essential property as the things usually designated by that name. . . . Exclusive of all his external property, every man is worth something."[5]

The Death of Human Capital? Phillip Brown, Hugh Lauder, and Sin Yi Cheung, Oxford University Press (2020).
© Oxford University Press. DOI: 10.1093/oso/9780190644307.001.0001

In *Two Treatises of Government*, John Locke, a major philosopher of the Enlightenment of the late seventeenth and early eighteenth century, expounded a similar view in recognizing that the ability to rise out of a state of nature depends on human industry: "I think it will be but a very modest computation to say, that of the products of the earth useful to the life of man, nine-tenths are the effects of labour."[6] In making the connection between nature and human labor, Locke proposed that what people put in they should get out. Private property resulting from our own efforts is a natural condition of a just society: "Man (by being master of himself, and proprietor of his own person, and the actions or labour of it) had still in himself the great foundation of property; and that which made up the great part of what he applied to the support or comfort of his being, when invention and arts had improved the conveniences of life, was perfectly his own, and did not belong in common to others."[7]

Such ideas on private property became increasing influential as they contributed to what Max Weber later called "the disenchantment of the world," with the breakdown of feudal ties and relations leading to the rise of market capitalism and the "right to create private property by the sweat of one's own brow."[8] If the idea of individual property rights and the rights of individuals to own their "means of production" in the form of labor was to become a founding principle of orthodox human capital theory, it was also understood that improvements in the conveniences of life would come to depend on advances in the division of labor.

Adam Smith: Humans as Expensive Machines

Adam Smith, widely recognized as an influential figure in the development of human capital theory, thought that what matters is not only the quantity of land or labor utilized in production but whether the workforce is organized along the lines of an efficient division of labor. Here he was prescient in his understanding that through the specialization of tasks, productivity could be increased. To make this point he used the example of a pin factory in which "one man draws out the wire, another straightens it, a third cuts it, a fourth points it, a fifth grinds it at the top for receiving the head. . . . In this manner [the process is] divided into about eighteen distinct operations."[9] Smith recognized that the division of labor required people in different occupations, some of which demanded extended periods of training. Therefore the wages attached to different categories of labor reflected the ease or difficulty, along with associated costs of "learning the business." Skilled workers requiring a significant investment in education could, Smith argued, be compared to "expensive machines": "A man educated at the expence of much labour and time to any of those employments which require extraordinary dexterity and skill, may be compared to one of those expensive machines."[10]

Within economics, Smith is widely acknowledged for extending Locke's idea of labor as private property by including an explanation of economic behavior based on the rational pursuit of self-interest. Edwin Cannan, who edited Smith's magnum opus, *The Wealth of Nations*, called Smith the economist's Shakespeare in providing pithy quotations. Perhaps the most popular describes the core assumption of *Homo economicus*: "Man has almost constant occasion for the help of his brethren, and it is vain for him to expect it from their benevolence only. He will be more likely to prevail if he can interest their self-love in his favour, and show them that it is for their own advantage to do for him what he requires of them. . . . It is not from the benevolence of the butcher, the brewer, or the baker, that we can expect our dinner, but from their regard to their own interest."[11]

The fact that neoclassical economists focused only on "self-interest" rather than "benevolence" will be explored in the final section of the book, but Smith also had something interesting to say about the impact of the division of labor on education and rational action. While there was an increasing need for managers and professionals to organize the production system, the vast majority of the workforce were stuck in mundane and mind-numbingly boring jobs "confined to a few simple operations." For most, the role of education served to compensate for the realities of employment rather than being a preparation for it: "The understandings of the great part of men are necessarily formed by their ordinary employments. The man whose life is spent in performing a few simple operations . . . has no occasion to exert his understanding, or to exercise his invention. . . . He naturally loses, therefore, the habit of such exertion, and generally becomes as stupid and ignorant as it is possible for a human creature to become."[12] Without the compensation of education most of the workforce were not capable of rational behavior, not because of the laws of nature but due to the realities of the division of labor.[13]

Alfred Marshall's Personal Capital

Treating humans as capital was challenged in some quarters because it robbed people of their common humanity, especially given political sensitivities around the abolition of slavery in Europe and North America. These debates centered on a crucial distinction between the liberty of free men and women as opposed to the lack of liberty of a slave.[14] It is worth reflecting on the fact that the slave trade—as the most obvious form of treating labor as the property of others—did not end without huge sums being paid to slave owners. Historical records show that in the United Kingdom an astonishing forty-six thousand slave owners were paid compensation. These included a Mr. John Austin who owned 415 slaves, for which he received compensation of £20,511, a sum worth nearly £17 million today.[15]

In 1848, around the time of abolition, J. S. Mill argued, "The human being himself . . . I do not class as wealth. He is the purpose for which wealth exists." It is humans' acquired capacities, when utilized in labor, that Mill regarded as wealth.[16] But despite the tripling of national wealth between 1845 and 1865, there was little recognition beyond a rudimentary division of labor that investing in human skills could be a source of productivity. Mill was closely associated with the "wage fund theory" that assumed the "fund" or "capital" available to pay wages was fixed, so that any increase in population would result in lower wages for the masses. This chimes with Ricardo's "law of diminishing returns" and Malthus's "iron law of wages," that wages can never rise beyond subsistence level because if the welfare of the poor is increased above subsistence, they will have more sex and increase the population faster than the rate of growth.[17] Even Smith envisaged a situation in which a nation might enter a "stationary" state when it is "fully stocked" with physical capital and "fully peopled." Of such a nation he had this to say: "Both the wages of labour and the profits of stock (capital) would probably be very low. In a country fully peopled in proportion to what either its territory could maintain or its stock employ, the competition for employment would necessarily be so great as to reduce the wages of labour to what was barely sufficient to keep up the number of labourers."[18]

Indeed the economic depression of 1866–67 served as a wake-up call to liberal elites as it was not only Marx's lumpenproletariat or underclass who were thrown upon the mercy of the workhouse but the working poor. The Liberal reformer Henry Fawcett, a professor of political economy at Cambridge University, wrote, "Visit the greatest centres of commerce and trade, and what will be observed? The direst poverty always accompanying the greatest wealth."[19] While this led some to call for the overthrow of capitalism, liberal-minded reformers—having absorbed the lessons of Darwin's *On the Origins of Species* (1859), popularized by Herbert Spencer (1862) as "survival of the fittest"—turned to become "missionaries in their own land." The salvation of the poor depended on converting them to middle-class values and habits.[20]

Alfred Marshall, widely regarded as the founder of modern economics, was also interested in what he saw as a central paradox of "poverty amid plenty." Why, he asked, has the Industrial Revolution not freed the working class "from misery and vice"? While acknowledging that the chief cause of poverty was low wages, unlike his illustrious predecessors he did not believe that poverty conformed to the laws of nature or that the only solution was a Marxist revolution. His visits to factories and offices in both Britain and America convinced him that the problem was low productivity. Therefore "the chief remedy . . . for low wages is better education."[21] He observed that employers were willing to pay higher wages for specialized skills linked to productive contribution. This observation held out the prospect of using new technologies, changing work practices, and a more highly skilled workforce to transform all men, including the working classes, into "Gentleman." "The aim of social endeavor must be to increase the number of those who are capable of the more difficult work of the world, and to diminish the number of those who can do only unintelligent work, or who perhaps cannot do even that."[22]

Marshall outlined all the ingredients of a nascent theory of human capital. He accepted Smith's argument that educated people could be compared to an expensive machine; he recognized skills upgrading as a way of improving job quality and industrial wages; he described how professional families were constantly alert to opportunities to invest capital in their children to secure the best occupations; he was also aware that the lower classes had fewer resources and were less inclined to make investments in their children. He even defined what he called "personal capital": "We have already defined Personal wealth to consist firstly of those energies, faculties and habits which directly contribute to making people industrially efficient. . . . If they are to be reckoned as wealth at all, they are also to be reckoned as capital. Thus Personal wealth and Personal capital are convertible; and it seems best to follow here the same course as in the case of wealth . . . to raise no objection to an occasional broad use of the term [capital], in which it is explicitly stated to include Personal capital."[23]

But rather than be crowned the true founder of human capital theory, Marshall deleted this paragraph from his classic work, *Principles of Economics,* and rejected the definition of human capital as "unrealistic."[24] Given his standing in economics at the time, Marshall was later identified as the person who killed off interest in ideas relating to human capital until well into the twentieth century. But this would be a misreading of Marshall's ideas, as he continued to address the workings of business to improve living standards for both workers and consumers through rising productivity. Richard Blandy notes that his rejection of human capital "was definitional, not conceptual," and in Mark Blaug's assessment, Marshall rejected only the "idea of including the acquired skills of a population in the measurement of the 'wealth' and 'capital' of an economy."[25] But a fully fledged theory of human capital did not emerge until seventy years after the publication of Marshall's *Principles of Economics* (1890).

Theodore Schultz: Investment in Human Capital

We started this book with reference to Schultz's presidential address to the American Economic Association in St. Louis in December 1960. It was entitled "Investment in Human Capital." As he rose to give the address, he would have found it hard to imagine the impact his speech would have. It is not often that abstract economic concepts get widely discussed, let alone come to redefine the role of education and economic policy around the world. Schultz opened with this statement: "Although it is obvious that people acquire useful skills and knowledge, it is not obvious that these skills and knowledge are a form of capital, that this capital is in substantial part a product of deliberate investment, that it has grown in Western societies at a much faster rate than conventional (nonhuman) capital, and that its growth may well be the most distinctive feature of the economic system."[26] He argued that economists should put the past behind them as it was no longer morally suspect to treat humans as capital, slavery had been abolished, and the rise of industrial capitalism was transforming the economic role of labor. He also rejected the "lump of coal" view of a homogeneous workforce.[27] Labor could no longer be treated as a factor of production, like land or investment capital, as differences in the quality of skills, along with the acquisition of technical knowledge, were becoming key to productivity and economic growth. Treating humans as capital was not to treat people as economic slaves but to highlight an extension of human freedom and social possibilities. Mass society was now invited into the world of the capitalist, to stand shoulder to shoulder in pursuit of their private interests, in a new industrial order in which Marx never existed: "Laborers have become capitalists not from a diffusion of the ownership of corporation stocks . . . but from the acquisition of knowledge and skill that have economic value. This knowledge and skill are in great part the product of investment and, combined with other human investment, predominantly account for the productive superiority of the technically advanced countries."[28]

In setting out this view, he pulled off a masterstroke that appeared to resolve a problem that had long vexed the great classical political economists. This was the problem of the conflict that they saw as endemic within capitalism. In their different ways, Karl Marx, Adam Smith, and David Riccardo all pointed to conflict over the distribution of profits between land and factory owners as opposed to the laboring classes, a conflict later defined by John Maynard Keynes as the key question of human society: how to reconcile efficiency, justice, and liberty. By sleight of hand this perennial class war found a peaceful solution. Echoing Marshall, Schultz claimed the answer was by enhancing the skills of the workforce, to increase the wealth of nations, so that a large share of the benefits of economic growth would go to the workforce in recognition of their contribution to productivity gains.

Schultz took it for granted that individual skills, efforts, and labor were private property in which people invest, as capitalists invested in factories and "expensive machines." This led Blaug to subsequently define human capital as "the present value of past investments in the skills of people, not the value of people themselves," as under slavery.[29]

Distributional issues were to be addressed through wage distribution and through transforming the social distribution of educational opportunity. Ideas about "who should be educated" based on class, race, or gender were not only outdated and unjust but under an investment model of educational development they were defined as economically inefficient.[30] So capitalism could be seen as a system in which everyone gained so long as they were prepared to invest in themselves.

Education as Investment

Schultz treated education as investment capital, dedicated to increasing wages and economic growth, rather than "education for its own sake" or "education as a pure luxury."[31] But he saw that not all education expenditure can be classed as pure investment or pure consumption, as it included elements of both, such as when someone signs up for a bachelor's degree in history because they really like the subject at the same time as wanting to improve their job prospects. Schultz concedes that the most relevant activities are partly consumption and partly investment, "which is why the task of identifying each component is so formidable and why the measurement of capital formation by expenditure is less useful for human investment than for investment in physical goods."[32]

Schultz's seemingly straightforward answer to this problem was to look for an alternative measure. In doing so he contributed, along with Becker, Jacob Mincer, and others, to making a decisive break with classical economics. Human capital theory followed the orthodox turn in economics, rejecting the established focus on the act, art, and value of labor within production: "In principle there is an alternative method for estimating human investment, namely by its yield rather than by its cost. While any capability produced by human investment becomes a part of the human agent and hence cannot be sold; it is nevertheless 'in touch with the market place' by affecting the wages and salaries the human agent can earn. The resulting increase in earnings is the yield on the investment."[33] Rather than attempt to measure investment in education or the value of what workers produce by using higher levels of skill, Schultz's focus was on the *yield* or *rate of return* from investments in education.[34] The focus on yield is perhaps unsurprising given that he was part of the Chicago school of economics that expounded orthodox approaches to economics.[35] The yield (rate of return) is used in the same way as orthodox economists use *prices* at the heart of their theory. Wages are taken as a proxy for investments in human capital, given that they are viewed as an expression of how employers value the contribution of individual employees, in the same way that individuals are believed to be driven by the price mechanism when attaching value to different goods and services.

Schultz also distinguished private rates of return for individuals from public rates of return for national governments, where the yield can be measured by economic growth rates. Equally, if governments can be encouraged to view tax dollars as investment rather than consumption, there is the prospect of increasing public support for educational expansion as a key investment for economic growth. Such investment was no different from investing in transportation infrastructure or new technologies, based on Schultz's assumption that human beings could be studied as part of an extended definition of technology as "an all-inclusive concept . . . including the innate abilities of man."[36] This is not without its dangers: first, anything that can't be justified on economic grounds looks like consumption and is of little value; second, if the economy takes a downturn, education is in the front line for reform because its rationale is to deliver economic growth; third, if individuals can be seen as the major beneficiaries of educational investments then there is some justification for a "use pays" model of funding.

Therefore, in taking the orthodox approach now associated with neoliberal political economy, Schultz and others were making a value judgment. For them what really matters in thinking about education and its relationship to the economy are those aspects of individual experience that are in touch with the marketplace and which can be captured by measurements of yield (rate of return). Here the value of education and an individual's contribution to society can be measured by the size of their paycheck. As Andrew Gamble observes in intellectual terms, the consequences of taking an orthodox approach as opposed to the approach of classical political economy (with its focus on a labor theory of value) was "to shift economics decisively from a multi-disciplinary study concerned with economic systems or, as Adam Smith put it, with the nature and causes of the wealth of nations, to a more specialized discipline dealing with a particular aspect of human behavior. Here we see one of the fundamental tensions in economics between understanding economic behavior as relative to particular historical contexts and understanding it as a universal attribute of human action found in all societies in all historical periods."[37]

While Shultz was prominent in developing the orthodox view of human capital, he was also concerned with historical and economic context. He was interested in the dynamics of change, which is most clearly expressed in his paper on disequilibrium in markets.[38] He noted, in a study of the economic histories of the agricultural regions of California, Brazil, and Canada, that how farmers adapted to change depended on their education. He also found that women's education was important in their choice of partner, birth rates, and ability to adapt to change. In his historical and comparative approach he attempted to bridge classical political economy and orthodox economics. But in Becker we see orthodox economics being crystallized in his focus on economic behavior, which he considered universal.

Gary Becker's Universal Appeal

It is Gary S. Becker rather than Theodore W. Schultz who is recognized by many economists as the dominant figure in the development of orthodox human capital theory. Both were professors at the University of Chicago, and both were awarded the Nobel Prize for Economics, but it is Becker's "economic approach," founded on what were believed to be universal laws of economic behavior and market competition, that ultimately captured the aspirations of a profession and put education at the heart of national economic policy. Becker brushed aside the conceptual and practical difficulties that accompanied Schultz's description of human capital, envisaging a new orthodox economics based on a science of human behavior, abstracted from the real world but in which its general principles would have application to all societies.[39]

Becker defined human capital as a product of market investment, whereby individuals make rational investment decisions about how much education or training to buy, or for governments, how much they should invest in human capital to stimulate economic growth.

He therefore defines human capital in much the same way as Schultz and Mincer, as "a person accumulating capital."[40] He also wrote that "persons investing in human capital can be considered 'firms' that combine such capital perhaps with other resources to produce earning power."[41] Becker also recognized that human capital was different from other kinds of capital due to diminishing laws of return, as people can absorb only so much knowledge and memorize only so many facts: "Since the memory capacity, physical size, etc. of each investor is limited, eventually diminishing returns set in from producing additional capital."[42] Again, this view is consistent with Smith's view of humans as "expensive machines" that require initial investment but will ultimately wear out.

On reflecting on the human capital revolution in the 1950s and 1960s Becker describes not only a universal theory of economic behavior but an almost exclusive focus on supply-side economics and the key role of human capital investment: "I began to realize that the human capital approach provides an entirely new way of looking at labor markets. Instead of assuming that differences in earnings mainly reflected whether workers held 'good' or 'bad' jobs, the human capital approach assumed that earnings mainly measure how much workers had invested in their skills and knowledge. According to this view, earnings would rise with the amount of investment in education and training. On this interpretation, good jobs are mainly jobs held by workers who have invested a lot in their human capital."[43] This approach further distanced the development of human capital theory from the classical political economy focus on what people do for a living rather than simply what they earn from doing it (the labor theory of value). With "years of education" (i.e., high school or college education) being a measure of labor supply, and "wages" being a measure of demand, Becker proposed a universal theory within which the social world is flattened into a common currency. Each unit of education or training, such as years of education, is treated as equivalent, rather like in a money economy where a dollar is a dollar is a dollar, regardless of how it is acquired or utilized. Becker's reliance on an orthodox theory of competitive markets—closely associated with Milton Friedman, Friedrich von Hayek, and others at the University of Chicago—meant that no distinction is made between good money and bad money, good human capital and bad human capital; there is only more or less of it depending on how much is invested. The more you have, the higher your income is likely to be, given an increase in an individual's market value.[44] Equally, the more governments invest in workforce education and training, the more productive and prosperous the population due to employers seeking to exploit new knowledge and skills to improve productivity or launch higher-value products or services.

What Becker called the "economic approach" is based on three pillars: utility-maximizing behavior, stable preferences, and market equilibrium.[45] Utility-maximizing behavior derives from a model of *Homo economicus* that views humans as solitary seekers of material happiness and bodily security—maximizing pleasure and minimizing pain—or what one economist called "calculating pleasure machines."[46] It assumes a view of human nature that is consistent with the much-quoted passage from Smith reproduced earlier, which claims that individuals are fundamentally self-interested and make rational choices to achieve their ends. Central to rational choice is the idea of utility maximization, in which consumers have stable preferences about their wants. The choices are rational because people make opportunity-cost assessments of means and ends in their own interest. For Becker, "self-interest is assumed to dominate all other motives."[47] In other words, people are hardwired to make rational choices that maximize their utility.[48] Becker's *praxeology* (science of rational action) is applied not only to education and wage distribution but also to criminal behavior, racial discrimination, and marriage. He suggests that women and men decide to marry, have children, or divorce based on an attempt to maximize their utility by comparing costs and benefits.[49]

Stable preferences rest on the idea that what people desire does not change substantially over time or change in different social or cultural settings. In a disarmingly candid statement, Becker observes "Economists generally have had little to contribute, especially in recent times, to the understanding of how preferences are formed, preferences are assumed not to change substantially over time, nor to be very different between wealthy and poor persons, or even between persons in different societies and cultures."[50]

He distinguishes between individual preferences for everyday market goods and services, such as a preference for oranges over other fruits or for a particular make of automobile, from those "fundamental aspects of life, such as health, prestige, sensual pleasure, benevolence or envy."[51] He asserts that these stable preferences are "present and equally potent in all human beings. What differs are the ways they choose to fulfill those desires."[52] This view of individual preferences is an integral part of his economic approach because it provides "a stable foundation for generating prediction" and prevents the analyst from succumbing to the temptation of simply using differences in individual preferences to explain findings that do not match the analyst's predictions.[53] If this were the case, there would be a need for detailed contextual studies into the nature of individual preferences or social identities that do not fit with the statistical application of Becker's general theory.

The third pillar describes how human preferences based on self-interest are coordinated through competitive "free" markets, along with the related idea of "market equilibrium." In Becker's own words, "The economic approach assumes the existence of markets that with varying degrees of efficiency coordinate the actions of different participants—individuals, firms, even nations—so that their behavior becomes mutually consistent. . . . Prices and other market instruments allocate the scarce resources within a society and thereby constrain the desires of participants and coordinate their actions. In the economic approach these instruments perform most, if not all, of the functions assigned to 'structure' in sociological theories."[54]

Here the market is seen as a way of allocating scarce resources without the conflict, strife, or inefficiencies assumed in Marxist analysis of market capitalism. Prices replace pistols as the way of regulating desire, as all surrender to market forces and obey the law of utility maximization, and in doing so ensure that "everyone receives mutual and just recompense for their efforts and investments."[55]

In this orthodox economic world, the laws by which resources could be rationally allocated were built on a particular account of human nature and its relationship to the market. But to achieve a universal theory of human capital linked to the real world through statistical measures of rates of return, Becker ignored the caveats that characterized Schultz's initial account of human capital development to present a simplified model based on a number of *as if*'s: human beings are treated as if they are capital; education is treated as if it is an investment; consumption is treated as if it is psychic income (to fit his theory of utility maximization); wages are treated as if they are a measure of individual productive contribution; years of education are treated as if they are a common measure of skill; the labor market is treated as if it doesn't matter as supply creates its own demand; income inequalities are treated as if they are both efficient and fair; conflict is treated as if it has been resolved through market competition; and economic growth is treated as if it's a matter of educational investment and reform.

It would seem therefore that Becker was following Milton Friedman's lead in suggesting that *as if* statements should be seen as an aid to prediction. As Friedman noted, "The question whether a theory is realistic 'enough' can be settled only by seeing whether it yields predictions that are good enough for the purpose in hand or that are better than predictions from alternative theories."[56] At times Becker seemed to think that these assumptions were convenient fictions in the aid of prediction, as in the case of stable preferences, at others that they reflected reality, as in his view that humans were hardwired to maximize their utility. By the time he had written *The Economic Approach to Human Behavior*, it appeared that he was taking these founding assumptions as reflecting key dimensions of reality.

What is also clear is that, as the French philosopher Michel Foucault noted in a lecture on human capital theory, the *what if* assumptions were also seen by policymakers as reflecting reality as the assumptions became hardwired into the policy processes of neoliberalism, as we will go onto explain.[57] As Becker later reflected, "Human capital is so uncontroversial nowadays that it may be difficult to appreciate the hostility in the 1950s and 1960s towards the approach that went with the term. . . . Only gradually did economists, let alone others, accept the concept of human capital as a valuable tool in the analysis of various economic and social issues."[58]

The Early Development of a Research Program

The early research program is not simply of historical interest, part of the genealogy of human capital ideas; it is important because it came to shape the research and policy parameters that will be reevaluated in this book. A significant feature of the research program was to normalize the idea of human capital investment being analyzed, measured, and understood as a key factor of production, if not the most important driver of individual prosperity and economic growth. Here we briefly highlight four aspects of the program: first, that human capital investment could be analyzed and understood in the same way that investments in physical capital, such as factory equipment, land usage, etc., are measured. The result has been endless attempts to test and refine statistical measures of rates of return, from which the policy equation "learning equals earning" is derived. A second aspect is the key differences between investments in what Becker called "general" and "specific" skills, which provide the backdrop to more recent discussions about who gains from education and who should pay, and the shifting needs of employers for people who are job ready rather than simply certified as trainable. Today this discussion centers on various combinations of hard and soft skills (or what are defined as noncognitive skills). A third aspect is human capital explanations for enduring wage inequalities based on differences in productive contribution. This poses a research question of significant interest to both Becker and Schultz of how to account for income inequalities based on gender and race, even with the same level of human capital investment. The fourth and final aspect of the program is the role of orthodox theory for the study of development economics.

Rates of Return

Just as economists study inputs and outputs to measure the productivity of land, factories, or machines, in the early research program they applied the same approach to the study of human capital investment. Inputs could be measured by GDP per capita spent on education or years of schooling, and outputs (or returns on investment) could be measured by wages. Along with other orthodox theorists, Becker focused much of his attention on developing statistical models to predict private and public rates of return. Where private rates of return depended on statistical proxies for learning such as years of education or level of certification, and earnings based on wages, public rates of return were measured by comparing overall expenditure on education and training against indicators of national economic growth.

Widely recognized problems with using years of schooling as a measure of human capital investment, given its failure to account for the quality of educational experience, include what students actually learned in school, college, or university. This led to attempts to incorporate other measures, such as the role of job-related experience, on lifetime earnings. Mincer pointed to research evidence showing that it was not only the starting incomes of those who had gained skills in schools or colleges that were important, but that we need to take account of the impact of work experience on wages over time. Mincer was able to show that employee salaries would continue to rise because performance on the job is a function of formal training plus experience. He started his doctoral thesis at the University of Chicago but moved to Columbia University in New York for personal reasons. However, he maintained contact with Schultz and returned to Chicago for a postdoctoral fellowship at Schultz's invitation.[59] This coincided with the publication of Mincer's classic article "Investment in Human Capital and Personal Income Distribution" (1958). In extending the concept of investment in human capital to include experience on the job, he attempted to model "life paths of income," showing that in many occupations, earnings rise with skill and experience. The life cycle of earnings is revealed to be an inverted U-shaped pattern as wages start declining when workers hit their fifties, reflecting what Mincer sees through youthful eyes as a deterioration in productive performance.[60] His findings were replicated many times and entered into what has become the pantheon of human capital truisms, which will be examined in a later chapter.

Who Should Pay for Education and Training? Generic and Specific Skills

Mincer's focus on investments in on-the-job training and productivity linked to years of experience rather than years of education highlights a related area of human capital research based on the distinction between general and specific skills.[61] This might seem like an arcane distinction to nonspecialists, but it relates to two overlapping debates that have set the policy framework for the funding of education. The first and most general of these concerns the question of what is a public and what is a private good. The standard, orthodox economist's way of answering this question is to ask: Who gains from education? If it is the society, then education is seen as a public good; if it is the individual, then it is a private good. Whoever benefits should pay, and if there is a shared benefit, then some formula must be devised to apportion costs.

Secondly Becker asked the more specific question: Who gains from training? In order to answer this deceptively simple question, he starts with the assumption of a competitive labor market in which there is perfect knowledge between firms and individuals. He distinguishes general from specific skills, defining general skills as those that all employers will find useful and that benefit workers because they can sell these general skills to a range of employers. In today's terms, general skills contribute to an individual's overall employability. But these skills allow workers to be poached or to move at will, and if employers invest in workers' general skills they may well lose their investment. In contrast, specific skills are those from which only a particular employer can benefit, so that it is worth the employer's investing in these specific skills.

Becker went on to argue that there would be no market failure in the funding of both general and specific training skills because workers would borrow funds for general skills training since they would gain from their improved productivity and rewards. If the employer invested in firm-specific skills, then this investment strategy would be optimal for both parties.[62] From this analysis it is easy to see how it is possible to justify charging students for four-year college degrees: because they constitute general skills. In developing this analysis, it is also worth remembering that Friedman—a major influence on Becker at Chicago and who became a trusted advisor in the Reagan and Thatcher years—believed that a person's human capital is nontransferable, and since they gain from the capital they acquire, they should pay for it.[63]

That said, the distinction between general and specific training that appeared relatively clear in the 1960s is not clear now. What we've seen more recently are employers demanding that more of the specific training along with general training be transferred to the education system because they want to hire people who are job ready rather than simply trainable.

Wages and Productivity: Explaining Gender and Racial Income Inequalities

Since the 1950s, human capital theory has been widely cited as an explanation of inequalities in earnings. Most of this research has pointed to differences in schooling and training as inequalities are primarily explained by differences in human capital investment. Mincer, echoing Smith, sees labor as subdivided by occupations that have different skill and training requirements. Therefore "the level of earnings in the hierarchy of occupations [is] due to differences in training required by them."[64] In a similar vein, Becker argues that the growth in earnings inequalities in the United States during the 1980s was "largely explained by higher returns to the more educated and better trained."[65]

Therefore the link between education, productivity, and earnings is central to the orthodox account (see Figure 2.1), as individual marginal productivity is used to explain differences in earnings, which reflect differences in individual economic contribution resulting from differences in human capital investment. It could reasonably be assumed that orthodox theorists have some means of showing, through their empirical research, whether wages are determined by a person's productivity. The answer given by Melvin Reder, who offers an insider's account of the Chicago school, was that "in applications of human capital theory, one does not usually measure the marginal productivity of labor directly but assumes it to be equal to the relevant wage rate."[66]

Here is a major *as if* assumption at the very heart of orthodox theory, which has also been used to explain differences in earnings. From this perspective, workers with the same skills should earn the same wages because they will be equally productive. But data on earnings inequality have consistently shown that women with the same education level as men earn less than men. Becker acknowledged this trend and considered it "an embarrassment to the human capital interpretation of sexual earnings."[67]

His response rested on the assumption that women with the same educational qualifications as men could receive a lower wage than men only if they were less productive. He then looked for why women might be less productive and came up with the conclusion that women were less productive in paid work than men because they had multiple roles to fulfill outside of work, whereas men did not. But even at the time when Becker was developing his approach there was a resurgent feminism that he and his colleagues chose to ignore, showing how powerful these *as if* assumptions are because they close the world to alternative interpretations. For Becker and other orthodox theorists, the explanation for these inequalities had to be found in the individual, not in social institutions or economic structures of inequality.

Just as Becker accepted the controversial notion of IQ as an indicator of intelligence, he also asserted that "the approach of sociobiologists is highly congenial to economists since they rely on competition, the allocation of limited resources . . . efficient adaption to the environment and other concepts also used by economists."[68] In sociobiology Becker found an additional explanation for why women had multiple domestic roles while men did not.[69] This sociobiological account is so deep-rooted that when David Deming found that women gain a premium for their social interaction skills when compared to men, he explained the difference in the skills of men and women

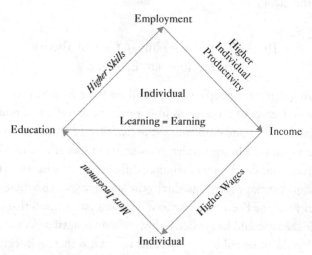

FIGURE 2.1 The orthodox model of human capital investment.

as follows: "Sex differences in sociability and social perceptiveness have been shown to have biological origins, with differences appearing in infancy and higher levels of fetal testosterone associated with lower scores on tests of social intelligence."[70] Not only does this make the role of education problematic, but it infers that progressive change, which is not predetermined, is difficult, if not impossible, to achieve.[71]

Germane to this discussion is the fact that Becker wrote his doctoral thesis on racial discrimination, which subsequently attracted attention and notoriety of the kind that followed his analysis of gender inequalities. He refers to racial discrimination as "taste" in which employers and workers, for whatever reason, have the "taste" of being prejudiced. Here it is the individual who has a preference for racism, with no explanation given for it.[72] He described the approach in his Nobel Prize–winning speech: "Instead of making the common assumptions that employers only consider the productivity of employees, that workers ignore the characteristics of those with whom they work, and that customers only care about the quality of the goods and services provided, discrimination coefficients incorporate the influence of race, gender, and other personal characteristics on tastes and attitudes."[73] This passage tells us much about Becker's orthodox approach because although he recognizes that employers, employees, and customers may all have a role in discrimination, wider cultural, political, and institutional structures of direct and indirect discrimination cannot be incorporated into his theory because he is unable to see beyond the horizons of "methodological individualism."[74] This analytic approach to gender and race raises fundamental questions about some of the limits of the theory.

The Application of Human Capital Theory to Development Economics

In observing that most people in the world are poor, Schultz concludes that "the decisive factors of production in improving the welfare of poor people are not space, energy and cropland; the decisive factor is the improvement in population quality." He argued that economists mistakenly believed that the study of economic development required different approaches from those applied in more developed settings. But by the late 1970s, when Schultz received his Nobel Prize for Economics, he found greater recognition that orthodox economic theory could be applied to low-income countries: "A fundamental proposition documented by much recent research is that an integral part of the modernization of the economies of low income countries is *the decline in the economic importance of farmland and a rise in that of human capital—skills and knowledge."*[75]

Schultz suggested that education accounts for much of the improvement in population quality and that the cost of schooling must be seen as an investment by families as well as governments. Even for very young children, parents have to forgo or sacrifice the value of the work that they would otherwise perform if not in school. Likewise longer lifespans resulting from improvements in health care "provide additional incentives to acquire more education, as investments in future earnings."[76]

Schultz's reflections on the potential of the theory to contribute to development economics were farsighted; for example, the theory became the foundation for much of the World Bank's development education policy throughout the 1980s to the present day. Although initially the World Bank took little interest in education because it was not seen as important to economic development, gradually an interest emerged in relation to technical and vocational education and then in relation to primary education.[77] In 1981 the World Bank appointed George Psacharopoulos head of the Education Department's Research Unit, leading to a number of highly influential studies on education investment in developing countries. As a result orthodox theory took center stage in the Bank's global development strategy, to which we will return.

For present purposes, the application of orthodox human capital theory to developing economies served to add to the credibility of Becker's claim to a universal theory of economic behavior. An analysis of institutions would confound the orthodox aim of producing universal laws by making economic claims specific to particular contexts, but in the comparative study of education and rates of return, there was little need to take account of differences in national cultures, histories, or institutional arrangements. Indeed any apparent failure of the economy to respond to human capital investment was interpreted as evidence of governmental failure to apply the proper economic approach.

Conclusion

It will be evident from the core *what if* assumptions developed by Shultz, Mincer, and most prominently Becker, that they were able to extend their analysis to a wide range of issues concerning the relationship between education and the labor market. In turn, they were able to influence policy in such powerful ways that their legacy remains. Above all, their influence shaped the way education is viewed in many countries: as an investment in the economic fortunes of the individual and the nation. It took some time for this dominant view to emerge, but it was triumphantly sealed by the advent of neoliberalism in the 1980s. It is to this episode in the history of the theory that we now turn.

3

The High Tide

MANY THEORIES ABOUT the social and economic world have a short life cycle. Things change unexpectedly, such as the Wall Street Crash, the collapse of the Soviet Union, Great Recession or more recently a global pandemic. Following such events new perspectives often grab the attention of pundits and scholars, consigning previously held theories to intellectual obscurity. The question is why that has not happened to orthodox human capital theory. To understand its enduring appeal, and why we believe it to be mortally flawed, this chapter looks at the reasons why, in the life cycle of theories, it reached its high tide before the global financial crisis in 2007 but continues to enjoy widespread policy appeal.

Two closely related themes or narratives in the 1980s gave some credence to Becker's claim that we had entered an "age of human capital," at least in terms of education and economic policy, if not economic reality.[1] First, this chapter will describe the political ascendency of neoliberalism, which shares common ground with Becker's economic approach. Paradoxically, the initial appeal of human capital theory in the 1960s had little to do with Becker's theory of economic behavior; rather it was the reinterpretation of education as investment, offering a key to economic development and individual opportunity, that brought the theory to prominence. The wider policy and political context in which Schultz gave his presidential address on human capital development was characterized by "economic nationalism," not free-market capitalism.[2]

Second, what made neoliberalism a viable, if inherently flawed approach to public policy was the idea of a fundamental transformation in economic organization, wherein human capital is viewed as the most important driver of economic development. This chapter will consider how these themes were taken up and developed into an international framework of human capital

The Death of Human Capital? Phillip Brown, Hugh Lauder, and Sin Yi Cheung, Oxford University Press (2020).
© Oxford University Press. DOI: 10.1093/oso/9780190644307.001.0001

development, perpetuating the view that education and the skills upgrading of the workforce remain the key to individual prosperity, improved productivity, and economic growth.

From Economic Nationalism to Neoliberalism

When human capital theory came to prominence in the early 1960s, it was in a political and economic context defined by the experiences of the Great Depression of the 1930s and the ashes of World War II. At that time Western nations were committed to achieving social progress for workers and their families. This was widely believed to require the resolution of two fundamental tensions endemic to capitalism: its tendency to distribute rewards unfairly and its chronic instability, which required government intervention as the market mechanism could not be the "sole director of the fate of human beings."[3]

The appeal of human capital during this period of economic nationalism was linked to the view of education as an investment contributing to economic efficiency, national growth, and individual opportunity. But unlike Becker's economic approach, human capital theory was part of a secular trinity of prosperity, security, and opportunity, where prosperity was to be achieved through the state regulation of trade, currencies, and markets (including labor markets). Fordist systems of mass production also created a mass market for consumer goods, bought by workers who were paid enough to buy them. Security was achieved by a commitment to full employment and through social security and healthcare provision for those who could not engage in paid employment. At the same time opportunity was to be delivered through new investment and reform of education, as the ranks of white-collar workers increased, so education was seen as both an avenue for upward social mobility and a way of increasing productivity and individual prosperity. Equally, in most countries higher education was state funded; going to college was free, although limited to a relatively small proportion of the age cohort.[4]

Here it is worth reiterating that a key reason for the success of economic nationalism at the time was that the state acted as the broker between capital and labor, providing the checks and balances required to deliver shared prosperity and social cohesion. Output in the advanced capitalist countries was 180 percent higher in 1973 than it had been twenty-three years earlier. For workers, this boom meant a rise in real wages of some 3.5 percent a year. If the population grew at 1 percent a year, each generation could expect to be twice as well off as their parents and four times as well off as their grandparents.[5]

Between 1950 and 1973 the average level of growth of the advanced economies was 4.9 percent, the number of jobs created increased by 29 percent,[6] and the average level of unemployment was 4.8 percent in America and 2.7 percent in Britain.[7] But this period of rising economic prosperity—which was not without its discontents—was unsustainable, and with its demise it transformed the fortunes of orthodox human capital theory.[8]

Orthodox Theory Comes of Age

The crisis of economic nationalism in the 1970s championed the ideas of neoliberal economists, including Milton Friedman, Friedrich von Hayek, George Stigler, and James Buchanan, who argued that market competition and individual freedoms were being hindered by state interference, stultifying market individualism and economic behavior, ideas consistent with Becker's economic approach and naked version of human capital, leaving people exposed to the full force of market competition with little social security.

The breakdown of economic nationalism was symbolized by the oil crisis in the early 1970s, growing industrial unrest, and rising inflation.[9] But it was the political interpretation of the failure of economic nationalism that contributed to the high tide of orthodox human capital theory. The resurgence of neoliberalism resulted in the election of Ronald Reagan in America (1980) and Margaret Thatcher in Britain (1979). Both identified the state as an impediment to economic growth and prosperity. It was blamed for inhibiting personal initiative and enterprise. Proponents of neoliberalism also claimed that nothing less than a major program of market deregulation was required to free people from the shackles of bureaucratic inertia and a culture of dependency resulting from the interventions of big government.

Reagan and Thatcher presented free-market economics as a way of reversing the economic decline of their "once great nations", as Japan and the Asian Tiger economies emerged as serious economic competitors, bringing new techniques of flexible mass production that highlighted a loss of Western enterprise and innovation. Drawing on the tenets of neoliberalism, Reagan argued for "an economy that [was] historically revitalized not by government but by people free of government interference, needless regulation, crippling inflation, high taxes and unemployment." Thatcher decried an overbearing state that had crushed the spirit of free enterprise: "I used to have a nightmare for the first six years in office that when I had got the finances right, when I had got the law right, the deregulation etc., that the British sense of enterprise and initiative would have been killed off by socialism."[10]

Much has been written about neoliberalism, but we need to see how it links to orthodox human capital theory if we are to understand its failed promise. There are several elements to this collection of economic ideas that are relevant to understanding Becker's theory of economic behavior. These include the following ideas:[11]

- The economic system works best when individuals are free to seek their private interests and are free to maximize their utility through market competition. *Homo economicus* fosters entrepreneurial innovation, and the operation of the market will lead to outcomes superior to those achieved through government planning. Hence Becker argued that the best industrial policy is no industrial policy.
- Individual economic freedom is sacrosanct, and the state should not try to intervene in the interests of any social group, rich or poor. The market should be left to determine what is of value and rewarded through the price mechanism, operating under the laws of supply and demand. The state's role should be to enforce legal contracts and guarantee that the rights of others are not infringed. It should limit itself to addressing areas of market failure, such as policing, armed forces, and transportation infrastructure.
- There are natural differences in individual intelligence, motivation, and moral character. Therefore any attempt by the state to engineer equality of opportunity, let alone equality of outcome, will inevitably fail. Individual qualities will be revealed and nurtured through the rigors of market competition. It is the qualities based on intelligence and motivation that determine who wins and loses in the supply-side competition for credentials.
- Labor market flexibility is required for companies to innovate and workers to adapt or develop their marketable skills to changing market conditions. Rigid labor markets result in the inefficient allocation of labor as rigidities corrupt the signaling function of wage differentials (the price mechanism).
- The best way to organize education and training is through market mechanisms because these will always be more efficient than state provision. The only form of equality that is sanctioned is equality of access to a market competition for credentials, enabling talent to rise to the top.
- Those unfit for this competition should receive only minimal state support, otherwise a culture of dependency will develop among the poor that weakens incentives for economic self-sufficiency, leading to an ever-increasing burden on the more energetic and deserving.

The rise of neoliberalism transformed the policy significance of orthodox human capital theory. The idea of education as an investment became the cornerstone of supply-side economic policy. By investing in themselves individuals were free to compete in a market-based *skills competition* that would reward them according to their individual marginal productivity. The focus on individual responsibility for human capital creation was given added impetus by the removal of the social and economic safety net in neoliberal societies, aimed at increasing market incentives for individual enterprise.

The high tide of orthodox theory also reflected the global ambitions of neoliberalism. In addition to reforms aimed at market deregulation at the national level, neoliberalism in the 1980s was also directed at the deregulation of global finance, trade, and labor markets. When looking back on this period, Reagan claimed, with considerable hubris and some justification, "We meant to change a nation, and instead we changed a world."[12] Chronicling the politics behind the rise of the global economy, Patricia Marchak describes the "sudden and spontaneous development, [when] business leaders and politicians around the world began using a whole new vocabulary . . . to promote a new agenda."[13] Alongside the Mont Pelerin Society and other established free-market organizations were influential think tanks such at the Trilateral Commission, established in 1973 by David Rockefeller, the incumbent CEO of the Chase Manhattan Bank. Members included former presidents and prime ministers as well as international business elites, its purpose to advance a general program for achieving a liberal integrated world economic system, to alleviate what was seen as protectionist disruption and domestic upheaval in America and other developed nations.[14] The "domestic upheaval" took the form of declining corporate profits, inflationary pressures, and what they saw as the unacceptable power of the trade unions.

Globalization was viewed as a policy instrument to undermine the power base of national trade unions because it gave companies the freedom to set up production in low-cost offshore locations. The extension of market competition also forced American and British workers into a global competition for jobs and wages with Mexican, Chinese, and Indian workers. Under these conditions, the only refuge or market shelter was to be found in investments in human capital. The global appeal of orthodox theory was therefore premised on the view that national governments could no longer protect workers within their domestic economies from foreign competition; individuals, firms, and nations all had to compete in a global skills competition in which investment in human capital was viewed as decisive.

The Knowledge Economy and Skills-Biased Technological Change

The neoliberal assault on the principles of economic nationalism only partly explains the high tide of orthodox human capital theory. Integral to the theory's appeal is the related idea of a rapid transformation in the role of human capital investment in a knowledge-driven economy. Again, this is based on a number of related ideas that elevated orthodox theory to the core of worldwide economic policy.

- *An economy increasingly dependent on knowledge and innovation.*

The work of the early human capital theorists pointed to a more extensive role for education, training, and credentials in a technologically driven economy.[15] Other economists at the time, including Robert Solow, argued that economic growth is explained by the external rate of technological progress, resulting in an increasing demand for skilled labor in response to an increase in the technical requirements of new areas of work. Fritz Machlup began the painstaking task of mapping the production and distribution of knowledge. He calculated that by the late 1950s, 29 percent of GNP in the United States had been produced in knowledge industries.[16]

Peter Drucker is widely credited with coining the phrase "knowledge economy" in the late 1960s to describe the enhanced role that knowledge would come to play in the economy, including the transformation of the occupational structure. He described how productivity and wealth creation depended on the manipulation of symbols, knowledge, and ideas rather than on physical labor or craft skills. Knowledge, previously applied to the organization of factory production (and office work) in the industrial era, now depended on the application of "knowledge to knowledge" as the key source of innovative goods and services.[17]

In the early 1970s Daniel Bell published an influential account called *The Coming of Post-Industrial Society*. It signaled a steep change in the nature of capitalism. Bell argued that the classical economic view was outdated; rather than the standard factors of production, scientific knowledge and certified expertise were the sources of economic innovation. Bell pointed to the increasing numbers of professional workers, including scientists, along with increasing private- and public-sector expenditure on research and development. Postindustrial societies, characterized by a shift in occupational structure from manufacturing to service industries, are, he believed, increasingly meritocratic, as "differential status and differential income are based on technical skills and higher education. Without those achievements one cannot fulfil the requirements of the new social division of labor which is a feature of that society."[18]

These early accounts of the knowledge economy gained growing public attention due to rapid advances in information and communication technologies, associated with the spread of personal computers and the internet. Silicon Valley in California and Route 126 in Massachusetts came to symbolize a new technological revolution. Manuel Castells, a leading theorist of the information society, describes the impact of that revolution: "The internet is the fabric of our lives. If information technology is the present-day equivalent of electricity in the industrial era, in our age the internet could be likened to both the electrical grid and the electric engine because of its ability to distribute the power of information throughout the entire realm of human activity."[19]

• *Technological change accelerating the demand for high-skilled workers.*

The assumption that the demand for skilled workers is driven by new technology stands at the heart of orthodox human capital's close cousin, skill-biased technological change (SBTC).[20] Its fundamental proposition is that the general-purpose technologies associated with information and digital technologies (e.g., computers and the internet) are skill biased rather than skill replacing; in other words, new technology increases the demand for higher skills rather than replacing skills with machines. It is argued that across the twentieth century, technology demanded increasing numbers of educated workers, a trend that SBTC's proponents assumed would continue, if not accelerate, in advanced knowledge economies.[21] Its policy significance lies in the support that it has provided for the rapid expansion of university education, while assuming that technology will drive the corresponding organizational and economic changes to utilize the skills students and employees acquire.

The Dutch economist Jan Tinbergen formulated the hypothesis that there is a race between education and technology, in which the challenge to education is to supply enough workers to meet the demands of technology. This led Claudia Goldin and Lawrence Katz to undertake a historical analysis of this race in the United States, after which they concluded, "In the race between technological change and education, education ran faster during the first half of the century and technology sprinted ahead of limping education in the last 30 years. The race produced economic expansion and also determined which groups received the fruits of growth." They therefore suggest that "most of the variation in educational wage differentials can be explained by a simple supply and demand framework."[22] Their policy solution is to advocate increasing the numbers earning a college degree as a way of narrowing these wage differentials.[23]

While this offered a justification for a focus on supply-side investment in human capital, perhaps of even greater significance in explaining the rising tide of orthodox theory in the 1980s was the idea of "endogenous growth," which challenged Solow's established account of economic growth, driven by the external rate of technological progress. Supporters of endogenous growth claimed that human capital investment was not just a response to an accelerating rate of technological progress but was now the driver of technological progress.

A major conclusion of Paul Romer's widely cited account of endogenous technological change is that "the stock of human capital determines the rate of growth."[24] It is a view elaborated by Daron Acemoglu, who claimed to show there is an endogenous relationship between new technology and the demand for skilled workers. Technological innovation, he suggests, does not simply drive the demand for education; by increasing the supply of skills, it leads firms to invest in new technologies in order to benefit from the productivity gains achieved with a more skilled workforce. Acemoglu explains, "New technologies have become more skill-biased throughout most of the twentieth century because the supply of skilled workers has grown steadily. This perspective also suggests that a faster increase in the supply of skills can lead to an acceleration in the demand for skills . . . so the timing of the increases in supply and demand is not a coincidence—instead it reflects technology responding to the supply of skills."[25] This view provides a causal explanation for how the productive potential of technology is translated via employers into the demand for more highly skilled workers.[26]

More recently three prominent skill-biased theorists—David Autor, Frank Levy, and Richard Murnane—acknowledged that computer technology may raise the demand not for all skills but only those that computers cannot replace.[27] Computers can undertake routine tasks; however, the skills demanded for nonroutine tasks are considered complementary to the technology and require high-level skills.[28] While these authors paid attention to the changing structure of labor demand, their policy prescriptions remained on the supply side, as they argued that students need to focus on acquiring those higher-level skills less likely to be replaced by algorithms.

- *A change in the historical relationship between capital and labor.*

The neoliberal ideas that inform orthodox theorists also include a new understanding of capital and labor. Accounts of an emerging knowledge economy, endogenous growth, and SBTC all contributed to the view that ownership of land, machines, and property is secondary to knowledge as the decisive economic asset. To support this view, various sources of evidence are used; for example, in 1920 more than 85 percent of the cost of a car went to pay routine laborers and investors, but by 1990 these two groups received less than 60 percent. Similarly, of the cost of a computer chip, 15 percent is divided among the owners of the raw material, equipment, production facilities, and routine labor, and the other 85 percent goes to educated labor, including designers, engineers, and patent attorneys.[29]

Drucker portrayed business owners as losing control of the means of production "because knowledge workers own their knowledge and can take it with them wherever they go."[30] And if knowledge, not laboring bodies, is the source of value, the historical relationship between capital and labor shifts in favor of those willing and able to invest in their human capital.

By implication, the only thing that holds people back is a lack of human capital. Good jobs follow human capital investment, transforming the role of the labor market. In the knowledge economy, labor markets should be deregulated to increase innovation and flexible employment. There is no longer a historical need for a protective system of social security. Those who cannot find employment or exist on poverty wages do not need state support but to be rescued from a culture of dependence by being given market incentives to train and find employment (of whatever kind).

Therefore the sole means by which people, young and old, can improve their life chances is through education, training, and the labor market: the state has little role in supporting workers through social insurance and welfare programs. This is human capital in the raw; without it, the chances of thriving in a neoliberal society are remote. Students and workers are to stand naked in the market, save for their credentials.

The Globalization of Human Capital

A cross current contributing to the high tide was the globalization of human capital, which added support to Becker's claim that his theory is universally applicable. The economic nationalism of the past, characterized by walled economies, imposed strict barriers to international trade, finance transactions, and the movement of labor. This was now viewed as artificially restricting economic enterprise as the competition for jobs depended on holding an appropriate passport.

The globalization of the economy, driven by market deregulation, enabled major North American, European, and Japanese companies to extend their global reach. It further transformed the labor market and its relationship to human capital investment. Perhaps the most influential account of this transformation was Robert Reich's *The Work of Nations*. American workers, he argued, were no longer judged by national criteria of education, training, or job performance. The appropriate benchmark for human capital investment was defined in relationship to the global labor market: "The standard of living of a nation's people increasingly depends on what they contribute to the world economy—on the value of their skills and insights."[31]

Reich used this insight to explain rising wage inequalities, highlighting the contrasting fates of production workers exposed to growing international cost competition. Those working in service occupations, including restaurants and retail stores, were largely dependent on the disposable incomes of individual knowledge workers who traded on their knowledge and skills worldwide. While this posed a fundamental challenge to the American economy in general, and the education system in particular, Reich repeated the argument at the time that there was no scarcity of good jobs but rather an undersupply of Americans to do the world's thinking. Describing the "upside" of the globalized economy, he writes, "Unlike America's old hierarchy and somewhat isolated economy, whose white-collar jobs were necessarily limited in proportion to the number of blue-collar jobs beneath them, the global economy imposes no particular limit upon the number of Americans who can sell symbolic-analytical services worldwide. In principle, all of America's routine production workers could become symbolic analysts and let their old jobs drift overseas to developing nations. The worldwide demand for symbolic analysts is growing so briskly that even under these circumstances real wages would still move steadily upwards."[32]

Although Reich is far from a neoliberal economist, he shared the view that because of the superior educational, corporate, technological, and innovation systems in America and Britain, they had a significant advantage in the global knowledge wars.[33] Globalization would contribute to an expanded demand for American knowledge workers, while standardized manufacturing would be done in third world countries. It is a race between education and technology and also one between education and the demands of global competition. As Richard Rosecrance put it, "Nations can transfer most of their material production thousands of miles away, centering their attention on research and development and product design at home. The result is a new productive partnership between 'head' nations, which design products, and 'body' nations, which manufacture them."[34]

National Policy and the Role of Education

For both developed and emerging economies the central message was that investment in human capital, combined with market-friendly policies, held the key to prosperity and economic growth. This took educational reform to the heart of economic policy. But it was not only the performance of individual students that was being assessed; the quality of national systems of education and training, now shifting to the front line of economic competition, was under review.

Faith in education to deliver significant returns to human capital was matched by the belief that education systems were not fit for purpose, often because they were not sufficiently based on market models of service delivery, requiring greater parental choice, deregulation of state schooling, and internal competition between educational providers.[35] If governments, firms, and families were being asked to invest more in human capital, following its leitmotif of "learning equals earning" (whether in the form of individual wages, company profits, or national economic growth), they had a right to expect education to deliver.

In America the National Commission on Excellence in Education in the early 1980s published *A Nation at Risk*, which was widely debated and left Americans in little doubt of where they stood in terms of the changing realities of the global knowledge economy:

> History is not kind to idlers. The time is long past when America's destiny was assured simply by an abundance of natural resources and inexhaustible human enthusiasm, and by our relative isolation from the malignant problems of older civilizations. The world is indeed one

global village. We live among determined, well-educated, and strongly motivated competitors. We compete with them for international standing and markets, not only with products but also with the ideas of our laboratories and neighborhood workshops. America's position in the world may once have been reasonably secure with only a few exceptionally well-trained men and women. It is no longer.[36]

The belief that Western nations were in urgent need of improving the quality of their stock of human capital was equally in vogue on the other side of the Atlantic. In 1993 an influential report from the National Commission on Education in the United Kingdom concluded, "For us, knowledge and skills will be central. In an era of world-wide competition and low-cost global communications, no country like ours will be able to maintain its standard of living, let alone improve it, on the basis of cheap labor and low-tech products and services. There will be too many millions of workers and too many employers in too many countries who will be able and willing to do that kind of work fully as well as we or people in any other developed country could do it—and at a fraction of the cost."[37]

The National Commission on Education's conclusions coincided with a World Bank policy research report titled *The East Asian Miracle*. It revealed that between 1965 and 1990 real per capita income growth rates in Japan and the four Asian Tiger economies of Hong Kong, Singapore, Taiwan, and the Republic of Korea were double the rates achieved in economies in the Organization for Economic Cooperation and Development (OECD).[38] The story told about East Asia was also of interest because the high-performing economies identified in the report were also characterized by high growth and declining inequality, which were of particular interest given growing income inequalities in America and Britain. The problem is that the East Asian models of economic development did not conform to a neoliberal view given evidence of active state intervention. But this did not prevent the World Bank from concluding that "what appeared to be a miracle was not that 'miraculous' because it was largely due to superior accumulation of physical and human capital," combined with "market-friendly" policies, where "the appropriate role of government is to ensure adequate investment in people, provide a competitive climate for private enterprise, keep the economy open to international trade, and maintain a stable macroeconomy. Beyond these roles . . . governments are likely to do more harm than good, unless interventions are market friendly."[39]

The subsequent education explosion in both emerging and developed economies was extraordinary, if not miraculous. An analysis of enrollment

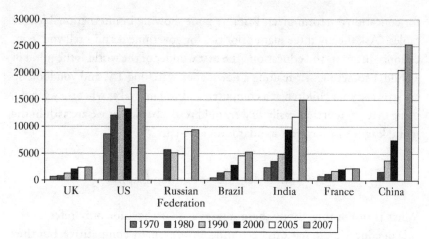

FIGURE 3.1 The expansion of higher education in selected emerging and developed economies (enrollments) in thousands.
Source: Lauder Brown and Ashton, *The Global Auction* (New York: Oxford University Press, 2011), Figure 3.2, 32.

figures for 113 emerging and developed countries reveals a doubling in undergraduate and postgraduate enrollment within a decade, from 72.5 million in 1996 to 136.1 million in 2007. By the time of the financial crash in 2007 China had over 7 million more students in higher education that the United States and ten times as many students as Britain.[40]

Politicians and policymakers of all political persuasions agreed that in this global competition, countries with the best education system would win. In 1990 President George H. W. Bush argued, "Education is the one investment that means more for our future because it means the most for our children.... By the year 2000, US students must be the first in the world in math and science achievement.... Every American adult must be a skilled, literate worker and citizen.... The nation will not accept anything less than excellence in education."[41]

His successor, President Bill Clinton, also spoke of the importance of education to America's competitiveness: "The currency of national strength in this new era will be denominated not only in ships and tanks and planes, but in diplomas and patents and paychecks."[42] And President Barack Obama was in no doubt that, "in the 21st century—when so many jobs will require a bachelor's degree or more, when countries that out-educate us today will outcompete us tomorrow—a world-class education is a prerequisite for success."[43]

In Britain one the best known quotations from Prime Minister Tony Blair highlighted the central role of education to government policy and the need for educational reform given Britain's poor showing in international league tables: "Ask me my three main priorities for government and I tell you: education, education and education. The first wonder of the world is the mind of a child. I sometimes sit reading a newspaper, watching TV, and you look up and you see your children at a computer, and you marvel at what they can do, using that computer as easily as we would read a book. Yet we are 35th in the world league of education standards today—35th."[44]

A Global Measure of Human Capital

What is interesting about these quotes is that they not only refer to the role of education in nations becoming more globally competitive, but they do so by benchmarking national standards against international league tables of educational performance. Their high profile demonstrates how far politicians and policymakers around the world have bought into a view of global market competition drawing on league tables that now shape and define education and human capital.[45] In turn, the intellectual justification for this new institutional and social technology for reconstructing the significance and nature of human capital emerged out of Becker's idea that it was possible to use a measure of education, such as years of schooling, to compare the performance of different countries. It was also augmented by the theories of endogenous growth and SBTC, which perpetuated the view that investment in human capital was the major determinant of economic growth.

The OECD, a Paris-based think tank funded by thirty-four major economies to promote global economic growth, prosperity, and sustainable development, is the chief propagandist of international league tables. It also became the champion of human capital and has had a global influence on national governments.[46] The OECD produces an annual flagship report, *Education at a Glance*, offering an extensive analysis of educational trends and policy initiatives in the developed world and leading emerging counties. The report of 2014 is indicative of the orthodox assumptions that shape its interpretation of educational data: "The economies of OECD countries depend on a sufficient supply of high-skilled workers. Educational qualifications are frequently used to measure human capital and the level of an individual's skills. In most OECD countries people with high qualifications have the highest employment rates. At the same time, people with the lowest educational qualifications are at greater risk of being unemployed. Given the technological advances that have been transforming the needs of the global labor market, people with higher or specific skills are in strong demand."[47]

But the OECD has gone much further, initiating new ways of measuring the value of education to the economy by developing a variety of international tests. These have been widely adopted by policymakers as a legitimate response to the difficulties of benchmarking or harmonizing national qualification systems that have institutional histories linked to different cultural, political, and economic priorities.[48] For instance, because educational experiences in Brazil, Britain, and Botswana are very different, using years of schooling as a measure reveals little about the knowledge, skills, or competences acquired in each country.

Another reason these new measures have been embraced is to maintain the policy relevance of educational performance in light of disappointing results. Eric Hanushek and Ludger Woessmann, proponents of the OECD's approach, suggest that while the centrality of human capital to economic growth and development is not in doubt, "few have not been at least somewhat disappointed by the results of the time, energy, and resources that have been devoted to improve human capital. Development simply has not proceeded at the pace many expected, given the sizable expansion of schooling in the depressed countries and regions of the world."[49] Rather than challenge the veracity of the standard orthodox model, they support the OECD's view that the main problem is finding more suitable indicators of educational performance. This has led to the development of comparative measures of skills and competences rather than relying on a worker's years of schooling or level of qualification.

Through its Program for International Student Assessment (PISA), the OECD purports to have established a sound comparative methodology by which students' performance at the end of compulsory schooling can be judged across countries.[50] But the effects have been to change classroom practice, assessment methods, and the wider purposes of education. Now a nation's human capital stock is judged by performance in benchmark tests compiled in international league tables. For these league tables to be comparable, a standardized measure of performance is required by which students, schools, and nations can be judged. In other words, these league tables are being used to define educational excellence.

In some countries the means and ends of education are defined in the currency of league tables, which include world rankings of colleges and universities. In America and Britain high-stakes national testing is widely used to drive up standards, and students come to understand the benefits of rote learning as an acquisitive game, to which we will return in later chapters. Of course, just as there have been cogent critiques of the PISA methodology, so there have been policy academics who have pointed out the inconvenient truth that national test scores do not always correlate with periods of intellectual and technological creativity.[51]

Perhaps even more perilous is that national testing perpetuates the standard view that the whole economy is based on a skills competition, in which the art of government is to reform education to address any mismatch between the stock of human capital and employer statements of need. Such is the enduring faith in human capital theory that Hanushek and Woessmann claim, "Even with very conservative assumptions . . . improvements in school outcomes lead to added GDP growth that could dramatically change the future prosperity of a country." On the basis of different education reform scenarios that calculate the impact of increasing PISA scores for national economic growth, they assert that a twenty-five-point increase in US PISA results would contribute $43.8 billion in future GDP until 2090.[52]

Conclusion

We can see how alluring this vision of human capital investment and the knowledge economy was to students, parents, and policy advisors. For students, the future looked bright and worth investment in the promise of well-paid jobs and personal fulfillment because firms depended on their brain power. For policymakers, it appeared that economic growth could be achieved through educational reform, where mass higher education was required to fulfill the demands of the knowledge economy. All they needed to do is provide access to a college education and the magic of the markets would do the rest. It is as if policymakers had found the philosopher's stone in the Chicago school of economics: a win-win in which, so long as students earned a college education, they would be guaranteed well-paid, interesting jobs, and as an added bonus, national competitiveness and wealth would rise. In part II we describe the unraveling of the orthodox approach and present a revisionist account of human capital development.

PART II

The Failed Promise

4

Learning Isn't Earning

TO WHAT EXTENT have we entered an age of human capital? There is no doubt that billions of dollars of private and public money continue to be spent on education and training. Attracted by the promises of a good job that education can deliver, parents make all sorts of investment in their children and send them to college in droves. Access to postsecondary education has never been easier. The number of students continuing on to some form of tertiary education has rocketed. Over 50 percent of birth cohorts in most industrialized countries go to college or university.[1]

But this does not make it an age of human capital, as presented by Gary Becker and other orthodox theorists. Of the central tenets of orthodox theory outlined previously, perhaps the most important is a causal relationship between learning and earning. It is causal in the sense that economic returns, measured by earnings in the labor market, are predicted to be proportional to the amount of human capital invested, on the assumption that employers are willing to pay a higher price for better-trained people given higher individual productivity. Moreover, as the demand for high-skilled workers increases, the value of human capital will continue to increase over time, making it profitable for individuals to make further investments.

To what extent is learning equal to earning? In rapidly changing technological and market circumstances, do all college graduates earn a premium over and above what high school leavers get? In other words, do wages reflect investments in education? Do graduates with the same level of education (credentials) have equal opportunities in the competition for jobs, as a result of the race between education and technology?[2]

In this chapter we offer a systematic review of the evidence used to support the key claims of orthodox theory. These include the body of literature claiming that investment in education and skills has become more valuable

The Death of Human Capital? Phillip Brown, Hugh Lauder, and Sin Yi Cheung, Oxford University Press (2020).
© Oxford University Press. DOI: 10.1093/oso/9780190644307.001.0001

over time as technologically advanced economies come to depend on the brainpower of the workforce.[3] To support this view, orthodox theorists typically compare average rates of return between college and non-college students.

There are a number of propositions that can be tested to determine if learning equals earning. First, wages reflect human capital investments in education. Second, the value of human capital increases over time. Third, learning equals earnings in all countries. Fourth, reward in the labor market is biased toward the most highly educated workers who will attract higher wages. Some of these points will be addressed in the next chapter, but here we begin with the central question of whether learning equals earning.

We take the United States and the United Kingdom as examples to assess the claim of a graduate premium. Using data from the US censuses of 1970 and 1990 and the American Community Survey 2010, along with the UK Labor Force Survey in the latter years,[4] we conduct new analyses of private rates of return to education in America over a forty-year period of significant economic, technological, and social change. These data challenge the central claim that learning equals earning by highlighting a real-term decline in earnings for many college-educated workers and increasing income inequalities that cannot be explained by differences in investments in education.

To support the "learning equals earning" argument orthodox economists have tended to measure investment by number of years of education completed, or the level of educational attainment, e.g., college degrees as opposed to high school diplomas. To show that more education yields higher returns, they compare the average (mean) wages of college and high school graduates.[5] But it has been widely established that mean labor income does not tell the whole story and in fact masks much of the rising inequalities heavily skewed toward the 1 percent of top earners.[6]

Until recently many economists treated the relationship between education and earnings in a linear fashion, taking average earnings as a measure of labor market returns. Indeed if we take averages we find that there is a graduate premium when compared to the average earnings of nongraduates. However, this kind of linearity is flawed for three reasons. First, simply looking at the level of education masks a great deal of hidden inequality, including internal stratification between different types of education and institutions. Second, the labor market is equally stratified and segregated by class, gender, race, ethnicity, industry, and occupation. Third, due to extreme outliers (i.e., the top 1 percent of high earners), a great deal of within-group inequalities by education and occupation is hidden even when median earnings are examined. To properly understand the link between education and labor market returns, we need a much more nuanced approach that disaggregates the data by gender, racial, and ethnic group as well as occupation, in addition to the level of education received.[7] Where possible, we draw on published sources and add new analysis only when direct between-groups and within-groups comparison are not available.

Using the US census and American Community Survey data over four decades at three time points—1970, 1990, and 2010—we compare college graduates' labor income to that of high school graduates.[8] Instead of using the overall mean or median income, we scrutinize the top and bottom end of the income distribution. This is similar to Jan Pen's imagery of an "income parade" to graphically depict income inequality, in which he postulates people's height to be proportional to their income. If everyone in the economy is lined up in a parade according to their height, what we will see is not a picture of a lot of people with average height but a parade of those of diminutive stature at one end and a few giants at the other.[9] As our analysis will show, the income distribution in the United States since the 1970s is startlingly similar to this.

How Much Does Higher Education Pay?

Average wages by level of education, as used in typical econometric analyses, generally show an apparent graduate premium. At first glance, as shown in Figure 4.1, college graduates do appear to, *on average*, earn considerably more than high school leavers per hour (in 2009 dollars) in 1970, 1990, and 2010. Immediately apparent is the fact that the mean gives a vastly overinflated average of earnings due to extreme outliers compared to the median. It is also clear that earnings for both college and high school graduates remain stagnant in real terms over time. To be sure, the gap in median hourly earnings between college and high school graduates increased over time, from 39 percent in 1970 to 41 percent in 1990 and 45 percent in 2010. However, *average* earnings, even measured by the median, typically hide an enormous amount of internal stratification and earnings polarization.[10] As we will show in our analysis, measuring the so-called yield or rate of return is not straightforward. How it is measured can lead to very different conclusions.

Figure 4.1 shows that the general trend of wages in the United States since the 1970s is one of stagnation, and once adjusted for inflation labor income for the majority has not grown over time; indeed some groups have experienced a wage decline, as we will describe. Using data from the US Bureau of Labor Statistics, the Economic Policy Institute (EPI) has also shown a decline in young graduates' earnings since 2000 (Figure 4.2). This may not come as a surprise, given the fact that in 1970 only 13 percent of all employees in the

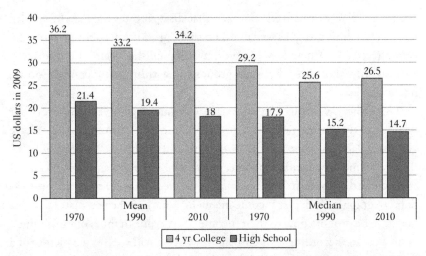

FIGURE 4.1 Mean and median hourly earnings (in 2009 USD) for college and high school graduates.

Sources: IPUMS USA US census 1970,1990 1% metro sample; the American Community Survey (ACS) 2010, (weighted), Ages 18–64.

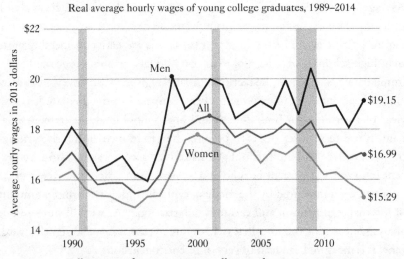

FIGURE 4.2 Falling rates of return to young college graduates since 2000.

Source: Economic Policy Institute, *The Top 10 Charts of 2014* (Washington, D. C., December 18, 2014), 8.[11]

US labor force had a four-year college degree. Rapid expansion in higher education meant that the supply of graduate workers shot up to 23 percent in 1990, and by 2010 34 percent of the workforce had a four-year college degree.[12] Figure 4.2 also shows that despite being equally qualified, women earn consistently less than men over the entire twenty-year period.

To give a more nuanced account of the rates of private returns to human capital, we examine the hourly wages of college and high school graduates in the entire wage distribution using income deciles. We divide wage earners into ten equal parts, ranging from the 10th, 20th, 30th, to 90th deciles. We compare the inflation-adjusted hourly earnings (in 2009 dollars) of college graduates in the top and bottom deciles to those of high school diploma graduates in 1970, 1990, and 2010. Figure 4.3 presents the results. College graduates in the top 90th decile (College H) earned consistently higher hourly wages compared to all other graduates and high school leavers. However, what is even more striking is that the 90th decile high school diploma graduates (High School H) earned more than college graduates with median earnings (College M), and this pattern is remarkably consistent over

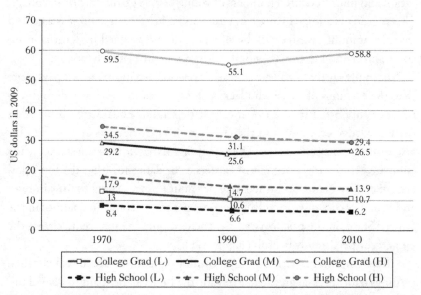

FIGURE 4.3 US hourly earnings (in 2009 USD) of high school and four-year college graduates in 1970, 1990, and 2010.

Source: IPUMS USA US Census 1970, 1990 1% metro sample; the ACS 2010, (weighted), Ages 18–64.

Key: (L) = bottom decile (10%), (M) = median (50%), (H) = top decile (90%).

time. The same is observable for high school graduates whose median hourly earnings (High School M) were consistently higher than college graduates in the bottom 10th decile.[13]

Two key messages emerge from Figure 4.3. First, only the top decile of college graduates who attended for four years clearly benefit from their investment in education. The average college graduate in 2010 made less than $27 an hour, lower than a high school graduate in the top decile, who earned nearly $30. Worse than that, the median hourly earnings for a high school graduate in 2010 was around $14, much higher than the bottom decile (10%) of college graduates, who scraped by with around $10 per hour.

Second, labor income flatlines or stagnates for most in real terms since 1970, with earnings being higher for most in real terms in 1970 than in 1990 and 2010. This is plausible given that a much lower proportion (approximately 10 percent) attended postsecondary education back then, and college graduates would have been a more highly selected group, as compared to around 27 percent in 2010. In short, the picture is plain: for the majority, investment in a college education has not resulted in parallel income growth over time. That is against the background of massive expansion in higher education and unprecedented numbers of young people graduating from college. This represents a huge increase in educational investment, and it is assumed that the amount invested will be significantly outweighed by returns in income and economic growth, a point we examine in a later chapter.

To simply say that a college education is worth having because it pays more than the earnings of those who lack such an education is clearly dubious, as it is not supported by the evidence just presented. Equally, the promise of the knowledge economy and the claims of SBTC theorists appear false for low-earning college graduates. The extent of polarization is even starker when compared to the top 1 percent of earners. Our data show that the top 1 percent of college graduates earned $159 per hour in 1970, rising to $165 in 1990 and $162 in 2010, mirroring Pen's income parade: income inequalities in the United States in the past forty years benefited only the 1 percent, leaving the 99 percent persistently behind (Figure 4.4).

These important within-groups earning disparities are revealed when earnings data are disaggregated, exposing the high salaries paid to a small minority and the misfortunes of the majority, who are unable to capitalize on similar levels of educational investment. Meanwhile college graduates at the bottom decile of the wage distribution earned consistently less than median high school leavers. Thus neither those at the top nor those at the bottom conform to the prediction of orthodox theory. As we will argue in the final

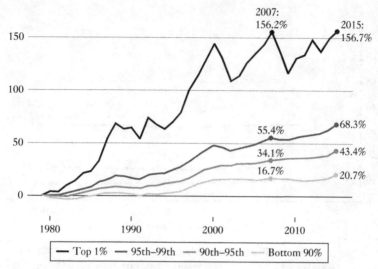

FIGURE 4.4 Cumulative percentage change in annual wages by wage group, 1979–2015. Source: EPI analysis of Wojciech Kopczuk, Emmanuel Saez, and Jae Song (2010, Table A3); US Social Security Administration wage statistics.[14]

section of the book, orthodox theory has contributed to this situation because it sets no moral limits to how much individuals should earn. Orthodox theory simply suggests that people should maximize their return on investment rather than doing something worthwhile to be paid a fair day's wage for a fair day's work.

If technological advances demand more highly educated workers, it should follow that investment in higher degrees would bring lucrative economic returns in the labor market. Figure 4.5 shows the earnings deciles for graduates with master's and PhD degrees compared with those of graduates with some college education over the same forty-year period.[15] "Some college" is defined as anything between one to three years of college education, most likely obtained from a wide range of public and private community colleges.

In contrast to orthodox predictions, investment in higher degrees is not necessarily matched with the anticipated returns. The pattern is in fact remarkably similar to that shown in Figure 4.3 in that only those in the top decile benefit with real wage growth over time. The earning profile of the majority of workers with postgraduate degrees is much closer to that of community college graduates. In fact the $32 median hourly earnings of these master's and PhD graduates in 2010 were only a couple of dollars more than high school leavers in the top decile (Figure 4.3: $29 High School (H) in 2010). In other

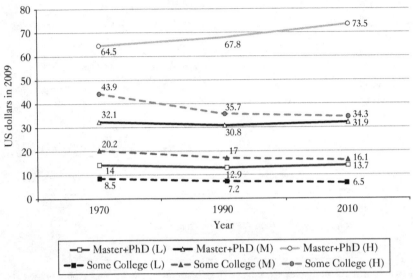

FIGURE 4.5 Earnings (in 2009 USD) of graduates with Master's and PhD degrees and graduates with some college in 1970, 1990, and 2010.

Source: IPUMS USA US Census 1970, 1990 1% metro sample; 2010 ACS (weighted), ages 18–64.

Key: (L) = bottom decile (10%), (M) = median (50%), (H) = top decile (90%).

words, the investment in an extra four to five years of advanced education has not paid off. Importantly, the value of these postgraduate qualifications has not increased over time either, except for those in the top decile. Since medical and legal training in the United States is available only in graduate school, these high earners are likely to be graduates with specialties in medicine, business, or law. With the average cost of a master's degree in the United States is approximately $30,000 for private universities,[16] the evidence shown here casts serious doubt on whether a higher degree is actually worth the time and investment, in terms of yielding monetary returns, for the majority of college graduates.

The message for community college graduates (those with up to three years of college education) is even starker, as those in the bottom decile have an earnings profile much closer to that of their counterparts with a high school diploma (see Figure 4.2). Meanwhile the proportion of community college graduates has expanded from 16 percent in 1970 to 31 percent in 2010. Since 2008 the proportion of community college students from low-income family backgrounds has risen from 30 percent to nearly 50 percent and in some cases 60 percent. The pressure of going to college has driven an increasing number of low-income families to invest a significant amount of money, often beyond their means, in the form of sizable education loans and personal debt, in private for-profit colleges, where students gain no positional advantage in the labor market.[17] It is these investments that are least likely to attract the kind of labor market return orthodox theorists predicted. To this group of students, learning is definitely far from earnings.

What Difference Does Age Make?

It is widely assumed that younger college graduates earn less due to their lack of labor market experience and that earnings will rise over time as they gain more experience. Orthodox theorists routinely treat age as a proxy for labor market experience, as is shown by the widely adopted Mincer model, in which "human capital earnings function" models the linear relationship between years of education and earnings, taking into account potential labor market experience.[18] At first glance it appears that employees are rewarded for experience since older workers earn more than younger ones. However, when we build in the rising costs of a college education, to say nothing of forgone earnings, things look pretty stark for many college graduates, and for orthodox theory. We will return to the rising costs of college education in chapter 6. Here we further disaggregate the analysis by age. First, the pattern of hourly earnings shown in Figures 4.6 to 4.8 resembles the big picture observed in Figure 4.3. Median graduate earners with college degrees earn consistently less than top-decile high school leavers; this is the case for all age groups, and the pattern is consistent over time from 1970 to 2010. Second, older graduates with more labor market experience do not earn more than their younger peers, as suggested by the flat lines across age groups in all three graphs. The only exceptions are college graduates in the top decile, where age does appear to pay since rates of private returns are higher for those in their thirties and older (Figure 4.6). In reality it may not be work experience but accumulated social and professional networks that matter most. However, even this trend flatlines in 2010 (Figure 4.8), where hourly wages remain stagnant for those in their forties, fifties, and sixties. This flatlining pattern is remarkably persistent over time in the three periods our data cover.

As can be seen in Figure 4.8, workers' median earnings at each educational level are highest when they are in their forties, but it is also in this age group that income plateaus. Even the most rudimentary understanding of work organization would include the fact that someone able to do a job is more valuable to an employer than someone who is untrained or new to the task. However, what is surprising is how we have moved away from the widely held

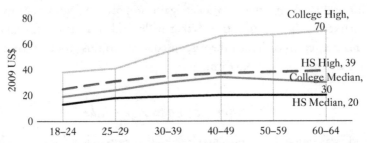

FIGURE 4.6 Hourly earnings (in 2009 USD) for college and high school graduates by age groups in 1970.

Source: IPUMS USA US Census 1970 1% Metro sample (weighted), ages 18–64.

Key: HS = high school; High = top decile (90%).

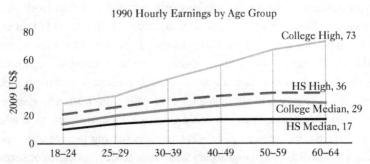

FIGURE 4.7 Hourly earnings (in 2009 USD) for college and high school graduates by age groups in 1990.

Source: IPUMS USA US Census 1990 1% metro sample (weighted), ages 18–64.

Key: HS = high school; High = top decile (90%).

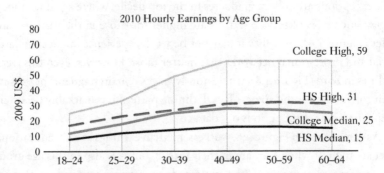

FIGURE 4.8 Hourly earnings (in 2009 USD) for college and high school graduates by age groups in 2010.

Source: IPUMS USA American Community Survey 2010 (weighted), ages 18–64.

Key: HS = high school; High = top decile (90%).

idea that an occupational career involves incremental increases in income rather than simply a wage for the job. In the past twenty years corporate remuneration has switched from incremental rises in wages reflecting assumed increases in productivity to flatter wages and annual bonuses, conditional on meeting performance targets.

This shows that the relationship between education and the labor market is much more complex than the linear picture orthodox theorists portray. Using advanced statistical analysis, labor economists and some stratification sociologists have long documented the highly diverse economic returns to college education, controlling for students' ability and propensity to attend and complete college. Both positive and negative selections are at play. Matt Dickson and Franz Buscha challenge the claim that more education and investment in human capital implies people earn higher salaries. They found that leaving school early to gain labor market experience pays more in lifetime earnings than time invested in a university education.[19]

Occupation Income Inequality

One of the key features of conventional thought about advanced capitalist economies is that they are distinguished by rising demand for a highly skilled workforce, which in turn has resulted in an increase in managerial and professional occupations and a decline in the demand for manual and unskilled work. But this account is not supported by research evidence showing the median earnings of graduates has not tracked the rise in technical, managerial, and professional employment.

This challenges Claudia Goldin and Lawrence Katz's argument that rising income inequalities are explained by the failure of the education system to produce enough skilled people.[20] If private rates of return to human capital investment are biased toward technologically advanced sectors or occupations, we would expect wages to be higher for graduates in these occupations over time. In Figure 4.9 we show low, median, and high decile earnings for a number of occupations, which offer little evidence of rising incomes reflecting more college graduates entering these occupations between 1970 and 2010.

Another explanation is that labor market structures have changed so that while the number in professional and managerial occupations has risen, this fails to tell the story that only some under these headings have good jobs and, above all, a decent income, as part of the core of an organization, while others in peripheral roles are on short-term or inferior contracts. This will be examined in a later chapter as we are witnessing increasing segmentation, stratification,

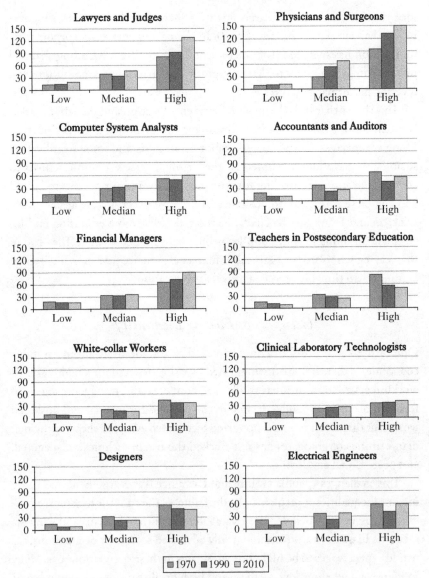

FIGURE 4.9 Hourly earnings (in 2009 USD) for US low (10%), middle (50%), and high (90%) graduate earners in selected occupations in 1970, 1990, and 2010.

Source: IPUMS USA 1970 Census 1% metro sample and 1990 Census 5% sample; 2010 American Community Survey, ages 18–64.

and in some cases polarization within and between occupations. What the evidence seems to show is that the growth in occupational wage inequalities cannot be explained in orthodox terms. In other words, it has more to do with the character of employment than the character or skills of workers.

To give a sense of the very mixed fortunes of knowledge workers or those in graduate occupations over time, we compared the hourly pay for managerial and professional occupations, typically requiring at least a four-year college education: lawyers and judges, physicians and surgeons, computer system analysts, accountants and auditors, financial managers, teachers in postsecondary education, white-collar workers, clinical laboratory technologists, designers, and electrical engineers. Low, middle, and high earners are represented by the bottom decile, median, and top decile earners in the data.[21]

Figure 4.9 shows the hourly income in 2009 US dollars for college graduates in these ten occupations in 1970, 1990, and 2010. It tells an important story about between- and within-occupation inequalities and differential income growth over time. The standardized scale on the *y* axis allows us to see an immediately striking picture of who the winners and losers are: lawyers and judges, physicians and surgeons at the top and white-collar workers and clinical laboratory technologists at the bottom. In 2010 the top decile of lawyers and judges enjoyed an hourly rate of over $120, while the same top 10 percent of physicians and surgeons made around $150 per hour. In stark contrast, top-decile highly skilled clinical laboratory technologists made only around $40 an hour.

These charts clearly show that the financial fate of those employed in different occupations points to a complex set of institutional and market relationships that have worked to the advantage of some occupational groups over others, regardless of their level of human capital investment. A second kind of inequality exists within occupations. Despite being in the same profession, top-decile lawyers and surgeons made six to ten times more than their colleagues in the bottom decile, and this gap appears to have increased toward the end of the forty-year period. Given the cost of time and training, it would appear that the within-occupation earnings gap is greater than the one between occupations, as anticipated by orthodox theory. Top-decile lawyers and physicians, and to a less extent financial managers, were the only groups who benefited from any real income growth over time. For the majority of graduates, the story is one of income stagnation.

Our evidence suggests that the weakening US economy at the end of the 1980s appears to have affected some occupations more than others. Labor income in real terms saw a much sharper decline for accountants and auditors, designers, and electrical engineers, and only electrical engineers and the top-decile accountants managed to reverse this decline in 2010. The apparent unusual wage premium among the highest earning (90th percentile) postsecondary teachers in 1970 is due to the changing composition of this group of graduates. In 1970 an exceptionally higher proportion (87 percent) of this group had five or more years of college education (equivalent to having a master's or doctoral degree). Twenty years later only 59 percent of this group had a master's or doctoral degree, and this proportion declines further to 35 percent in 2010. This is also likely due to the rapid expansion in postsecondary education since the 1990s, when a great many college professors were employed in community colleges with much lower wages. It is of no comfort that our findings are echoed by a 2016 article in *Nature* which highlighted growing and severe income polarization among scientists in the United States since 1973. Only the top 1 percent of elite scientists continue to enjoy lucrative returns and soaring income, moving them into the ranks of the superrich, while the majority of highly trained and highly skilled scientists are left behind to endure the consequence of stagnant income growth.[22]

Of course the pattern of income stratification and polarization between and within occupations shown in Figure 4.9 could be the result of age and gender inequalities, to which we will return in the next chapter. However, what remains unequivocal is that the same level of human capital investment does not yield the same labor market returns, even for those who invested in a high-skilled occupation, such as computer system analysts and clinical laboratory technologists. With the exception of the top-decile earners, the majority of highly skilled college graduates have not escaped the fate of income stagnation over time or rising income inequalities. What is more troubling is that technological advance has not brought the graduate premium promised to the majority of aspiring students and parents who have invested large sums of money, time, and effort, probably only to be disappointed with meager returns. The relationship between education and overall wage returns has not grown or increased for most people over time, whereas inequalities within and between qualifications and between occupations have grown over time.

The Global Landscape: Returns to Education in OECD Countries

Evidence from other OECD countries shows a very mixed picture on the returns to higher education and casts another direct challenge to the central claim that human capital investment is universal in the labor market. Even the most cursory analysis points to the importance of "varieties of capitalism" that cannot be reduced to national differences in supply and demand.[23]

In Figure 4.10 we can see that the average premium for a bachelor's degree is 148 percent of a high school diploma (upper secondary education) in all OECD countries.[24] However, this tells us only about relative differences; it says nothing about the actual earnings of someone with an upper secondary education, especially when we disaggregate into top and bottom deciles in the earning distribution, as we have in the evidence presented earlier. The patterns for the United Kingdom (149 percent) and Germany (152 percent) are very similar, whereas figures are slightly higher in the United States (160 percent) than in other OECD economies. Figures for France and Sweden are much lower at 124 and 123 percent, compared to the much higher "graduate premium" in developing economies such as Chile and Brazil. In countries where data are disaggregated further, master's and PhD degrees appear to yield an even higher premium.

If the universal value of human capital is consistent, as orthodox theorists claim, we would expect returns to educational investment to be universally uniform in all OECD countries where demand for a highly skilled workforce is biased toward the technologically advanced. That said, these data need to be treated with some caution. The graduate premium needs to be placed within the context of the industrial and educational structures of different countries

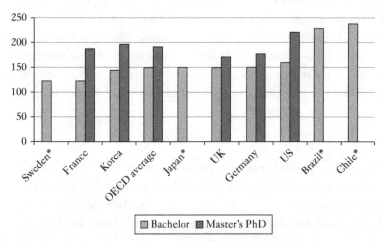

FIGURE 4.10 Relative earnings of graduates working full time in select OECD countries, 2014.
Note: * denotes only "all tertiary education" available in Sweden, Japan, Brazil, and Chile.
Source: OECD, *Education at a Glance*, 2016, Figure A6.1.

or varieties of capitalism. In Sweden, for instance, nongraduate jobs are much better paid than in the United Kingdom or United States, hence the lower graduate premium. We must also note that the apparent graduate premium is based on average income from employment and should likewise be interpreted with caution. These headline figures tell us nothing about the within-group difference in graduates' ability to capitalize on their educational investments. Further analysis such as we presented earlier in this chapter is needed to get a more accurate picture in each of these countries. Nonetheless, while these figures may give an overall impression that higher education pays, we need to take account of overall income distribution and the extent of graduate unemployment and underemployment in these countries. Simply comparing average wages can give a very misleading picture of the graduate premium, as noted. Moreover, in Thomas Piketty's analysis of the rapidly widening income inequalities in countries like the United States and the United Kingdom, the graduate premium reflects structural inequalities, which cannot be explained by orthodox theory.[25] With the rising cost of college education in both the United States and the United Kingdom, the actual cost of failure, including the forgone labor market experience, could not be more obvious.[26]

In contrast to the prediction of orthodox theorists, income inequality has not been alleviated with the expansion of higher education. In fact the opposite is true: the forty-year period 1970 to 2010 saw the sharpest rise in income inequality in both the United States and the United Kingdom.[27] Additionally the race between education and technology simply cannot be the explanation for rising inequality, as our data show. According to orthodox theories, the expansion in college education in both countries should drive down graduate returns, but the top-decile income share has risen from 33 to 48 percent in the United States and from 28 to 42 percent in the United Kingdom.

Conclusion

In this chapter we challenged the central arguments in orthodox theory that more investment in education leads to higher earnings and that the value of human capital increases over time as societies become more technologically advanced. So what does the data presented here tell us? First, once we disaggregate the data on the returns to education, the question of causality, which is at the heart of the theory, becomes much more complicated than orthodox theorists suggest. If the only measures of the returns to education are the average or median returns for graduate and nongraduate workers, then a clear and plausible causal inference can be drawn. But when the data are disaggregated the causal story breaks down, presenting a far more complex picture showing that for many learning doesn't equal earning. Second, at best, this outdated theory of the relationship between education and the economy applies only to the golden era of the pre-1973 recession, as shown in our data in 1970, when income inequality was much less severe and only a small proportion of the workforce received a college education.

Third, our evidence demonstrates that the early promise of orthodox theory applies only to the privileged few. Becker's central idea is that the value of human capital theory is that wages reflect investments in education, not that those on higher wages typically have a bachelor's degree. This is a subtle but crucial difference. It is one thing to say that a lot of people who earn high wages have higher levels of education, and it is quite another that everyone with a higher education has a high income relative to those who have less education. It is the latter statement that defines a key claim in orthodox theory. If the former statement is true, then human capital theory loses much of its explanatory power.

However, recent attempts have been made to defend the basic tenets of orthodox theory by retreating from the general claim of the link between learning and earning and arguing for a more nuanced understanding that acknowledges that general investment in education may be less important than specific skill sets which remain highly valued by employers. They argue that top income earners have special skills that mark them out for such high rewards; in corporate-speak, they are "talent" that needs to be highly rewarded because of their superior productivity.[28] But such arguments fail to take account of the changing occupational structure or new patterns of work, requiring a theoretical account of the demand as well as the supply side of the labor market.

It is the industrial and occupational structure of countries that determines the distribution of wages. Even Goldin and Katz, who are leading proponents of SBTC, have shown that Harvard graduates in economics and finance earn extraordinary salaries presumably because of the Wall Street effect rather than the extraordinary skills or talent of these employees.[29] When we consider the oligopolistic nature of the finance industry, as with many other industries, we can see how excess profits are generated and then pocketed by top-decile earners. The wages of many graduates may also be depressed by the global auction for high-skilled as well as low-skilled jobs, in which there is a price competition driven by the growth in college-educated workers in low-income locations, again pointing to fundamental changes in the relationship between education, employment, and incomes.[30]

Evidence from the Bank of England on the declining effect of qualifications on wage growth is testament to an increasing number of economists coming to terms with the lack of purchasing power of human capital.[31] Even those with master's and doctoral degrees on both sides of the Atlantic make about the same amount or in some cases significantly less than the top-earning high school leavers. The stark reality is that this situation is much worse for those from working-class backgrounds, especially women and ethnic minorities, who consistently get lower returns for their investment in higher education.[32]

5

Winners and Losers

THIS CHAPTER ASKS who wins and who loses in the distribution of credentials, jobs, and wages. Orthodox theorists argue that human capital is the most important form of capital in modern economies, so by investing in education individuals can earn the returns on their rising productivity.[1] This led to the view that knowledge workers would be the key beneficiaries of today's economy, as they would supersede traditional capitalists as wealth creators.

Human capital investment was also seen to address arbitrary inequalities in education, employment, and income. It is assumed that market competition has become more meritocratic because in order to ensure recruitment of workers with the highest productive potential, managers are required to appoint on merit rather than class background, gender, or race.[2] For Gary Becker, who was wedded to explanations of human action that were determined by IQ and sociobiology (especially the genetic elements to behavior), the links between education and labor market fortunes were clear. Individuals could invest in the development of their human capital and receive their rewards based on merit in the labor market.

In the previous chapter we raised the question of how best to explain the differences in returns to education, particularly for the top-decile wage earners. Here we present evidence of who have been the real winners and losers in Becker's "age of human capital." We will show how rates of return reflect social inequalities of class, gender, and ethnicity. This analysis challenges three key tenets of orthodox theory, first, the contention that human capital has become the most important source of capital as industries become more knowledge intensive and a greater share of the profits goes to high-skilled workers. The reality is that productivity capture far exceeds labor compensation over time. Whereas in orthodox theory, incomes are assumed to reflect

The Death of Human Capital? Phillip Brown, Hugh Lauder, and Sin Yi Cheung, Oxford University Press (2020).
© Oxford University Press. DOI: 10.1093/oso/9780190644307.001.0001

productive contribution—wages rise in harmony with improvements in productivity—the reality is most of the benefits of increasing productivity are captured by shareholders and senior executives.[3]

Second, orthodox theory teaches that wages reflect individual productivity linked to human capital investment. However, the picture we witness is one of a winner-takes-all concentration of higher earners at the top of the income distribution. A third tenet of orthodox theory is that the distribution of opportunities and rewards becomes more meritocratic over time. In other words, any differences between winners and losers should reflect differences in human capital investment, ability, and performance: people get what they deserve. However, in the past forty years the United States has been characterized by persistent and unmerited inequalities.

Productivity Gains: Winners and Losers

When we look at who is winning and who losing it is clear that until 1973, orthodox theorists had a plausible case in thinking that income would rise as workers' productivity increased. But after 1973 there is increasing divergence between productivity and wage growth. Despite a steep rise of 74 percent in productivity, hourly compensation (Figure 5.1) went up by only about 8 percent.

These trends are not unique to the United States. A similar picture emerges from Britain, although it has not achieved the same levels of productivity growth.[4] While the link between productivity and earning has been broken, the proportion of the workforce gaining higher levels of educational qualification has risen dramatically. This is certainly not a scenario orthodox theorists would predict. The question is: Who gained? Researchers at the Economic Policy Institute (EPI) in Washington show that since the late 1970s the top 5 percent of earners were the clear winners, with a 41 percent increase in real wages, compared to only 6 percent of the average median wage worker. Those in the bottom 10 percent of wage distribution actually see a decrease in real wages by 5 percent (see Figure 5.2).

This evidence is consistent with the work of political economists who have charted the increasing polarization of income, particularly Thomas Piketty.[5] Based on historical data, he argued that, under normal conditions, the returns to capital always outstrip those of wage earners, resulting in a polarization in income between those at the top of the income and wealth parade and ordinary workers. This is because the capitalist class has found ways to change the rules of the game, including the relationship between education and income.

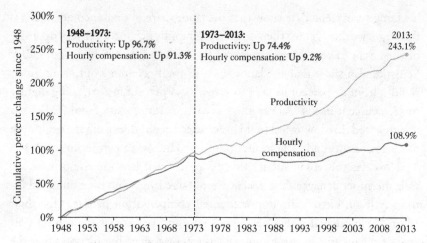

FIGURE 5.1 Productivity and reward in the United States, 1948–2013.

Source: EPI analysis of Bureau of Labor Statistics and Bureau of Economic Analysis data. *Raising America's Pay Economic Policy Institute. Why It's Our Central Economic Policy Challenge*, Josh Bivens, Elise Gould, Lawrence Mishel, and Heidi Shierholz (Washington D.C.: Economic Policy Institute) June 4, 2014. Figure A.[6]

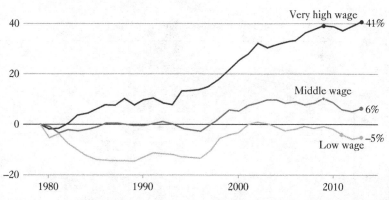

FIGURE 5.2 Cumulative change in real hourly wages of all workers, by wage percentile, 1979–2013.

Note: Low wage is 10th percentile; middle wage is 50th percentile; very high wage is 95th percentile.

Source: EPI analysis of Current Population Survey Outgoing Rotation Group microdata. *Why America's Workers Need Faster Wage Growth – And What We can Do About It* (Washington, D.C.: Economic Policy Institute, 2014). Figure F.[7]

Long-term trend data show that the labor share of total income, which is the wages workers get for their output, has rapidly declined, the very opposite of what Schultz and others expected.[8] Figures from the US Bureau of Labor Statistics also show that the labor share of total economic output declined rapidly, from 66 percent in 1947 to as low as 56 percent in 2011, rising slightly to 58.4 percent in 2016.[9] Even the International Monetary Fund (IMF) has documented this downward trend in advanced economies from the beginning of the 1980s at round 54 percent, declining to below 40 percent in 2008–9.[10]

How has this come about? Piketty argues that it is the rise of what he calls the supermanager, "top executives of large firms who have obtained extremely high, historically unprecedented compensation packages for their labor."[11] He calculates that between 60 and 70 percent of the top 0.1 percent of the income hierarchy consists of top managers. But he notes that the phenomenon of the supermanager is largely confined to the United States, Britain, Canada, and Australia. When income inequality in these countries is compared to that in continental Europe and Japan, his argument is clear. While the top percentile in these countries has increased their share, it is only by a relatively small percentage compared to the English-speaking countries (Figure 5.3).[12] Nevertheless the reemergence of the superrich is a global phenomenon. The wealth of the richest 1 percent of people in the world amounts

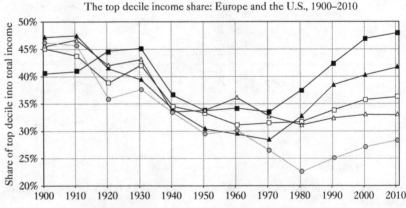

FIGURE 5.3 Income inequalities in five Western economies, 1900–2010.
Source: Thomas Piketty, *Capital in the Twenty-First Century* (Cambridge, MA: Harvard University Press, 2014), Figure 9.7.

to \$110 trillion; that's sixty-five times the total wealth of the bottom half of the world's population.[13]

The proposition that there are a few top talent or supermanagers whose productivity is far superior to any other worker is dubious; therefore country comparisons are important. It may be that these figures reflect the self-serving ideology of the supermanager: if top managers have the highest marginal productivity compared to everyone else, the disproportionally high returns rewarded to them are legitimized. This reflects, at one level, a form of extreme individualism coupled with a kind of cartoonish superhero mentality. Piketty refers to the "illusion of marginal productivity" as it is almost impossible to calculate the marginal productivity of those whose jobs are unique.[14] We can give an estimate of the marginal product that would be gained by adding an extra worker to a production line but not for work involving a complex hierarchy of decision-making.

Partly this is because new technologies permit market players to emerge without requiring huge initial start-up costs. With relatively small numbers of employees they can build hugely profitable businesses, relative to setting up factories. Obvious examples in the high-tech sector are Bill Gates (Microsoft), Mark Zuckerberg (Facebook), and Jack Ma (Alibaba), but another extraordinary example relates to Apple Corporation, cofounded by Steve Jobs. Indonesia and Thailand's combined market capitalization of all listed firms was \$780 billion in 2012, close to Apple's market capitalization of \$765 billion in 2015, with a full-time equivalent workforce of just ninety-three thousand. It is difficult to imagine that such figures reflect differences in individual marginal productivity.[15]

Piketty suggests that the notion of the greater marginal productivity of the rich "comes close to a pure ideological construct on the basis of which a justification for higher status can be elaborated."[16] To this can be added the explicit ideology of "talent," which McKinsey and other consultancy companies have argued marks out the talented few capable of running global corporations.[17] The upshot of these arguments is that it is far more likely that national institutions and political cultures matter in determining the wages of occupational elites rather than their contribution to productivity.[18]

Others have been more trenchant about the strategies by which the superrich add to their fortunes. James Galbraith argues that it involves the predatory looting of corporate and public wealth. Joseph Stiglitz suggests that the 2008 financial crisis revealed that "it was *not* contribution to society that determined relative pay, but something else: bankers received large rewards, though their contribution to society—and even to their firms—had been *negative.* The wealth given to the elites and to the bankers seemed to arise out of their ability and willingness to take advantage of others."[19]

There is yet another sting in the tail. It could be argued that the rise of the superrich will lead them to invest their profits in business innovation, thereby creating more jobs. But as Jose Gabriel Palmer has shown, entrepreneurs and supermanagers in the United States have reaped the benefits of their workers' productivity while failing to invest the surplus in their businesses. The same analysis can be applied to the United Kingdom. In both cases managers have simply pocketed the profits.[20]

In short, orthodox theory is conceptually blind to inequalities in power that shape both the market rules of the game and the relative chances of individuals winning or losing. The increasing concentration of market power in the hands of elites is central to understanding the great reversal in the fortunes of human capital theory we will describe. The previous analysis also points to significant social class inequalities, which enables the winners to capture most of the benefits from productivity growth and to translate this into a massive advantage for their children.

Economic globalization has enabled the superrich to add to their wealth and has translated into privilege in education. In turn, this has meant reduced opportunities for those without the financial means to access opportunities to enter private schooling and elite universities.[21] This has intensified the competition for credentials within national systems, spurred on by secretaries and ministers of education who hold out the illusion of well-paid, high-quality jobs, if only students work hard enough.

Mounting evidence shows that access to prestigious universities is by no means equal. Vikki Boliver found compelling evidence of unfair access to research-intensive universities in the United Kingdom, where students from lower social class and ethnic minority backgrounds were less likely to apply or receive an offer.[22] In the United States, Jennie Brand and Yu Xie found evidence of negative selection, whereby those who are least likely to attend college benefit most if they do.[23] Moreover the opportunity cost of noncompletion of college is disproportionately higher for working-class students.[24] Florencia Torche finds a strong intergenerational association among those with lower attainment. This relationship between class and attainment weakens for those with a bachelor's degree but reemerges among those with advanced degrees.[25]

In the United States it has been conventional wisdom that inequalities in education relate to people of color, that color is a proxy for class.[26] But the two are interrelated. In the most comprehensive survey of who wins and loses in American education and why, Greg Duncan, Richard Murnane, and their colleagues examined the processes that have overturned conventional wisdom as the education–labor market relationship is fundamentally changing.[27] What did they find? First, as incomes in society polarize, segregation between schools widens. It was once the case, as John Dewey noted, that schools were one of the few places where rich and poor met. Now that is increasingly unlikely. Residential segregation is reflected in segregation within schools, highlighting considerable overlap between race and social class.[28] At the same time, inequalities in income determine the resources that parents can devote to their children's education. Duncan and Murnane's study shows that investments in books, recreation activities, and childcare rise dramatically with income.

For those who experience poverty, the problem for children is exacerbated by unstable household employment, which can affect school performance in part because children in poor families are more likely to move from one area to another. Changing schools frequently has been shown to have a detrimental impact on educational progress.[29] There is little doubt that high levels of poverty and highly insecure employment do not encourage educational achievement for those at the bottom of the labor market. Orthodox theorists would respond to such dire circumstances by calling for educational reform. This is something we agree on, but even with more credentials the social distance to travel in order to achieve social mobility has increased, and it may do little to alleviate the plight of those who are losing out.

Losing Out

Today we frequently hear "We are the 99 percent," as distinct from the 1 percent of clear winners in terms of income and wealth. But if the rest of the workforce is losing out, it is those most disadvantaged in education and the job market who are the biggest losers. Despite all the talk about the rise of mass higher education, it's worth remembering that 35 percent of Americans between the ages of twenty-four and twenty-nine have a high school diploma or less, and another 30.8 percent have some college but not a bachelor's degree or higher (34.2 percent have at least a bachelor's degree).[30] The less qualified are more likely to be unemployed. For example, the unemployment rate for high school graduates not enrolled in additional study increased from 15.9 percent in 2007 to a peak of 28.1 percent in 2010, following the Great Recession, but has since declined to 17.9 percent in 2016. Young college graduates between the ages of twenty-one and twenty-four have fared better, as the unemployment rate peaked at 9.9 percent in 2011 and dropped to 5.6 percent in 2016.[31]

While educational qualifications do not offer an insurance policy against unemployment, it is the case that average unemployment rates internationally are lower for those with a bachelor's degree compared to those with a high school education.[32] Therefore, according to orthodox theory, the logical solution is to give the losers access to marketable skills by extending educational opportunities. But those losing out in today's economy are not only paying an educational penalty, they are also paying the price for changes in the job market.

Figures on the relationship between education and unemployment tell us nothing about the kinds of jobs people with a high school diploma or a bachelor's degree are entering. Economic growth may well increase the number of jobs available, but the key questions are: What kinds of jobs are people with different levels of qualification getting, and how much they are earning for what they contribute?[33] While those with higher levels of credentials are, on average, less likely to be unemployed, there is extensive evidence of underemployment.[34] Here a distinction can be drawn between hours-based underemployment (say, when someone is in involuntary part-time employment because they cannot find a full-time job) and skills-based or education-based underemployment (when employees are better qualified and skilled than their jobs require, such as someone with a bachelor's degree in law training to be a barista rather than a barrister).

The evidence suggests that in many countries, including the United States and Britain, significant proportions of college graduates are doing subgraduate work. Jaison Abel and Richard Deitz found that 44 percent of college graduates between the ages of twenty-two and twenty-seven who entered the American labor market between 2011 and 2014 were underemployed.[35] These findings, they suggest, are consistent with the thesis that there has been a reversal in the demand for cognitive skills since 2000.[36] They also found significant differences in relation to gender and ethnicity, consistent with our analysis, outlined later. There were more women (55 percent) underemployed than men (44 percent). Black and American Indian graduates were 17 percent more likely to be working in a non-graduate job than whites, and Hispanics are also overrepresented among the underemployed, with 31 percent more likely than non-Hispanics to be working in low-skilled service jobs. In commenting on this research, Richard Vedder pointed out that these findings are underestimates since they fail to consider the 40 percent of students who enroll in college but never graduate.[37] In Britain the Office for National Statistics reports that underemployment among graduates rose from 37 percent in 2001 to 47 percent in June 2013.[38]

In citing these statistics, we should not lose sight of what underemployment means for those experiencing it. Kody Steffy has talked to both those who considered themselves voluntarily underemployed, who tended to be middle class, and those who thought of themselves as involuntarily underemployed. Here is what some of the involuntarily underemployed told him.[39]

> A telecommunications male graduate now working as a line cook: "I must have sent over 100 applications. . . . I kid you not, I was sending applications out to everybody and my main problem was they all wanted experience."
>
> A working-class female East Asian languages and cultures major, after having applied for many jobs, said of her present job as an administrative assistant, "Its just unfulfilling. . . . I email people. Like literally a high school student could do my job. Sometimes I shred paper for 30 minutes. And I'm just like, 'oh man . . .'. I actually liked waitressing more. . . . I think I used more brain power as a server."
>
> A working-class male graduate now working as a barista: "I mean I'm not really happy where I am. . . . I have a lot of anxiety because of more or less the job." When asked if he was looking for another job, he replied, "Yes I'm looking here and there. I don't know I kind of get, not really depressed, its just kind of like, I just feel hopeless to even look any more for jobs."
>
> A triple major in Spanish, sociology, and criminal justice (with a 4.0 GPA) working in a cafeteria felt she had to lie about her degree: "Sometimes, I especially at the beginning I would just lie, say, "Yeah I'm a student." And just pretend I didn't graduate. And my friends would be like, 'You graduated from college, you should be proud of that!' And I'm like, 'But I'm not.' I don't know."

What comes across in these snippets and from Steffy's study is the waste of talent that these young people represent. But that wastage extends right down the labor market. As a result, those at the bottom are losing out because of bumping down. The top squeezes out the middle, and the middle, those beneath them. Giving those at the bottom more skills may help an individual to compete, but it does nothing to resolve the basic problem: the scarcity of decent job opportunities, not a lack of skills. Human capital policies have inadvertently imposed additional barriers to employment and the occupational mobility prospects of those with fewer credentials at the wrong end of the labor market.

Bumping down makes it difficult for people with few qualifications to find meaningful employment, even though they may be perfectly capable of doing the job in question. And without high-quality work to do, they can't proving themselves on the job. Employers prefer to hire graduates rather than nongraduates for lower-wage work, according to the screening hypothesis.[40] This hypothesis suggests that employers use credentials not as an indication of potential productivity, as human capital theorists assume, but as a way of identifying those that are likely to be reliable, punctual, and well disciplined.[41]

This reasoning seems plausible because there is a limit to how much productivity improvement there can be in many low-wage jobs: how many beers can be poured in an hour? To this we can add another dimension when hiring for low-paid service work, which is that it often requires emotional labor.[42] Graduates are desirable for this low-paid work because higher education socializes students into expressing themselves in ways that involve the public display of interpersonal skills in seminars and student presentations.

The combination of perceived reliability and emotional labor may lie at the heart of these recruitment decisions, but it is also the case that employers are prepared to pay a small premium for graduate workers when they undertake the same jobs as nongraduates.[43] It may also be the case that employers believe graduates want flexible hours or to move on more quickly, seeking better jobs, thereby giving employers even greater flexibility.

When those with few formal qualifications and even those with some college education but without a bachelor's degree are losing out because of negative signaling in the job market, Lester Thurow calls this situation "statistical discrimination." This "occurs whenever an individual is judged on the basis of the average characteristics of the group, or groups, to which he or she belongs rather than upon his or her own personal characteristics." It is not that nongraduate job applicants are not up to the job, but they are rejected by virtue of being a nongraduate or unqualified.[44] In the 1970s Ivar Berg argued that the increasing importance attached to credentials in hiring decisions was nothing less than a "great training robbery," consigning a large number of people with few formal qualifications to "a social limbo defined by low-skilled, no-opportunity jobs in the 'peripheral labor market.' "[45] Therefore, as Ewart Keep and Ken Mayhew write, "given the current social-class composition of higher education entry, there are significant risks that yet greater expansion, unless it is attended by a fundamental redistribution of access opportunities, will lead to further declines in social mobility."[46]

When we examine the real world rather than the idealized account given by orthodox theorists, we find that the polarization of income and wealth has had a profound impact on individual life-chances. This contradicts the proposition that differences between winners and losers reflect differences in human capital investment, ability, and performance. But to what extent does it challenge the view that gender and racial background are less important in an "age of human capital"? This is an important part of our analysis, as many women and men from different racial, ethnic, and social class backgrounds have invested in education to make a better life. Do they benefit from the same returns in the labor market?

The Rise of Women?

Over the past two decades, women have made significant gains in educational attainment. The gender gap in access to college education has virtually closed and even reversed, with women outperforming their male counterparts.[47] As can be seen in Figure 5.4, in 1970 just over 8 percent of women obtained a four-year college education (including master's and PhD degrees), compared to 13.3 percent of men. In 2010 women surpassed men, with 30 percent

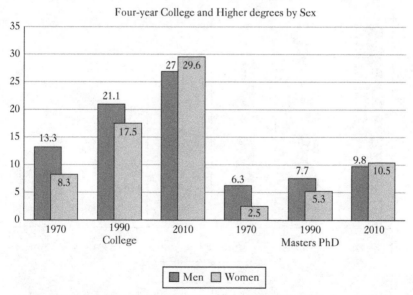

Four-year College and Higher degrees by Sex

FIGURE 5.4 Percentage obtaining four-year college and higher (Masters PhD) degrees by sex in 1970, 1990, and 2010.

Source: IPUMS USA US Census 1970; 1990 1% metro sample; ACS 2010 (weighted), ages 18–64.

obtaining four or more years of college education compared to 27 percent of men. During this period women made even more remarkable progress in gaining graduate qualifications. In 1990 the proportion of women obtaining a master's or PhD degree doubled that of 1970, from 2.5 to 5.3 percent. In 2010 this rate doubled again to 10.5 percent, higher than the rate for men. In sum, by 2010 women had outperformed men in achieving both undergraduate and graduate degrees.

At the same time, female labor market participation also increased during the forty-year period. In 1970 fewer than 45 percent of women were in employment; by 2010 that figure had risen to 63 percent. Female inactivity rate had also fallen sharply, from 53 percent in 1970 to only 31 percent in 2010. The trend in male labor market participation and economic inactivity is reversed. The proportion of employed men dropped to 69 percent in 2010 from 81 percent in 1970, and the corresponding inactivity rate rose to 23 percent from 16 percent.

Figure 5.5 shows that women are now increasingly just as likely as men to be active in the labor market. If human capital, as Becker argues, is the most important of all forms of capital, we should expect to see a greater share of

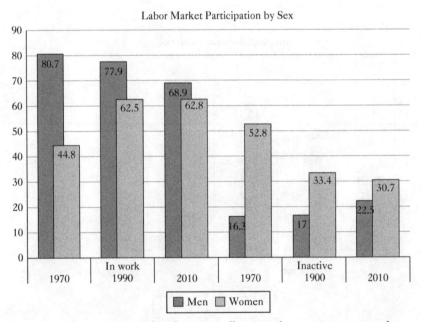

Labor Market Participation by Sex

FIGURE 5.5 Percentage in work and economically inactive by sex in 1970, 1990, and 2010. Source: IPUMS USA US Census 1970; 1990 1% metro sample; ACS 2010 (weighted), ages 18–64.

this human capital investment in the form of wage compensation for both women and men. However, the evidence is pointing in the opposite direction. Women's success in higher education has not been mirrored by rates of return similar to those enjoyed by men. Instead women with the same qualification earn markedly less.

Figure 5.6 compares the hourly earnings of male and female college graduates and high school leavers. It is immediately clear that women college graduates earned significantly less than men even when we take into account "work intensity," dividing their annual labor income by the number of hours worked and the number of weeks per year in employment. Women with a college degree in the top decile earned $48 (2009 USD) per hour in 1970 while their male counterparts earned $64, making the gross hourly gender pay gap 25 percent. This gap widened to 35 percent in 1990 for the top-decile graduate earners and was at 32 percent in 2010. A similar pattern can be seen for high school leavers. Top-decile female high school leavers earned 30 percent less than men, at just under $26 per hour in 1970, compared to just over $37 for their male counterparts. This gap too remains persistent at 29 percent in 1990 through to 2010 at 25 percent.

To a large extent, British data support the US pattern (Figures 5.7 and 5.8) for returns to education by gender. We should note that, as in the United States, older British knowledge workers are not rewarded more because of increased labor market experience, so that even older male degree holders do not earn more than their peers in the forty-to–forty-nine age group. Again the exception is the top 10 percent of degree holders. The older graduates in both countries are a more positively selected group, as they will have obtained their degrees before higher education expansion, when a much lower proportion of the population went to university.

Women's earnings on average flatten out even sooner in their thirties. But it is doubtful whether this can be explained by employment interruptions, which is the typical orthodox economist's hypothesis, as women in Britain on average have their first child at age thirty-five. However, the issue of potential pregnancy does appear to influence employers' recruitment strategies, which may then be related to wages: an unlawful prejudice.[48] In these figures the British designation A-Level is the equivalent of the top-decile US "High School High" graduates.

The data on gender differences in wages in the United States and Britain show that after decades of struggle for equal wages this gap is still huge at all educational levels.

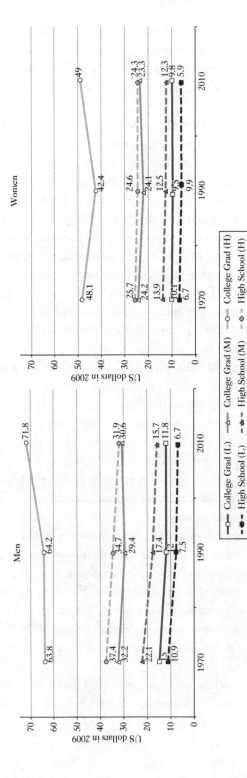

FIGURE 5.6 Hourly earnings (in 2009 USD) for US high school and four-year college male and female graduates, 1970, 1990, and 2010.

Source: IPUMS USA US Census 1970; 1990 1% metro sample; ACS 2010 (weighted), ages 18–64. Key: (L) = bottom decile (10%), (M) = median (50%), (H) = top decile (90%).

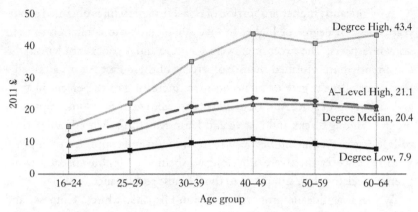

FIGURE 5.7 UK male A-level and degree graduates' hourly earnings (in 2011£), 2009–11.
Source: Quarterly Labour Force Survey 2009–11 pooled samples weighted by piwt10 and CPI adjusted to 2011£.
Key: Degree and A-Level High = 90th percentile; Degree Low = 10th percentile.

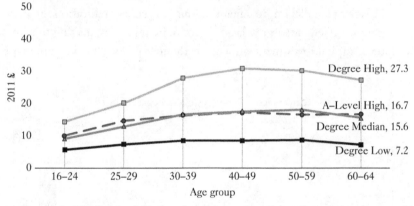

FIGURE 5.8 UK female A-level and degree graduates' hourly earnings (in 2011£), 2009–11.
Source: Quarterly Labour Force Survey 2009–11 pooled samples weighted by piwt10 and CPI adjusted to 2011£.
Key: Degree and A-Level High = 90th percentile; Degree Low = 10th percentile.

Race and Human Capital Investment

Do we see higher wage returns in line with improved productivity for racial minorities who invested in education? Despite rapid expansion in postsecondary education (Figure 5.4), racial and ethnic minorities are still less likely than whites to attain a college education. Rapid expansion in higher education since the late 1980s did not benefit all racial groups equally.

A significantly higher proportion of non-Hispanic whites obtained a four-year college or degree or higher in 1970, 1990, and 2010 compared to their nonwhite peers. The exceptions were Chinese and Japanese students, who consistently outperformed them: 20 percent of these East Asians attained a four-year college degree or higher in 1970, increasing to 38 percent in 1990 and 54 percent in 2010. At the bottom of the scale we witness some impressive progress among blacks and Native and Latin Americans, who doubled their college degree attainment between 1970 and 1990 and continued to improve in 2010. However, they were still a long way behind their non-Hispanic white peers, especially when compared to the Chinese and Japanese.

While a significant proportion of non-Hispanic whites, Chinese, and Japanese achieved a four-year college education (Figure 5.9), much of the expansion in postsecondary education has been in the community college sector, where racial minorities are overrepresented. Our data show that between 26 and 28 percent of black and Native American students had some to three years of college education in 1990, rising to 35 and 36 percent in 2010.

The lack of parallel improvement in four-year college education for all racial groups is likely due to the lack of economic resources, making this kind of human capital investment difficult in the first place. Not only are major

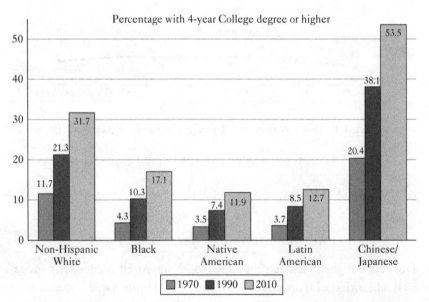

FIGURE 5.9 Percentage obtaining US Four-year college degrees or higher degrees by race in 1970, 1990, and 2010.

Source: IPUMS USA US Census 1970; 1990 1% metro sample; ACS 2010 (weighted), ages 18–64.

differences in academic performance linked to differences in expenditure in school districts in the United States, but even with the same credentials African Americans and Hispanics lose out. Even more striking, Chinese and Japanese, the best performers in college education, fare worse than non-Hispanic whites in graduate unemployment. It seems that they need more and better education just to be on a level playing field with white peers. So how easy is it for them to get a job in the first place, and what are the returns to their investment in a college education?

Before higher education expansion, having a college degree was almost a golden ticket to employment. As seen in Figure 5.10, there was almost full employment for college graduates in 1990, with around 1.5 percent of non-Hispanic whites, blacks, and Native Americans being out of work. Unemployment rates were slightly higher, at 2 percent, for Chinese and Japanese and nearly 3 percent for Latin Americans. Economic downturns do not always affect everyone equally; some escape the misfortune of being laid off, while others face unemployment. In 1990 graduate unemployment remained low for non-Hispanic whites, Chinese and Japanese, and Latin Americans, but the rates doubled for blacks and tripled for Native American college graduates.

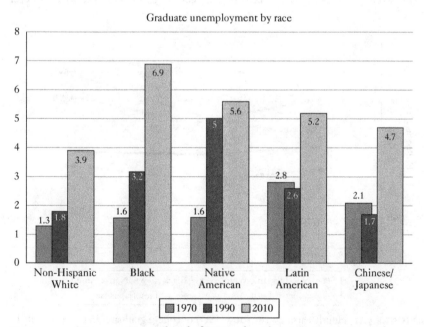

FIGURE 5.10 Percentage unemployed of US Graduate by race in 1970, 1990, and 2010.

By 2010 graduate unemployment had risen drastically for all groups, even for non-Hispanic whites and Chinese and Japanese. But the real losers were black college graduates and their Native and Latin American peers. Perhaps this should come as little surprise since rapid expansion in higher education had increased the supply of graduate labor. As discussed in the chapter 4, the proportion of college graduates in the labor force had risen sharply, from just 13 percent in 1970 to 34 percent in 2010. Every third worker in the labor force had a college degree in 2010. Competition for jobs had never been more intense. Technological advances clearly had not been able to absorb all the knowledge workers the higher education system produced.

Unequal Labor Market Returns by Race

A key message emerges from Figure 5.11, even among the top 10th earning decile, there is racial inequality in the returns to education. The winners appear to be Chinese and Japanese college graduates, whose earnings have the sharpest increase over time, when wage stagnation is the norm for most. In 2010 their earnings even surpassed those of the non-Hispanic whites. Interestingly, the race-wage gap was much larger in 1970 than in 2010. Although they are still very much the worst off, Native Americans have caught up by narrowing the wage gap in 2010. This mixed picture echoes earlier observations in Peter

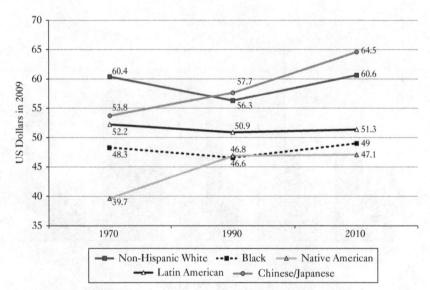

FIGURE 5.11 Hourly earnings (in 2009 USD) of college graduates in the top decile by race in 1970, 1990, and 2010.

Blau and Otis Duncan's classic sociological study of social stratification and inequalities in life chances: significant inequalities remain, particularly among black graduates.[49]

Immediately apparent from Figure 5.12 is that for the median college graduates, investment in education produces the opposite of what Blau and Duncan expected. Not only have they made far less than high school leavers in the top decile, but the racial gap in earnings is profound and has increased over time. Non-Hispanic whites and Chinese and Japanese consistently get more for their qualifications than blacks and other racial minority graduates.

When disaggregating further by gender and race, the real winners are the top 10 percent of college male graduates. It is here we can see the largest racial earnings gaps. Chinese and Japanese male graduates enjoyed income growth from 1970 to 2010, despite a lower starting point compared to non-Hispanic white male graduates, who also experienced steady income growth throughout the forty-year period. Black, Native American, and Latin American male graduates, even in the top 10 percent group, experienced

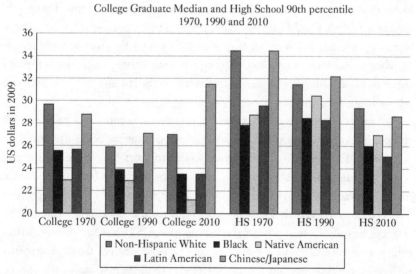

FIGURE 5.12 Hourly earnings (in 2009 USD), median college graduates and 90th percentile high school leavers.

Source: IPUMS USA US Census 1970; 1990 1% metro sample; ACS 2010 (weighted), ages 18–64.

Key: HS = High School

either only very modest (Native American) or no growth at all. For women, Chinese and Japanese graduates did best, far exceeding non-Hispanic white female graduates. Surprisingly the pattern for the top 10 percent of graduate women for all other racial groups is one of stagnation, mirroring that of their peers at the bottom 10 percent, placing them alongside the "losers" in the game of winner-takes-all.

Our evidence directly challenges the alleged linear relationship between productivity and labor income. Women and racial minorities' invested human capital yields far lower returns in the labor market, where non-Hispanic white men are the consistent winners. This picture of winners and losers means that competition for the limited number of desirable knowledge jobs is ever more intense.

In the United Kingdom the adverse effects of the 2008 financial crisis have affected ethnic minority university leavers much more severely compared to whites. Black and Asian graduates have fallen further behind in the job market over time. A study conducted by the Higher Education Funding Council for England shows the employment rates six months after graduation for all minority ethnic groups are substantively lower compared to their white peers.[50] By forty months after graduation, employment rates had improved for all groups except the Chinese graduates, who suffered a 2.8 percent decrease. Chinese, Indian, and Pakistani first-degree holders in 2008–9 all had lower professional employment rates six months after graduation. This gap is largest for black Caribbean students, whose professional employment rates were 9.3 percent lower than white graduates'. The situation worsened in 2010–11, when black African graduates had significantly lower professional employment rates, at only 65.9 percent, compared to Indian and white graduates, who achieved 78.7 percent.[51]

Research also shows graduate unemployment has gone back to pre-2008 recession levels and more university leavers are now working part time or engaged in further study. A study on school-to-work transition comparing university choices and social class and ethnic background found that ethnic minority graduates are between 5 and 15 percent less likely than their white peers to be employed six months after graduation, and many are unlikely to reach their full earnings potential even years after.[52] This study also finds that ethnic minority students were less likely to hold degrees from prestigious universities and on average have lower grades than their white counterparts. Many of them come from lower social class backgrounds and may not have access to the same level of financial and social resources that white students have. Importantly, three and a half years after graduation the ethnic earnings gap worsened especially for women. This may suggest that ethnic minority graduates are less successful in career progression compared to white British peers.

Conclusion

In asking the question who wins and who loses and why in the competition for credentials and income, we have shown that orthodox theory cannot address the key trends in education and the labor market and how they are structured. The winners are using their market power to their advantage, making it very difficult for others, including many of those from middle- and working-class backgrounds, to compete through education (human capital investment). We will offer a revisionist history of human capital development as a way of understanding the changing relationship between education, jobs, and rewards. These changes, at least in part, reflect power relations and the relative ability of different social groups to mobilize resources to win. Writing of the former Soviet Union, Daniel Bell described it as an "unjust meritocracy," what Thomas Jefferson called an "artificial aristocracy."[53] The same could now be said of many Western countries.

The decades between 1970 and 2010 are crucially important in the history of race and gender equality in the United States, for that period witnessed major civil rights victories and legislative attempts to outlaw discrimination. Against this background was also a period of rapid expansion and investment in higher education nationally and individually. Much of this was premised on the belief that technological changes demand a more knowledge-intensive workforce and that investment in education will enhance productivity and yield higher economic returns. However, our findings provide compelling evidence that investment in education does not pay equally, certainly not for all.

Our data show that only a minority of top earners are the winners and that the majority are losers in the race to the top. Contrary to orthodox theory's prediction of universal uniform returns to the same amount of investment, spending more years in college has not yielded proportional economic returns for the majority in the labor market. This is particularly the case for women and racial minorities. Racial minority students who made it through to postsecondary education are predominantly concentrated in two-year community colleges, often at a higher cost as many of these colleges are privately run. While this may not stop the parents of racial minorities from investing in their children's education, the returns to their investment are far less than what they might expect compared to the returns enjoyed by whites.

The middle groups—the majority of the qualified losers—faced with rising costs of investment, coupled with declining or stagnating returns, also confront being priced out of the competition when routes to any decent jobs have become heavily congested. Despite this, people are having to play for bigger stakes as those at the top are claiming most of the benefits of productivity, and the costs of losing have increased as the relationship between learning and earning has fundamentally changed. The IMF has acknowledged that wages have not caught up with productivity in many economies, leading to a decline of labor share of national income.[54]

Orthodox theorists have argued that top income earners have special skills that mark them out for such high rewards. But this seems implausible given Piketty's critique of the marginal productivity of supermanagers. We appear to be observing the outcomes of social class, gender, and ethnic forms of dominance. These forms of dominance are subject to change, and we have noted some improvement in the opportunities for women and some ethnic groups, but it is also clear that educational achievement does not translate into equal labor market opportunities. The next chapter explains why.

6

The Mirage of Opportunity

OUR EXPLORATION INTO the failures of orthodox theory needs to look beyond earnings data to understand the changing context of education and the job market. The relationship between education and paid work has never been straightforward. But there is no doubt that the human capital mantra of "learning equals earning" has fueled the expansion of higher education around the world.[1] Some of this growth has had a profound impact on people's lives, but its implications for individuals, families, neighborhoods, and societies depends on the ever-changing relationship between education and the job market.

Today the mismatch between supply and demand is not temporary but endemic. Advocating educational expansion without commensurate job opportunities results in increasingly wasteful competition. The point here is not that a college or university education is of little value, as it may be highly valued by students and have wider societal value, but unless the occupational structure can accommodate increasing numbers of better educated and more highly skilled workers, the expansion of education offers little more than a mirage of opportunity as defined by orthodox theory.

The view that learning equals earning has perpetuated a mirage that has exposed many job seekers and workers to the full force of market competition, stripped to little more than what they can earn from their labor, as welfare safety nets are threadbare, offering people little choice other than to invest in education as a route to economic salvation.[2] Without a labor market that can provide enough good jobs, the whole edifice of market economies, along with its supporting narrative encapsulated in the American Dream, is under threat. Without good jobs, people are unable to pay their way in the world and have little prospect of maintaining their living standard, let alone progressing to something better.[3]

The Death of Human Capital? Phillip Brown, Hugh Lauder, and Sin Yi Cheung, Oxford University Press (2020).
© Oxford University Press. DOI: 10.1093/oso/9780190644307.001.0001

This chapter shows how orthodox theory has contributed to the destruction of the neoliberal opportunity bargain and has become part of the problem rather than a policy solution. Beyond stagnant, if not declining incomes, there are three other symptoms, namely, credential inflation, elite closure, and a narrowing of academic purpose to "education for employability." Credential inflation is at the heart of a human capital currency crisis given a decline in the exchange value of credentials. The goal posts move with almost every graduation ceremony, and the rules of the game change as employers look beyond credentials in making their hiring decisions. Many people are being priced out of the market not because they are stupid or lack ambition but because they do not have the resources to stay in an extended competition; at the same time, elites are using their social advantage to win a competitive advantage by monopolizing elite institutions and accessing international networks.

Equally, when human capital assumptions are so imbued in public policy, the typical response to the evidence presented in previous chapters is to call for students, teachers, and educational administrators to double their efforts to raise educational standards and for policymakers to reform education and training systems rather than to challenge the assumptions on which orthodox theory rests. The wider the gap between learning and earning, the narrower the purpose of education becomes. All three symptoms—credential inflation, elite closure, and reducing education to employability—contribute to explaining why orthodox theory is not fit for purpose.

Credential Inflation: Devaluing Credentials as a Currency of Opportunity

In encouraging people to invest in themselves, human capital policies have fueled credential inflation rather than extended individual opportunity. These inflationary pressures diminish the value of individual and public investments when there is a significant mismatch between the requirements to do a job and the requirements to get a job. Credential inflation is akin to monetary inflation. When the supply of money is greater than the supply of goods and services, the result is an increase in the cost of those goods and services as sellers are able to secure higher prices. In other words, when sellers charge higher prices, buyers have to pay more, reducing the value of their wages. In the same way, if more people gain the qualifications previously required for technical, professional, or managerial jobs, and if the number of these jobs does not expand to meet this rise in supply of qualified people, the result will be inflation associated with a weakening in the exchange value of credentials on the job market.

Credential inflation therefore creates a mirage of opportunity in much the same way that financial inflation makes it seem as if people have got more money, when in fact their buying power is reduced because things cost more. It is a mirage because giving people greater access to education at all levels, reflected in rising levels of academic achievement, appears to create more opportunities for people to enter better jobs, but this holds true only if job entry requirements are held constant.[4]

In orthodox theory, the systematic forces leading to credential inflation are rarely considered because it is assumed that under normal market conditions there is a balance or equilibrium between supply and demand. Orthodox theorists argue that overqualification and underemployment are temporary issues, like graduate unemployment, because it takes time for people to respond to market signals, leading them to adjust their education and training investments in line with market demand. But this is to misunderstand the nature of labor markets. The belief that they return to a balance or equilibrium over time fails to take into account the way factors such as the polarization of earnings influence the labor market.

In *The Winner-Takes-All Society*, Robert Frank and Philip Cook describe how the glittering prizes held out to a few in high-profile occupations, including finance, fashion, and sport, result in wasteful competition for top vocational prizes, which attract large numbers of contestants. Many of these people could instead make a positive contribution in other areas of the economy, especially those characterized by labor shortages.[5] Likewise, in the maelstrom of the 2008 financial crisis Mervyn King, the governor of the Bank of England at the time, spoke out against the social and educational distortions caused by too many of Britain's most talented young people being lured into financial careers by the huge bonuses on offer at the time: "I do think it is rather unattractive that so many young people, when contemplating careers, look at the compensation packages available in the City and think that these dominate almost any other type of career."[6]

Although it is sometimes difficult to disentangle changes in job requirements resulting from increasing job complexity as opposed to changing requirements due to rising numbers of better qualified people, there is clear evidence of credential inflation reflected in high levels of underemployment, as previously noted.[7] This means that credentials as a currency of labor market opportunity are devalued as many high school and college graduates cannot buy into the kind of jobs that were previously associated with different levels of certification.[8] This reflects not only changes in labor supply, with a tripling of the numbers with a college education in the United States since 1970, but also the structure of labor demand (discussed in the final section of the book).[9]

Richard Vedder and his colleagues,[10] for instance, looked at six occupations that did not change significantly between 1970 and 2010; these included taxi drivers, sales clerks in the retail trade, firefighters, and bank tellers. They found that in 1970 only 1 percent of taxi drivers were college graduates, rising to 15 percent in 2010. For jobs in sales the figure was just under 5 percent in 1970 and increased to 25 percent.[11] Drawing on millions of job postings, Catherine Rampell found that in 2007, 12 percent of postings for dental laboratory technicians required a degree, but five years later this had increased to 30 percent of postings.[12] A report in the United Kingdom by the Institute for Labor Market Research on graduate incomes predicts that 34 percent of those in the lowest income decile will have tertiary qualifications.[13]

Social Congestion and the Red Queen Problem

In educational terms, these inflationary pressures lead to raising the bar of academic achievement, whether in respect to gaining access to highly ranked schools, colleges, or universities or getting hired in the labor market. Jobs that were previously open to people with a high school education now require a college degree. Randell Collins, who coined the term "credential inflation," observes how the increasing supply of credentials creates an inflationary spiral: "Students who want to get ahead are forced to go back to school for longer periods, to get advanced degrees and professional specializations. One can predict that the process will continue to repeat itself at a more advanced level too. If in the future everybody had a Ph.D., law degree, M.B.A., or the like, then these advanced degrees would be worth no more than a job in a fast food restaurant, and the competition would move on to still higher degrees."[14]

Where credential competition simply increases the requirements to stay in the game, individuals find themselves in the surreal world of the Red Queen's race. In *Through the Looking Glass and What Alice Found There*, Lewis Carroll describes Alice constantly running to keep up with the Red Queen but remaining on the same spot:

"Well, in our country," said Alice, still panting a little, "you'd generally get to somewhere else—if you run very fast for a long time, as we've been doing."

"A slow sort of country!" said the Queen. "Now, here, you see, it takes all the running you can do, to keep in the same place. If you want to get somewhere else, you must run at least twice as fast as that!"[15]

Running faster and longer becomes more expensive in time, effort, and money; it also changes the foundations of human capital investment. Orthodox theory assumes that people make an opportunity-cost assessment based on anticipated future earnings (learning equals earning). But in reality, much of today's expenditure is economically rational not in human capital terms but in terms of a positional logic. It is not simply a positive-sum investment but a defensive expenditure because failure to invest when others do reduces an individual's chance of finding a job compared to those investing in marketable skills.[16] This is a long way from the ideas of Becker and Schultz, as human capital investment is increasingly a response to the pressures of competition rather than a contribution to individual marginal productivity.[17]

This points to the fact that orthodox theory is based on the view that more competition is better because it raises standards and lowers prices. But competition operates very differently in different market circumstances.[18] Credential inflation is a symptom of social congestion resulting from a capacity problem involving too many people wanting to make the same educational or occupation journeys. In attempting to get ahead of the crowd it creates an opportunity trap, which is counterproductive for individuals, education, and the wider society.[19]

Therefore, when it comes to finding a job, people do not act alone, one at a time, as in a game of chess, because we are all in play at the same time.[20] Getting a college education or working harder for higher grades may have little impact on one's chances of getting ahead, unless one is better positioned than others, or there is an increasing number of good job openings. Indeed such actions can leave people worse off as the personal and financial costs of staying in the competition—investing in a higher degree—continue to mount as the sum of such individual acts do not improve the position of all individuals taken together. But people continue to invest not because they expect a commensurate rate of return but to stay in the game or to secure a positional advantage in the competition for jobs.[21]

Why the Best Jobs Remain Out of Reach

The mirage of opportunity not only results from people needing to meet higher entry requirements, but also from institutional changes in the rules of the game. When the scarcity value of a college education is under threat, social elites do not stand still; they double their efforts to maintain their distinction.[22] We are not suggesting that elites have undiluted power to rig human capital investments in their favor, but they are clearly able to manipulate currencies to their advantage. The mirage of opportunity reflects the way ranking tournaments, which determine who wins and loses in education, were previously organized as national competitions and have been increasingly subjected to the rigging behavior of social elites.[23] Ordinary families are being outclassed in the sense that elite families are best placed to meet the rising costs of a privileged education and to develop the cultural assets now associated with professional and managerial careers.

Entrance fees at private schools, colleges, and universities have risen steeply in the past thirty years. The tuition cost at private high schools in America has now reached the level of a college education; for instance, Salisbury School for boys in Connecticut costs a little over $49,000 for tuition and other fees and offers classes in Mandarin, robotics, and entrepreneurial studies.[24] The annual fees for a bachelor's degree at a private nonprofit four-year college in 2016–17 averaged $35,020, and 7 percent of those attending private colleges pay over $51,000. Although such fees are significantly higher than for public four-year institutions, the costs associated with going to a public four-year college or university have also increased to 3.1 times more than the costs in 1970, after adjusting for increases in the Consumer Price Index.[25]

Paul Campos calculates that if car prices in the United States over the same period rose as fast as tuition costs, the average new car would cost over $80,000.[26] He points out that enrollment in undergraduate, graduate, and professional programs has increased by almost 50 percent since 1995, resulting in $1.3 trillion in student loan debts, more than consumer debt on credit cards and auto loans before the 2020 global pandemic. Although bursaries, scholarships, and endowment funds help those from less affluent backgrounds meet the costs of higher education, the average student in the class of 2016 has $37,172 in student loan debt.[27]

In the United Kingdom the cost of private education has also exploded in recent decades, rising over two and a half times faster than the Consumer Price Index.[28] Middle-class families with children in private school confront average annual fees that are almost two-fifths of their average gross earnings, as fees have virtually doubled since 2003.[29] An analysis of the cost of private education found a dramatic change in who can now afford to send their children to such schools as salaries have failed to keep pace with rising fees: "The average doctor, accountant or professional is not the typical private-school parent—at least, not any longer."[30]

The introduction of a £9,000 annual tuition fee in English universities in 2012 left students with even higher individual debts than in America, averaging £44,500. By 2020 it is estimated that the government will be paying out £23 billion in cash and getting £3.2 billion in repayments. There are 4.6 million loans outstanding, and 1.9 million former students are not making any payments because they do not earn enough to trigger repayment.[31]

There are two more reasons why the best jobs may remain out of reach for many despite heavy investments in a college education. First, employers are using extended entry criteria, which is helping social elites to repackage their human capital investments to distance themselves from others. Second, educational performance is now judged on international league tables that render invisible students, colleges, and universities that fail to qualify as international centers of excellence.

Credentials and the Employable Self

Credentials as a currency of exchange now depend on the development of a wider personality package. This reflects changes in employer hiring practices, far removed from the original bureaucratic model of the role of credentials linking education to corporate employment. It involves more precise and codified ways of identifying talent because educational credentials on their own do not serve as a proxy for employability and productive performance.

Candidates need to present a winning personality commensurate with a competence profile that includes both hard currencies (including credentials, sporting achievements, music prizes, work experience) and soft currencies (including social confidence, interpersonal sensitivity, business awareness), packaged in a "narrative of employability."[32] In short, if the promise of human capital was that academic credentials would substitute certified expertise for social selection, it has failed, as many employers have made social selection an explicit part of their hiring criteria.

Inequalities in the everyday lives of candidates directly impact hiring decisions because employers look for demonstrable evidence of social competences, such as the confidence to effortlessly mingle with other candidates and hirers or to demonstrate what Pierre Bourdieu called "embodied cultural capital," including how a candidate looks, walks, talks, and thinks. This makes it more difficult for those who lack an appropriate cultural inheritance to hide behind certified technical expertise.[33]

It is therefore more difficult for people from disadvantaged backgrounds to demonstrate their employability as the classroom and lecture theater cease to be the dominant places of learning. This is not only because the period of learning has been extended into later life but also because it trespasses most of the institutional barriers between the family, education, work, and leisure. The boundaries between education and everyday life are collapsing. The economy of experience highlights the importance of capitalizing on extracurricular activities and social networks used to demonstrate the range of behavioral competences that organizations have benchmarked as indicative of managerial or professional employability. Even for those from more affluent backgrounds the economy of experience is no longer a passive consequence of living a privileged life or coming from a privileged background. It has to be worked at so that it can be packaged in a narrative of individual employability, often at the expense of intrinsic human experience.[34]

The economy of experience is global. International firms are looking for candidates who have exposed themselves to different cultural contexts or learned foreign languages. The nineteenth-century tour is back in fashion as it offers an additional way for elites to distinguish themselves in a world of mass higher education, although this may change in the aftermath of the Covid-19 global pandemic.

But as employers widen their recruitment criteria to include soft (social) as well as hard currencies of employability, any reference to class background, gender, ethnicity, or culture is typically discouraged in the hiring process because they are inadmissible as evidence of individual employability. All potential employees must be treated as equals until the inequalities in life experiences and opportunities are revealed in the form of individual (in)competence. But widening the currency of labor market exchange has enabled those from more privileged backgrounds to unleash a full panoply of capital assets, no longer limited to securing an advantage through the competition for credentials.

Lauren Rivera in her book *Pedigree* exposes the social class, ethnic, and gendered nature of recruitment by employers in the leading financial and legal corporations in New York.[35] Her insights on the way recruiters judge people according to class-based forms of presentation are consistent with Karen Ho's finding that in Wall Street hiring practices there are shared cultural experiences between occupational elites and those who attend the best schools, colleges, and universities.[36] C. Wright Mills asserts that it is difficult to avoid the simple conclusion that to access elite positions in public and corporate life, it greatly helps to "fit in" with those already at the top.[37] Is it because of their skill level or their social class privilege? These studies help to fill out the picture of why the system works in favor of graduates from privileged backgrounds who dominate elite colleges and access to top jobs.[38]

Changes in the rules of the game are not limited to the criteria employers use in making their recruitment decisions in the competition for managerial and professional employment. Companies have also responded to mass higher education by restratifying their occupational hierarchies. Suffice it to say that whereas the distinction between graduate and nongraduate or college and high school job-seekers was widely used to differentiate employees in respect to roles, rewards, and career opportunities, there is increasing segmentation of the college-educated workforce. Today the rhetoric of "talent management" is used to conjure something different from bureaucratic expertise or leadership. It involves reformulating the old hierarchy of certified achievement and incremental differences in pay related to expertise and experience. Undermining established models of occupational mobility in distancing the real talent from the rest adds a premium to attending high-ranked universities because these are where leading employers go to source high potential talent.[39]

The Elites' Monopoly of Educational Excellence

As more people get a college education and the job market is increasingly differentiated, access to elite schools, colleges, and universities is required to secure the grades and social trimmings to compete for tough-entry jobs. This is exemplified by the changing role of elite private schools in the United Kingdom, previously known for developing leadership skills for public life. When universities started lifting academic entry requirements in response to more high school students making the grade, the private schools turned themselves into credential factories, ensuring that students from fee-paying families got value for money—the grades required for Oxbridge or other leading universities around the world.[40]

The priority given to academic performance in UK elite private schools was also a response to increasing international demand to privately educate children from wealthy global elites alongside aspiring national elites. What characterizes these schools, as they establish branch campuses and introduce international marketing campaigns, is the apparent virtues of the British public school brand, although such activities have a long history dating back to the days of the British Empire, when the children from colonized elite families were educated to further the interests of the empire.[41]

International schools are also gaining in popularity.[42] These schools are typically privately run for profit, and their fees can be higher than those for elite schools such as Eton.[43] What makes them international are the qualifications they offer, which have global currency when it comes to access to elite universities.[44] The most prestigious cater for families of high ranking officials in transitional corporations, multinational agencies and international nongovernmental organizations. The number of international schools has risen rapidly, driven by national elites who are seeking advantage for their children in the global economy. In 2002 there were approximately three thousand such schools; by 2017 that figure had increased to more than eight thousand serving 4.5 million students.[45] Not all students who attend an international school will gain the results to enter a highly ranked university, but the investment is a risk that many parents who can afford it are prepared to take.

It should be noted that there is a significant democratic deficit in the international school system precisely because it is global and not accountable to any nation-state.[46] Access to these global schools is through the wealth and wishes of parents and not based on merit.[47] In other words, access to educationally privileged institutions is no longer subject to democratic accountability.

These schools are now linking into what has rapidly become a global higher education market. While the origins and destinations of those who attend these schools have not yet been studied, logic suggests that these students, who are typically multilingual and multicultural, will have a distinct advantage in accessing highly rated universities if they have the right grades.[48] And, as with many classed institutions and relationships, the links are not just based on qualifications. We know of one international school in Britain that is visited by deans from Harvard as part of their recruitment strategy, for these are precisely the overseas students who will apply to Ivy League universities.

In China, recruitment to top universities reflects the same social composition found in many other countries. China's National Higher Education Entrance Examination—commonly known as the Gaokao—involves millions of students competing for entry to highly ranked universities, but it continues to favor those from prosperous families, rich in cultural capital and with powerful social networks.[49] A similar process occurs in India, where top Indian institutes of technology and institutes of management are dominated by students from elite families, for whom the global labor market beckons.

While they embrace the policy rhetoric of widening participation, elite universities in the West are also concerned to preserve their brand value—the status of their degrees as a key differentiator in student and staff hiring in the competition for resources. Within an increasing market-based competition a status hierarchy of universities has been formalized through the creation of league tables for both teaching and research. Moreover these ranking tournaments are no longer limited to national contexts but are global, helping to create world-class universities, offering a new source of reputational capital in the competition for the best students and faculty regardless of nationality. Elite universities have formed exclusive members-only clubs and international alliances explicitly targeting other universities of equal status (if not higher) to benchmark academic brands.[50] The changing character of education and its relationship to job markets has important class consequences, extending the discussion of why it is very difficult for those from less privileged backgrounds to access world class universities.

As major companies introduce various systems of talent management, often on the flawed assumption that much of the value within organizations is created by a small cadre of professional and managerial talent, they target elite universities and ignore graduates from less prestigious universities and colleges, who are written off as having subprime credentials. These firms re-cruit from elite universities because their students are regarded as the best of the best and most likely to exude the personal chemistry and social fit re-quired for corporate success.

The same logic applies globally as companies internationalize talent man-agement. In hiring their future talent pool, corporations benchmark leading universities around the world, often based on their own formulations in conjunction with public rankings. Such rankings are compiled by Jiao Tong University in Shanghai and the World University Rankings by the *Times* newspaper group in the United Kingdom, which at the time of writing list Oxford, California Institute of Technology, Cambridge, Stanford and Massachusetts Institute of Technology as the global top five.[51]

In David Rothkopf's account of the new superclass, he notes that among the CEOs of America's leading corporations, 30 percent attended one of only twenty elite universities, led by Stanford, Harvard, and Chicago.[52] These universities provide the basis for forging networks between students and alumni; four Ivy League universities have endowments of $1.9 million for every full-time-equivalent student, offering an annual supplementary equiva-lent of $76,000 per student.[53]

Throughout the second half of the twentieth century the link between education (at all levels) and the labor market was based on the assump-tion that the hierarchy of educational credentials matched the hierarchy of occupations: those who had achieved the highest qualifications would be set on career ladders that enabled them to be upwardly mobile and to make a significant productive contribution. But orthodox theorists left unrecognized the positional power games that shape educational performance and occupational hiring.

Education for Employability

The mirage of opportunity is not limited to the declining exchange value of credentials. It is also evident in the narrowing of educational purpose; as a result education is failing to meet the needs of individuals rather than the imputed needs of industry. In the mid-twentieth century the development of credentials as a currency of exchange seemed to offer genuine prospects of better jobs and social mobility. It also preserved an institutional distance between education and the workplace, which permitted a wider conception of educational purpose.

The aims of higher education, for example, went far beyond seeing education and the labor market simply in financial terms: higher education institutions were established for wider reasons than just the economic. Nation-building and citizenship are but two justifications for the modern university. As Andy Green has argued, when the great universities of Europe and the United States were being established, nation-states were also being formed, and a major aim of universities was to help establish the modern welfare state and new models of citizenship.[54] In essence, higher education was not only about technical skills but was also about developing individual character: inculcating the dispositions and attitudes desired by the culture of the society.

Within this context, credentials signaled the value of investment in education by benchmarking technical competence in preparation for specific occupational fields, and by signaling the differential trainability of people entering the job market. But today the entire education system has become part of the currency of human capital, requiring accounting for the performance of students, teachers, schools, colleges, and universities. Employers have also become impatient with a currency that signals trainability rather than supplying people who are job-ready. Consequently there is a much greater focus on hiring people who already have marketable skills and experience that employers can plug in to add immediate value.

Faith in orthodox theory has also meant that stagnant incomes, overqualification, and stalled social mobility are not seen for what they are, symptoms of the transformation of global capitalism, but rather as failures to reform education (supply) to adjust to changing employer demands. The whole educational enterprise, including new investment, pedagogy, curriculum, and assessment, has been redefined and must be accounted for by the way it contributes to student employability. In the erroneously named *Fulfilling Our Potential* (2015), the British government set out its proposals for the reform of higher education to encourage universities "to provide degrees with lasting value to their recipients": "This will mean providers being open to involving employers and learned societies representing professions in curriculum design. It will also mean teaching students the transferrable work readiness skills that businesses need, including collaborative teamwork and the development of a positive work ethic, so that they can contribute more effectively to our efforts to boost the productivity of the UK economy."[55]

Here the aims of higher education are reduced to improving access, raising standards, and increasing social mobility by increasing competition and student choice. There has also been a decisive shift away from valuing the arts and humanities to focus on science, technology, engineering, and mathematics (STEM), subjects that are believed, again erroneously, to have more direct market value.[56] In a later chapter we will describe this as the banking model of education, in contrast to the individual growth model we propose under the *new* human capital. For present purposes it is clear that there is no reference to promoting the "general powers of mind," which the influential Robbins Committee defined as a key aim of higher education in Britain in the 1960s, at approximately the same time Theodore Schultz was unveiling the principles of human capital in his 1960 presidential address. As Robbins recognized, "the aim should be to produce not mere specialists but rather cultivated men and women. And it is the distinguishing characteristic of a healthy higher education that, even where it is concerned with practical techniques, it imparts them on a plane of generality that makes possible their application to many problems. . . . It is this that the world of affairs demands of the world of learning."[57]

But the narrowing of education purpose witnessed today involves a greater focus on marketable skills and education for employability. It is the result of various efforts to maintain a supply-side account of why education has failed to live up to the assumptions laid out in orthodox accounts. It is an example of where policy is made to fit the theory rather than the reality of the labor market. But if the theory is flawed, so will the policy recommendations that derive from it.[58]

If credentials are not delivering what employers need, the solution is to reengineer the relationship between learning and earning.[59] As a result, the education system is being reformed to directly supply the labor market with not only technically qualified people but people with a wider range of skills and competences matching the imputed needs of industry. By extending employability skills to include soft or generic skills, policymakers have unified the notion of skill and competence to encompass both mind and character.[60]

Various efforts are then made to get a better understanding of what firms want and then to tailor education and training provision to match them. This involves breaking down occupations into discrete activities to identify the specific and generic skills and competences required. The purpose of education can then be defined as delivering a set of quantifiable skills to be delivered to the labor market. So, for example, elements of character become a set of generic soft skills, such as personal drive, effective teamwork, and being a good communicator. This approach can also be used to identify any mismatch between the skill profiles of the education system and those anticipated by employers, involving ever-greater precision in the connections between education and the labor market by decomposing education and learners into a series of discreet skills. Elegant as some of these attempts have been, they represent a narrow-minded approach that cannot escape the realities of the changing relationship between education and the labor market.[61]

Many within the educational establishment have bought into the rhetoric of "generic skills," but it is not clear that the systems of thought characteristic of an induction into academic knowledge relate to many of the practical aspects of paid work. Problem-solving in the workplace, for instance, may take quite different forms from those relating to specific academic problems. It is also not clear how educational institutions can be reformed to meet rapidly changing industrial needs because labor markets are much more flexible than schools, especially in periods of economic volatility and workplace innovation. Even if desirable, it will take time to convert changing work practices into new curricula, and even longer for students to complete the necessary education or training. This highlights the problem of seeking to supply existing employer demand, as capitalism is not only in constant flux but employers are poor at articulating their needs beyond immediate requirements.[62]

Much of what constitutes effective performance at work is also context-specific, and the same is true of the education system. Basil Bernstein argues, "We cannot consider skills abstracted from the context of their transmission, for their relationships to each other and their function in creating, maintaining, modifying or changing a culture. Skills and their relationship to each other are culturally specific competences. The manner of their transmission and acquisition socializes the child into their contextual usages. Thus, the unit of analysis cannot simply be an abstracted specific competence like reading, writing, counting but the *structure* of social relationships which produces these specialized competences."[63]

Unequivocally, what is required to make people immediately employable is not the same as what is required for people to lead fulfilling and productive lives. Despite claims that there is little difference between teaching generic skills as marketable skills or life skills, when the focus is on meeting the needs of commerce, a premium is placed on those aspects of educational experience and performance that are judged to have market value. This overshadows or ignores those aspects of human knowledge, skills, and attributes not seen to be of direct relevance to the jobs people may enter after school or college, to say nothing of what they may do in later life.

Education is more than an investment in human capital. As we will argue, there are good social and economic reasons why education should not be reduced to tailoring behavioral standards or competences to the anticipated requirements for job market performance. Employers are primarily, if not exclusively, interested in the skills, knowledge, or personality traits believed to contribute to performance in particular jobs. This involves submitting to formal education and training to make oneself employable; as Alvin Gouldner observes, people "must submit to an education and to a socialization that early validates and cultivates only selected parts of [themselves], those that are expected to have subsequent utility."[64]

Conclusion

What education is offering to many is a mirage of opportunity, which has reshaped the education system to conform to orthodox ideas of efficiency and justice. This mirage shares some characteristics with the 2008 financial crisis. It took Britain hundreds of years to create the first trillion pounds of national wealth but just eight years to create the second trillion in the period leading up to the financial crisis. This wealth was not created by company profits deposited in banks; hard cash accounts for just 3 percent of the money supply in the economy. Most of the second trillion was created by bank lending, secured against leveraged debt from other banks, fueling a growth in sub-prime mortgages.[65] This has a striking resemblance to the massive increase in college diplomas and degrees that bear little relationship to the requirements of the economy but contributed to the myth that we had entered the "age of human capital."[66]

7

The Failed Promise of Development

IN THIS CHAPTER we examine the promise of human capital investment on economic growth and its consequences for developing countries.
Education investment as a way of increasing the stock of human capital remains a key part of the World Bank's approach to policy reform for so-called
developing countries.[1] We argue that such accounts fail to understand the
changing relationship between education, employment, and economic
growth. Notwithstanding the rapid economic advances made by some
emerging economies, most notably China and India, the experience of development has left many people within these countries stranded in the rubble
of modernization, while others, including those with a tertiary education,
struggle to find meaningful and sustainable employment.[2] Despite continuous national investment in education and economic liberalization, many
developing countries are falling further behind. We describe some of the
tensions and contradictions of development in emerging economies and how
they are fueled by the failed promise of orthodox theory.

Against the context of intense economic globalization and international
migration, we highlight the constant flows of highly skilled workers to developed countries. Many OECD countries actively recruit highly qualified
graduates from emerging economies to fill labor shortages. Classic examples
can be seen among doctors and nurses from the Asian subcontinent and the
Philippines in the National Health Service in the United Kingdom, and Asian
Indian software engineers in southern California. Much of the cost of education in these cases is borne by the sending countries, creating a so-called brain-
drain phenomenon. Some of these workers have been characterized as "the
new argonauts," repatriating knowledge and know-how to set up businesses
in their country of origin, yet brain circulation may represent an important
exception rather than a new model of development.[3]

The Death of Human Capital? Phillip Brown, Hugh Lauder, and Sin Yi Cheung, Oxford University Press (2020).
© Oxford University Press. DOI: 10.1093/oso/9780190644307.001.0001

Since the late 1980s, record numbers of international students have been studying outside their own country. The majority of these students are concentrated in affluent developed countries in North America and Europe, and more recently Australia. These receiving countries not only profit from high tuition fees, but many international students stay on after completing their studies; they find work in the local labor markets and pay taxes in these rich countries, exacerbating the brain-drain phenomenon from the developing world and casting doubt on the orthodox promise of national economic salvation.

Ha-Joon Chang describes a growth deceleration in emerging economies since the 1980s after the adoption of neoliberal programs.[4] Many face competition for jobs in which it is hard for them to win given what appear to be more attractive opportunities in other countries. Indeed perilous journeys to seek out a more prosperous future in the West are far removed from the image of human capital as a source of human dignity and economic freedom.

The benefits of brain circulation, return migration, and remittances are far outweighed by the hollowing-out effects of the brain drain in emerging economies and the brain gain in rich nations in the West. In this chapter we will examine orthodox accounts in the development literature. Drawing on recent statistical evidence, we will show the constant flow of highly qualified foreign-born nationals to OECD countries. This discussion contributes to a key argument in the book: that the world is creating vast numbers of qualified people for which there are not enough good jobs in today's global economy.

Human Capital Theory in the Development Literature

In his 1960 presidential address to the American Economic Association, Theodore Schulz highlighted the importance of human capital theory for economic development.[5] He believed that the link between economic growth and human capital could be applied to developing economies in the same way that it was applied to America and European countries. Schultz attributed the earning differentials between a farm laborer and an industrial worker to a "real" difference in productivity. He recognized that economic growth involved workers migrating from rural to urban locations to take advantage of changing job opportunities. Schultz's ideas sparked considerable policy interest and empirical research that provided the foundation for the World Bank's education and development policies. This includes further development of the "new growth theory" (also known as the endogenous growth model) by Robert Lucas in the late 1980s, which contends that economic growth is a direct result of the increasing returns associated with the creation of new knowledge.[6] In developing economies this was a particularly pressing issue given relatively low rates of educational participation. Education was presented as a way to improve the productive capacities of the nation's population and to drive economic growth.

Earlier we described how the World Bank showed little interest in education, which it did not consider important to economic development. Gradually an interest emerged in relation to technical and vocational education and then in relation to primary education. We also described how the analysis in 1981 of rate of returns to different levels of education in developing countries by the Bank's George Psacharopoulos proved highly influential.[7] What is also significant is that, by then, human capital theory was wrapped in the wider assumptions of the Washington Consensus. John Williamson summarizes the economic policies "that Washington urges on the rest of the world" as "prudent macroeconomic policies, outward orientation, and free-market capitalism."[8] This included opening countries to free trade; privatization of state assets; user-pays policies, especially in tertiary education; and state deregulation. The reason this list of policies is so significant is that the Washington Consensus tried to get developing countries to mimic the conditions of the competitive markets of orthodox economics. It assumed that the closer economies approximated to the strictures of neoclassical economics, the more efficient and productive they would be.

For countries forced to conform to the Washington Consensus to qualify for World Bank loans, these policies were the equivalent of being visited by a natural disaster.[9] So why did the World Bank pursue these policies? A short answer is that it suited political elites in the United States and in other developed countries to have developing economies open to trade in which wealthy countries held the advantage.[10] We need to look more closely at the World Bank's view of the role of human capital.

Education Investment and Economic Growth

Earlier chapters examined how orthodox economists have repeatedly attempted to establish a link between the accumulation of human capital of the workforce and labor market returns, measured by educational attainment and average earnings, assuming that earnings reflect productivity.

Evidence based on America and Britain clearly shows that for many learning isn't earning, so the question is whether human capital initiatives in developing economies have fared any better, especially given their connection with poverty reduction and the World Bank's promise of economic growth if orthodox policies were pursued.[11]

Fundamental problems with the application of orthodox theory to developing countries can be illustrated by drawing on the work of Eric Hanushek and Ludger Woessmann, two of the leading contemporary proponents of orthodox theory, whose work is embraced by the World Bank.[12] In their widely disseminated paper for the Bank, Hanushek and Woessmann assert that the "quality" of education can make a significant difference to a nation's future GDP. They calculate that if the educational reforms they recommend were implemented, GDP would rise in developing countries by 5 percent. In a later report they make more extravagant dollar estimates as to how much can be gained by improving education.[13] The powerful role of education, they assert, lies in its ability to increase the level of cognitive stock of economically productive human capability, and therefore the productivity and efficiency of the working population. They caution that improvements in school attainment alone are not enough to guarantee economic growth; rather it is the cognitive skills of the population that are "powerfully" linked to individual earnings and to economic growth.[14] Before we examine their theory in detail, we first look at the broader picture of the educational expenditure in select developing countries. Have they followed the World Bank injunction to grow economically by investing in education?

Figure 7.1 summarizes government expenditure in education from 1960 to 2010 in select countries. We can see that education investment in high-income countries was 5.2 percent of GDP in 1965, falling to around 5 percent between 1980 and 2000 before rising to 5.5 percent in 2010. In contrast, low- and middle-income countries such as Kenya, Malaysia, and Morocco have spent consistently more since 1980. But strong performing economies such as Taiwan, South Korea, India, and China spent far less during the same period. Even at the most basic level, it is clear from these figures that higher human capital investment does not guarantee economic growth. It certainly appears that the exceptional economic performance of Taiwan and South Korea cannot be explained by the relatively low level of education investment in these high-income countries. In fact the sharp increase in GDP per capita in many rich countries preceded rapid expansion in higher education. This casts serious doubt on the assumption and the direction of causality between investment in higher education and economic growth.[15]

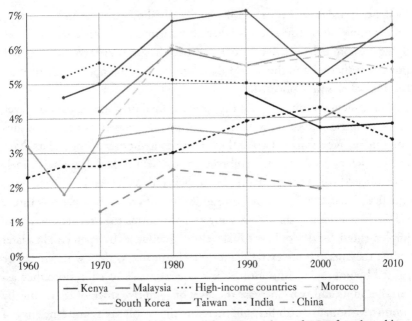

FIGURE 7.1 Government expenditure on education as share of GDP for selected low- and middle- income countries (plus average expenditure of high-income countries).

Source: Max Roser and Esteban Ortiz-Ospina, "Financing Education," *Our World in Data,* 2019.[16]

Importantly, investment in education to produce more qualified graduates does not create more desirable jobs in the economy, and this trend is particularly acute for developing countries. The global unemployment rate was 5.6 percent in 2017, adding 3.4 million jobless people to the 201 million unemployed since 2016. Even when the unemployment trend reversed in 2018, falling to 5.5 percent, this happened only in developed countries. An undesirable characteristic of joblessness is its concentration in the developing world in both emerging economies and middle-income countries: in Latin America and the Caribbean, unemployment rates rose significantly between 2014 and 2017, reaching as high as 12.9 percent in Brazil in 2017.[17]

This reflects the fact that jobs growth has failed to keep pace with the increase in labor supply, which disproportionately affects women and young people. Women in North Africa and the Arab states are twice as likely to be unemployed as men. Deeply troubling is the 13 percent of global youth (under twenty-five years old) who are unemployed, a rate three times higher than the adult rate (4.3 percent). The situation is especially severe in North Africa, where some 30 percent of young people are without a job. According to the International Labor Organization, the youth-to-adult unemployment ratio had reached a historical peak even before the recent global pandemic. For those who are lucky enough to be working, many are in vulnerable employment, with limited access to social security and employment benefits. Temporary, informal, and involuntary part-time employment are all on the rise. While some workers have to work excessive hours, others are subjected to time-related underemployment.[18]

Hanushek and Woessmann argue that low educational performance costs developing countries trillions of dollars in poorer economic growth: "The analysis . . . particularly concentrates on the role of human capital. Human capital has been a central focus of much of the recent growth modelling, and it is a standard element of any empirical work. Its importance from a policy perspective is clear and unquestionable."[19] This central argument is further developed in their book *The Knowledge Capital of Nations*, where they contend that "a country's rate of economic growth is a function of the skills of workers and other factors such as technology and economic institutions." They predict that nations with more human capital will make more productivity gains compared with nations with less human capital. By relating changes in GDP per capita to the *quality* of education, they claim that education will "affect long-term growth rates even when no additional education is added to the economy."[20]

Hanushek and Woessmann present this "knowledge capital," as they call it, as a superior measure of human capital that can be used across countries to solve a wide range of "development puzzles," such as the East Asia Miracle and the Latin American Growth Puzzle.[21] Mere investment in education by a nation is not enough; it is the quality of this investment that matters to economic growth. The authors have criticized traditional measures of human capital using school attendance for failing to capture "quality" issues in workforce development. Instead they seek to capture national differences in the quality of human capital, as the amount of learning achieved.

To develop a measure that "can equate knowledge of people across countries," they adopt a proxy for the "aggregate human capital of a nation": data from the International Student Achievement Tests, now widely known as PISA (Program for International Student Assessment).[22] PISA is a survey of educational achievement of fifteen-year-olds across OECD countries in three main subjects: math, science, and reading. Hanushek and Woessmann focus on the first two skills, which they relabel "cognitive skills." After aggregating the country-level data from 1964 to 2003 and modeling the effect of these cognitive skills on GDP per capita, they conclude that there is a causal link between cognitive skills and economic growth: "Our interpretation is based on our own view of what schooling does for individuals, and, by implication, for nations. Our measures focus on the development of general skills, which we see as key to how individuals adapt to new situations and how new ideas and approaches are developed. Countries whose people have more knowledge skills can keep improving their economic performance over time through new technologies, improved production processes, and enhanced economic operations."[23]

These arguments are highly dubious on at least four counts.

Count 1: The role of skills and wage growth depends upon the industrial development path taken. For example, we find radically different growth rates in Ireland and South Korea based on quite different models of skill formation and economic development.[24] This suggests that the relationships between the state, private enterprise, and education systems are crucial to understanding the different outcomes of such countries.

Not only do Hanushek and Woessmann assert a direct causal link between academic ability and economic growth, but they also assume open markets and free trade are desirable and even necessary. However, the Asian economies do not conform to a free market model.[25] The distribution of the supply of educational qualifications may be necessary, but it is not sufficient for economic development; it is the way those qualifications and the skills they denote are used that is crucial.[26] Economic development relies on a number of drivers, including fundamental changes in the (re)structuring of global value chains. This highlights an important limitation in the orthodox approach to development, as improving the overall educational standards of a nation is one thing, but when it comes to the creation of new employment opportunities, nations are in a global competition over which they have very limited control.[27]

Critics such as Chang point out that the pathways to development taken in East Asia departed radically from the Washington Consensus formula, including in education.[28] While the World Bank attributes the exceptional economic growth rates in the four Asian Tigers to neoliberal market-friendly policies, there is evidence that they required major state intervention in economic infrastructure and industrial policies and, in the case of Hong Kong and Singapore, a large state-funded public housing program.[29]

This highlights problems associated with the direction of causality in orthodox theories, an issue to which we shall return. Hanushek and Woessmann make the same mistake other orthodox theorists do in assuming that the increased supply of educated workers will generate labor demand; to translate the benefits of better educated workers into estimates of GDP requires a misguided act of faith that all that is lacking in developing economies is a better educated workforce rather than investment in infrastructure, technological innovation, and new job opportunities for higher-skilled workers.

In short, the causal assumption that orthodox theorists make lacks plausibility because they cannot theorize how demand for labor can be created. To illustrate the problem of determining whether investment in education is required to deliver economic growth or whether it is the fruits of economic development that fund the expansion of educational provision, Hong Kong is instructive. Government expenditure on education in Hong Kong in the early 1970s was 2.3 percent of GDP, rising to 3.9 percent in 2001. At the same time Boliva and Paraguay spent far more, 5.5 percent and 5.3 percent respectively, but without the kind of economic growth experienced in East Asia.[30] Importantly, educational reforms in primary and secondary levels, such as the introduction of free education for all, were slow to take off in East Asian Tigers economies, including Hong Kong, and rapid economic growth preceded the expansion in higher education in the 1990s. In the same way that there seems to be little systematic relationship between the proportion of GDP spent on education and national economic vitality, there is also little to support the claim that supply drives demand. At best, education is one of a number of "complementary conditions" on which economic development depends.[31]

Count 2: Hanushek and Woessmann make the assumption that educational institutions and cultures have little impact on the way students are taught and socialized and, consequently, on how educational experiences may impact skill utilization in employment. Yet we know that different schooling systems approach questions of knowledge, pedagogy, and learning quite differently, and this appears to impact the capacity for innovation and the application of skill. It is for this reason that many countries in East Asia, despite frequently topping the various international educational test league tables, worry about "chalk and talk" teaching and lack of creativity.[32]

Count 3: There is a problem with attributing causation to education systems. The PISA test scores for any given country (or major cities, in the case of China) are average scores for all students taking the test. It is a blunt tool to gauge educational quality. The highest-performing locations (Taipei, Singapore, South Korea, Hong Kong, Shanghai, and Japan) have wide disparities in test scores. In these locations students from advantaged socioeconomic backgrounds are two years ahead of their socially disadvantaged counterparts. PISA also tell us nothing about teaching methods adopted in these high-performing economic contexts.

Data from PISA 2012 actually show a link between long *out-of-school* study hours and high performance scores. It may be a culture of long hours of study rather than superior teaching methods in East Asia that is critical to achieving high test scores. This would also explain why there is a concern about the overemphasis on rote learning in countries like Singapore, because success in international tests like PISA does not automatically translates into the talent profiles of international companies. There is evidence of a gap between the "technicians" who are good at passing tests and the "talent" who drive transnational companies. This is a problem that Singapore, as one of the best PISA performers, is confronting.[33]

Count 4: Orthodox theory, as exemplified by Hanushek and Woessmann, takes little account of the global economy.[34] Orthodox theorists work with a very limited measure of "openness to trade" that tells us little about the effects of globalization on the economic structure of developing countries or the retention of high-skilled labor. Their strategy of calculating the benefits of education to GDP assumes a closed economy and that the future will be like the past, but if we know anything it is that in the current global upheavals the future will not be like the past. In an age of global production and cross-border activities, one nation's investment in cognitive skills could be contributing to another nation's rising GDP rather than its own. In short, Hanushek and Woessmann's studies of development underline the problems of seeking general law-like propositions that take no account of history or social context and, most important, the global dynamics of migration.

The Age of International Labor Migration

Just as goods and assets get traded internationally, people travel and cross borders. We live in an age of migration, when people are on the move more than ever. Almost 250 million international migrants lived outside their birth country in 2015. The global financial crisis did not halt the speed of global movement of humans and capital. While the demand for low-skilled workers to fill unwanted jobs in rich nations remains resilient, the global competition for talent has never been so intense. Virtually all OECD countries have some kind of immigration fast-track programs or a point or tier system to attract high-skilled professionals. In the academic year 2010–11, some 27 million immigrants in OECD countries were educated to tertiary level, an increase of 70 percent compared to the preceding decade. Among them, 11 percent of African-born immigrants had a tertiary diploma. Overall 30 percent of the 27 million immigrants were highly educated, and 20 percent originated from

China, India, or the Philippines. Emigration rates to OECD countries from Latin America and the Caribbean are also higher than ever before, at a rate almost seven times that for Asia.[35]

High-skilled migration is probably most pronounced in the United States. Data from the US Census Bureau and the American Community Survey show that nearly 50 percent of immigrants arriving in the United States between 2011 and 2015 were college graduates, an increase from 27 percent in 1990 (Figure 7.2).[36] The corresponding figures for US-born residents were 30 percent in 2015, rising from 20 percent in 1990. This persistent and growing human capital gap between recently arrived immigrants and native-born US residents is staggering. One in two immigrant college graduates in the United States is from Asia. India, the largest contributor, accounts for 1.6 million immigrants with college degrees out of the 11.1 million in 2015. The second largest supplier is China (including Hong Kong), followed by the Philippines, Mexico, and South Korea. These college-educated arrivals also have a much higher level of English proficiency compared to cohorts arriving in the previous two decades.[37] In 2000 over 97 percent of physicians trained in Grenada and Dominica emigrated overseas, followed by 66 percent in St. Lucia and over 54 percent in Cape Verde.[38] These figures reflect, on the one hand, rising levels of education investment in developing countries and, on the other hand, the intensification of brain drain across the globe in recent decades.

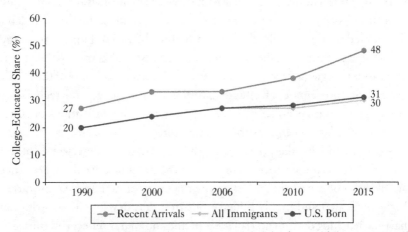

FIGURE 7.2 Share of college graduates among US adults (age 25+) by nativity and period of arrival (%), 1990–2015.

Source: Migration Policy Institute (MPI) tabulation of data from the U.S. Census Bureau 1990 and 2000 decennial census and 2006, 2010 and 2015 American Community Survey (ACS).

Brain Drain and Brain Circulation: Human Arbitrage in the Global Economy

One way of characterizing human capital in the global economy is with the idea of arbitrage, where corporations seek a cost advantage in relation to workers by sourcing the best skills for the lowest wages or by replacing skilled workers with automation. We will see in chapter 10 how corporations do this through a global auction, sourcing skills across the global labor market and through automation and digital Taylorism.[39]

For developing countries with strong educational institutions, there is no guarantee that their most successful students will remain to help develop their home countries when there are incentives for them to work overseas and to send back remittances. We know that remittances are a significant feature of the global economy. For example, US$48 billion were remitted from the United States, followed by US$26 billion from Saudi Arabia, and US$17 billion from Switzerland. While remittances may contribute to the country of origin economically, the medium-term construction of stable institutions such as those of education, law, and the state is in jeopardy because the expertise, institutional memory, and collective commitment are weakened.

There are exceptions. The migration of Chinese high-tech workers from the West Coast of America to Taiwan and then to China, and Indians in high-tech industries returning to Bangalore and Mumbai, are noteworthy examples, but they are few and far between. Many of these highly skilled professionals were once international students. AnnaLee Saxenian describes how "brain circulation" occurred when former foreign science and technology students first settled and worked in the United States, then took home capital and knowledge to form the Silicon Valley–Hsinchu-Shanghai transnational network and synergies for regional innovation.[40] It is true that some of the highly skilled entrepreneurs do facilitate transfers of knowledge and technology at a time when their home country does not have the institutions or infrastructure to train and employ their own scientists. But while some manage to stay connected with their place of origin via transnational networks, others are attracted to the magnet economies of the developed world, where they are likely to be a permanent loss to their country of heritage. An exodus of highly educated and highly skilled labor from less developed countries can have far-reaching detrimental socioeconomic and welfare effects on those left behind.[41]

International education has become a multibillion-dollar enterprise with mass global student migration. In 2008, 2.9 million higher education students were enrolled in a university abroad, compared to just 600,000 in 1975.[42] Sixty-two percent of them were studying in North America and Western Europe, and the top four most popular education destinations were the United States (624,474), the United Kingdom (341,791), France (243,436), and Australia (230,635).[43] International student mobility primarily flows from Asia and the Global South toward OECD countries, the main senders being China and India.

By 2008 China had become the largest supplier, sending over 441,186 students to the United States, Japan, Australia, United Kingdom, and South Korea. In second place, 170,256 Indian students were also studying abroad. These figures soared in 2016–17 with 351,800 Chinese students in the United States alone. During that time Asian students accounted for 61 percent of all international students in the United States.[44] Export education has become a lucrative business in many Western countries, not least because of the handsome revenue it generates for the host countries. In 2005 the education investment of these students totaled US$32.9 billion in revenue in OECD countries.[45] In Australia, education has become the third largest service export industry after tourism and transport, and a significant proportion of it is targeted at international students. Demand for export education is predicted to exceed 7 million students by 2025.[46]

International student mobility has become a new form of labor migration. This "study migration" satisfies many Western governments' desire to recruit the best scientists and engineers, particularly in fields related to information technology. Compared to traditional immigrants arriving directly from overseas, who commonly struggle with poor language skills and undervalued foreign qualifications, these young and well-qualified international students are highly attractive. Having spent time in the host country's educational institutions, they are already culturally adapted. With advanced language skills, training and experience relevant to the domestic labor market, and qualifications readily recognized by local employers, they are considered "work ready."

Crucially the majority of these students are self-funded. It is common for international students to have to take on low-skilled, low-paid, part-time jobs during their study to help pay for their education. Once they complete their education they become much more valuable economically to the host country. Conscious efforts in cultivating students into skilled migrants take various forms of post-study visa programs, semi-permanent work, and residency permits, all aimed to transition some of the best and the brightest into employment serving the host country's economy.

Both Australia and Canada rely heavily on points systems that give priority to skilled migration, particularly in engineering, information technology, and medicine. As early as 1991, 79 percent of Indians and 88 percent of Chinese who received science and engineering PhD degrees from US universities were working in the United States five years later.[47] Saxenian found that nearly 30 percent of Silicon Valley start-ups between 1995 and 1998 were founded by Chinese and Indians.[48] The biggest players—United States, United Kingdom, Australia, and Canada—were recently joined by Japan in the race for talent. These national policies serve no other purpose but to intensify persistent trends of brain drain.

International students turned professional migrants are a highly select group since only those who succeed in securing gainful employment can stay on. Nearly half of the professional workers in Australia and Canada were foreign-born in 2011. They are likely to be students with high academic attainment in their home country before pursuing higher education abroad. This radically departs from Hanushek and Woessmann's prediction of knowledge capital investment generating economic growth for the nation; even if that tenuous link were true, it could happen only in a world in which no one moves.

Unequal Rates of Return for Foreign- and Native-Born Workers

Tensions between economic globalization and international migration have cast further doubt on the claims made by orthodox theorists. In reality, returns to human capital investment rarely play out like this. The need for both low-skilled and highly educated workers in advanced economies continues to draw fresh waves of immigrants from the less-developed parts of the world. However, labor market returns to educational investment for immigrant workers, as we've seen for some native-born workers in previous chapters, is far from equitably distributed.

Although many highly educated international students choose to settle in the host country after completing their advanced degrees and training, the stark reality is that not all of them can find professional employment. There are significant gaps between foreign-born and native-born workers in terms of overqualification rates (Figure 7.3). Migrant workers are more likely to be overqualified in their jobs compared to native-born workers. The situation is particularly severe in certain Nordic countries, such as Sweden and Denmark, as well as Southern Mediterranean countries, such as Greece and Italy. Overqualification is also much more prevalent among new immigrants

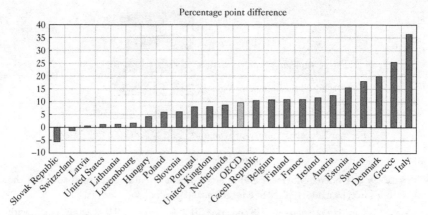

Percentage point difference

FIGURE 7.3 Differences in overqualification rates between foreign- and native-born workers ages 15 to 64 in select OECD countries, 2015.

Note: Data on the United States refer to 2016. The reference population are persons with a high education level aged 15-64 who are not in education.

Source: European countries: Labour Force Survey 2015 (Eurostat); United States: Current Population Survey 2016.

within five years upon arrival in the host country. In 2014–15 the rate among those arriving in the preceding five years was 10 percent higher compared to 2006–7.[49]

In European OECD countries, the unemployment rate in 2016 for foreign-born workers was as high as 14 percent, compared to 8 percent for the native-born. Similar trends can be found in the United States, where foreign-educated immigrant men and women were more likely to be underemployed or unemployed (Figure 7.4).[50] We have discussed how international students stay on after completing their higher education and in many cases advance degrees in the West. Their labor market fortunes may well be better than graduates who arrived after completing their education and training in their home countries. The lack of a degree from a recognized university can make foreign-educated graduates far less competitive in American and European labor markets, especially for jobs commensurate with their qualifications. Foreign-born US-educated graduates were slightly better off than their foreign-educated immigrant peers but still fared worse compared to their native counterparts, with 21 percent being unemployed or underemployed.

Figure 7.4 shows that migrants, particularly migrant women, do not have the same opportunities as indigenous workers. This suggests that there are forms of systematic discrimination based on a hierarchy of labor market opportunities that do not appear to have anything to do with the productivity of workers. But when we look more closely at some of the employment practices concerning migrant labor, we find practices that approximate to indentured labor.

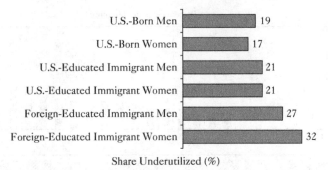

FIGURE 7.4 Underemployment and unemployment of college-educated adults in the US labor force, by nativity, place of education, and gender (%), 2009–13.

Source: MPI analysis of 2009–13 ACS and 2008 SIPP data from the U.S. Census Bureau, with legal status assignments by Bachmeier and Van Hook.

The H-1B visa in the United States is a clear example. Under this visa, migrant labor can be employed but only under strict conditions, which include companies paying these workers an annual salary of over $60,000. Foreign workers on this visa are not permitted to change jobs if applying for a Green card. There is therefore no incentive for corporations to increase their wages. The majority, 71 percent, are high-tech workers from India who have been sponsored by outsourcing companies like Infosys, Tata Consultancy, and Wipro. They are cheap labor. At $60,000 their wages are way below the market rate for American workers. One former H-1B worker described the scheme as indentured servitude.

When we reflect on the human capital assumption that people are free to choose jobs based on open and fair contracts of employment, such indentured schemes clearly fail to offer even basic freedoms, including the right to change jobs.[51] While we have highlighted this case because it is in a developed country, there is evidence of similar conditions, particularly for women locked in transnational supply chains.[52] It is also evident from the sheer size of remittances that many migrant workers are not motivated by gain for themselves but survival for their family networks and communities in their country of origin. To gain a more adequate understanding of the economic motivations and implications of remittances would require a far wider analysis than that offered by orthodox theory.

Conclusion

In this chapter we set out to ask if human capital investment lives up to its promises of economic growth and development. The inadequacies of orthodox theory in respect to development are underlined by the scale of the global employment challenge. Uneven economic recovery and downward economic growth projections have left millions of workers unemployed globally. In 2016 almost 202 million worldwide were without a job, an increase of 5 million from 2012. The recent global pandemic will make matters far worse. Equally, evidence we have reviewed on developing countries is not necessarily about the lack of educational investment but rather that the investment itself does not pay off in the ways orthodox theory predicts. Few would doubt the value of education in preparing individuals and nations to meet the challenges of rapid social and economic changes on a global scale. Education has played a part in lifting millions of people out of extreme poverty. But although the poverty rate since the 1990s has been halved, one in five were still living in poverty in 2013.[53] There has also been a major shift in the world economy wherein Asian countries such as China and India are becoming bigger players.

None of this can be explained by human capital theory. Orthodox theory assumed a central position in the Washington Consensus, but, as we have seen, it is wholly inadequate in guiding education and economic development policy. The causal claim that improving the stock of knowledge capital (measured by PISA score) would trigger boundless and long-term economic growth is at best dubious. And crucially, this causal claim is premised on the idea of a closed economy where people do not move. As we have seen, the education market is becoming more international than ever, and students, especially those studying for advanced degrees, are becoming more internationally mobile. Migration often contributes to the economic growth of different, often more affluent countries.

Both developed and developing countries confront the lack of good-quality job growth—especially the kinds of jobs that a more educated workforce might expect—as well as brain drain from developing countries. Orthodox theorists have failed to adequately recognize that labor markets are not simply based on skills competition but also rely on cost competition, where wage expectations of Western workers are misaligned with the price for the job within global markets. Moreover, contrary to orthodox theory, sustainable economic growth in developing countries involves the lasting political will of the state, active industrial policy, and cooperation between national governments. This has proved difficult with President Donald Trump in America and the United Kingdom's vote to leave the European Union (Brexit). It is difficult to say what will happen to trading relations and international migration. In Britain the borders are closing to many foreign workers, despite the rhetoric about "Global Britain." In America, Trump is more committed to building walls than bridges.

It could be argued that closing the borders to migrants will benefit their home countries by reversing some of the key elements of inequality in the labor market that migrants experience. But this is a superficial reaction: it tells us very little about the strong economic and social infrastructure all countries need and the lack of availability of good jobs in developing countries. At the same time, there is reason to doubt that the borders will be closed, as they were in the early part of the twentieth century; the power of transnational corporations and the global flow of knowledge will make that more difficult. What is more certain is that the failed promise of orthodox human capital theory needs to be addressed if we want to improve the quality of life for all rather than the few in both developed and emerging nations.

8

A Revisionist History

IN PREVIOUS CHAPTERS we described some of the ways in which investments in human capital have failed to deliver on their promise. Ultimately what we are witnessing is the death of human capital as it has been developed within orthodox economics. Our autopsy reconsiders a number of the *as if* assumptions that shaped the theory and the policy initiative developed around the world. More than a history of ideas, what is at stake here is how we understand the economic and social problems to be addressed, given fundamental structural changes in the relationship between education, jobs, and rewards.

The Happy Accident of Human Capital Development

While recognizing how investments in education and training contributed to the transformation of both economy and society, we reject the way proponents of the orthodox approach, most notably Gary Becker, view that transformation *as if* it has universal, law-like applicability. In the nineteenth century the French sociologist Auguste Comte shared Adam Smith's optimism that the rise of capitalism offered a route to social progress. He viewed the egotistical foundations of early capitalism as a "happy accident" because the increasing productivity at the time seemed to benefit workers as well as factory owners. But Comte worried that the primitive form of capitalism of the day, premised on self-interest and unregulated market competition, would erode the social fabric unless capitalism could be progressively reformed in the direction of altruism rather than self-interest.[1] The premise of a happy accident could equally be applied to orthodox theory in the twentieth century.

The Death of Human Capital? Phillip Brown, Hugh Lauder, and Sin Yi Cheung, Oxford University Press (2020). © Oxford University Press. DOI: 10.1093/oso/9780190644307.001.0001

We have shown that Becker's universal claims have been disproved by economic realities. Far from being a universal theory of economic development, the plausibility of orthodox theory depended on a particular set of circumstances, such as those pertaining to America and Europe in the era of mid- to late twentieth-century economic nationalism. We have described how in 1960s America, the growth of white-collar jobs in private- and public-sector bureaucracies, coupled with educational expansion such as greater opportunities for a college education, gave rise to a closer relationship between education, jobs, and incomes. With relatively small numbers in college, there was a rough correspondence between education level and job title. To be a university student was to be seen as part of an occupational elite. At the time bureaucratic career structures for white-collar workers were also characterized by incremental pay increases, giving some credence to Mincer's argument that the value of human capital increases with work experience.

Learning, both in the classroom and on the job, appeared to equal earning through progressive incremental pay raises rewarding experience as well as initial training. This led orthodox theorists to mistake a happy accident for a new economic theory.[2] The miracle seemed to be investment in education, but in reality it was the various strands of economic nationalism at the time, including the rise of office bureaucracy in both the private and public sectors that offer a more plausible account of the connection between learning and earning. In the 1990s we again saw the rise in demand for college graduates related to the high-tech revolution. But this too was due to specific economic and social conditions that have not been sustained, resulting in a financial crash, leaving many Western economies with huge national debts.

We have described how Adam Smith recognized the limits to universal theories of economic growth, as he viewed economic development in terms of "stocks" of people and physical capital that are filled up in spatial containers (countries) also encompassing natural resources in combination with national laws and institutions. When the spatial container is "under-peopled" or "under-stocked" with physical capital, there is potential for "progressive" growth; when the spatial container is "fully peopled" and "fully stocked," economies enter a "stationary state."[3] Although Smith did not anticipate the potential for new technologies and human skills to increase productivity and fuel economic growth, he did recognize the need for new ways to sustain growth. Giovanni Arrighi concludes that nowhere does Smith suggest that the invisible hand of the market acting on its own can get the economy unstuck from the trap of a stationary state: "If anything or anyone can, it is the visible hand of the government through suitable changes in laws and institutions."[4] If this account of the "happy accident" is correct, we need to rethink the allocation of scarce resources through market prices and look instead to the broader structural conditions of twenty-first-century capitalism.

The Creative Destruction of Skill-Biased Technological Change

Treating technological change *as if* it is skill-biased also ignores the realities of economic development under capitalism. If capitalism is driven by anything like a universal reality, it is simply that it never rests. Capitalism is characterized by "perpetual commotion," described by Schumpeter. Following Marx he observed that "capitalism . . . is by nature a form or method of economic change." It involves a relentless pursuit of new markets, new consumers, new goods, new ideas, new methods of production, new advances in transportation and logistics, new forms of work organization, in pursuit of capital accumulation and increasing profits. It is this perpetual commotion in doing "more with less" that highlights the analytical limitation of the orthodox approach, as "the problem that is usually being visualized is how capitalism administers existing structures, whereas the relevant problem is how it creates and destroys them. As long as this in not recognized, the investigator does a meaningless job. As soon as it is recognized, [their] outlook on capitalist practice and its social results changes considerably."[5]

The perpetual commotion, which Schumpeter described as the "gale of creative destruction," makes it clear that the wind does not always blow from the same direction. This seems particularly apposite in regard to the orthodox approach, which assumes a linear or one-directional approach to economic change, with a growing proportion of the workforce benefiting from the rising demand for skills. Although some workers would see their jobs disappear as a result of technological innovation, this is viewed as part of a virtuous cycle leading people to retrain for new, higher-skilled and better-paid job openings. These ideas contributed to the failed promise of the knowledge economy, which was supposed to accelerate the shift toward an age of human capital.

But it is clear that the orthodox approach has failed to offer a credible account of social and economic change given an inadequate theory of capitalism. There is no automatic association between technological innovation and the demand for skills. In the same way there is no automatic association between learning and earning, as it is the potential for people to capitalize on their skills and knowledge that needs to be explained in a fundamentally different economic and social context from the time when Schultz, Becker, and Mincer formulated their ideas about human capital. It is the perpetual creation and destruction of human capital that needs to be studied, including the relationship between skills innovation and skills obsolescence.

This warns of the dangers of defining economies and societies by dominant or emergent technologies or level of scientific knowledge, whatever label is applied: "industrial," "information," "knowledge," or "digital" economy. Although capitalism can change its spots, it's still capitalism. This is an important point when seeking a different understanding of human capital because it requires an institutional and dynamic approach, recognizing the policy limitations of investing in the knowledge and skills of individuals. The education system cannot compensate for market capitalism. At best, educational reforms are part of a solution that requires other institutional interventions that Western governments of neoliberal persuasions were reluctant to recognize in public policy debates before the 2020 pandemic.

The Contingent Relationship between Education (Learning) and Wages (Earning)

The orthodox approach treats investment in education and training *as if* it is a form of capital, revealed in differential wage rates paid to those with more or less education and training. Indeed the claim to a causal relationship between education (learning) and wages (earning) is at the heart of the theory's appeal. We have shown that what shapes the relationship between education and wages varies according to different versions of the theory. In its original formulation, it was assumed that investment in education would lead to higher wages because employers would respond to the productive potential of better-educated workers by using more advanced technologies to improve the market value of their goods or services. At the same time rising wages of college-educated workers signaled to students that they could earn higher returns with a college education, generating a virtuous circle of educational investment, technological innovation, and higher wages.[6]

This conformed to what is commonly known as Say's Law, in which the supply of educated labor elicits the demand. While Becker maintained that there is a causal relationship between education and wages, he seemed underdecided about the importance of technology. In his formal model it was supply in a context of rising skill demand that determined wages.[7] Therefore

Becker and others could assume that earnings mainly measure how much workers invest in their skills and knowledge, and at the same time "technology may be the driver of the modern economy, especially in the hi-tech sector, but human capital is certainly the fuel."[8]

Proponents of skill biased technological change (SBTC) did not share Becker's view on the role of technology, as they were in no doubt that changes in technology were the key driver of labor demand. This changed the direction of the causal relationship between education and wages, but not the basic tenets of a labor-scarcity model of human capital. Goldin and Katz used the skills-biased approach to argue that growing inequalities in the relationship between learning and earning were largely the result of the failure of education to keep pace with the demand for higher-skilled workers, causing firms to recognize their scarcity value. This explained why higher wages were being paid to high-skilled workers.[9]

In an attempt to maintain the integrity of orthodox claims to explain the relationship between learning and earning in light of increasing evidence of wage stagnation and concerns about the impact of automation on labor supply and demand, another argument was developed: that learning may equal earning only if people are trained with the employability skills that firms cannot replace with robots.

In different but related ways, these accounts of causation all point to how progress can be maintained through education, since it remains the key to raising wages. Without a labor-scarcity view of causation, orthodox economists might provide interesting relationships (correlations) between education and wages, but they would lose the claim to universal predictive powers and the idea of economic progress that they seek to maintain. It would also undermine much of its policy appeal if the relationship between learning and earning were shown to be contingent on historical, social, and market contexts. It would be especially damaging if it transpired that further investment in education and training may have a negligible impact on individual or national wage rates. Even more detrimental to orthodox theory, further investment may prove to be counterproductive, leading to wasteful positional competition, squandering vast public and private resources in the scramble to secure a decent job. We reject the claim that this undermines the value of education, but it does undermine the causal foundations of orthodox accounts.

The available evidence points to a contingent, although not arbitrary relationship between education and wages. Our data show that the wages of many of those with a college education have not increased and that the relationship between education and wages has not moved in consistent ways;

in fact much of the evidence points to significant wage differentials between those with the same level of education.[10] This again reveals that the orthodox approach does not reflect labor market reality. It is those at the top of the income parade who have increasingly distanced themselves from the rest, and the stagnant or declining returns for many are not simply a reflection of market failure but the new normal in a context of neoliberal, global market competition. Here higher-skilled jobs can be done for a lower price due to an expansion in national and global supply of college graduates and because employers can use new technologies to redesign jobs that make them less dependent on the brain power of employees. But we have also highlighted systematic inequalities in education and individual life-chances and inequalities in labor market power that have a crucial impact on the relationship between learning and earning.

We have shown that all workers' wages, except the top 10 percent, have either flatlined or declined between 1970 and 2010. At the same time, the debts associated with loans for college may contribute to the next financial crisis. And now we are confronted with the prospect of many jobs, including high-skilled jobs, being turned over to AI (discussed in chapter 11).

The Myth of Individual Marginal Productivity

Wages are treated *as if* they are a universal measure of individual productive contribution, and therefore income inequalities are treated *as if* they are both efficient and fair as employers pay people according to their individual marginal productivity. This is directly related to a theory of merit in which employers hire the more highly educated because of their superior productive potential. This false system of accounting is related to what Ivar Berg called a "great training robbery." We have described these *as if* assumptions about marginal productivity as little more than an act of faith because orthodox theorists have no direct measure of marginal productivity but simply assume that it is reflected in wage rates.

Those who claim that wages are determined by a worker's productivity need to be clear about the meaning and measurement of productivity. At the time of formulating the orthodox approach, most of the workforce performed clearly defined roles in factories or offices. As Thomas Piketty observes, "When a job is replicable, as in the case of the assembly-line worker or fast-food server, we can give an approximate estimate of the 'marginal product' that would be realized by adding one additional worker or waiter (albeit with a considerable margin of error in our estimate)."[11] Today calculating productivity is much more problematic. Indeed it is wage inequalities that need to be explained rather than assuming wages are determined by marginal productivity.[12]

In many areas of professional and managerial work there is considerable ambiguity in both the qualities and competences required to perform professional and managerial work, but it often involves impression management in influencing the perceptions and judgments of senior colleagues.[13] Daniel Kahneman, a Nobel Prize–winning economist, describes this ambiguity as the "illusion of skill" among financial fund managers; he shows that "the selection of stocks is more like rolling dice than like playing poker."[14] When the stocks' performance is examined over time, the correlation between the fund choices they make and increases in market price is not significant.

Piketty declares it naïve to think that the explosion of very top US incomes can be explained by objective measures of individual productivity. When an individual's job function involves a range of activities that typically include the management of other employees, "the very notion of 'individual marginal productivity' becomes hard to define.... It becomes something close to a pure ideological construct on the basis of which a justification for higher status can be elaborated."[15]

Amartya Sen, another Nobel Prize–winning economist, also rejects the marginal productivity view of how wages are determined. The "alleged fact" of wages reflecting marginal productivity, says Sen, is "a fiction, and while it might appear to be a convenient fiction, it is more convenient for some than for others."[16] It is certainly convenient for orthodox economists in need of a statistical measure that enables them to equate the relative value of labor, but is it equally convenient for those who seek to capture for themselves and fellow executives and shareholders the benefits of productivity gains, where the higher the wage, the greater the assumed contribution.

It is also more convenient for some rather than for others because it imposes no ethical foundations for restricting labor market power or salary hikes. This makes it easy for occupational elites to point to their inflated wages as a measure of their productive contribution and the market price for rare talent. But these wage inequalities often reflect differences in individual bargaining power rather than actual contribution.[17] The social norms that have been built around the private rates of return in America, Britain, and elsewhere resulted in a widening gap between rewards bearing little relationship to economic or social contribution. Today the incomes of many people both within and outside of the formal job market are not commensurate with their education, training, or contribution.

It is a mistake to believe that the individual marginal productivity of low-wage workers is easier to evaluate because they are often engaged in routine and low-skilled tasks. Extensive international research conducted by the Russell Sage Foundation reveals significant national differences in the quality of low-wage work and the well-being of low-wage workers, reflecting differences in income security, worker protection, and wider social benefits, which are all outside the remit of individual marginal productivity.[18]

Gender income inequalities show that much of the work performed by women is invisible in orthodox accounting systems. Katrine Marcal, following a long tradition of feminist writers, asserts that the market is built on a hidden economy in which a lot of work performed by women goes unnoticed and unrewarded: "Beyond the reach of the invisible hand there is the invisible sex." Remarking on who cooked Adam Smith's dinner, she writes, "Giving birth to babies, raising children, cultivating a garden, cooking food for her siblings, milking the family cow, making clothes for her relatives or taking care of Adam Smith so he can write *The Wealth of Nations*. None of this is counted as 'productive activity' in the standard economic model."[19]

Marilyn Waring, who has written extensively on this issue, states, "The lack of visibility of women's contribution to the economy results in policies which perpetuate economic, social and political inequality between women and men. There is a very simple equation operating here: if you are invisible as a producer in a nation's economy, you are invisible in the distribution of benefits (unless they label you a welfare 'problem' or 'burden')."[20]

Waring is referring to the costs of care and nurturing of children, early childhood education, and domestic labor. As early as 1941 Simon Kuznets drew attention to this problem, but orthodox theorists have paid attention only to the costs of investment in college education.[21] There can be many ideological reasons why this has been the case since women's work is often not counted in measures of individual marginal productivity; even within formal employment, when men and women do the same job, women typically receive inferior pay.[22]

These inequalities in market power and the wages it derives need to be accounted for in the *new* human capital.[23] We are not suggesting that individual productivity is irrelevant in wage settlements, but it is only part of the story. We have shown that income differences reflect positional inequalities rather than simply individual marginal productivity, as individuals and companies are involved in a permanent power struggle over the capitalization of human labor. Account needs to be taken of an inherent conflict of interest between individual workers and trade union representatives seeking to increase the value of labor, while companies seek to restrict or reduce labor costs. Who has the upper hand in this relationship at any particular time depends on the balance of market and political power.

When market power becomes a key source of income, rent-seeking behavior becomes inevitable.[24] Joseph Stiglitz has extended this argument to claim that America has become a rent-seeking society, as elites use political and economic power to get a larger share of the national pie rather than grow the national pie.[25]

The Failed Democratization of Capital

This discussion points to a fundamental paradox at the heart of Schultz and Becker's human capital revolution, presented *as if* we were witnessing a democratization of economic power through human capital investments in education. We have shown how labor ceased to be treated as a factor of production like land or investment capital because differences in the quality of skills, along with the acquisition of technical knowledge, were judged to be key to explaining economic growth. According to orthodox ideas, this shifted economic power to skilled workers, given their key role in the economy. It was predicted that a larger share of the profits would go to workers who were employed to think for a living, as they were driving growth. In sum, the general approach of orthodox writers was to see human capital as ever more important to the economy and as offering a route to individual and national prosperity.[26]

But Schultz and others failed to understand how attempts to democratize capital through education would ultimately bring working- and middle-class families into direct conflict with the interests of moneyed and business elites. When only a small minority entered the job market with a bachelor's degree, employers had relatively little problem absorbing them into their corporate ranks, especially in periods of economic growth. It was plausible to argue that by investing in education individuals and families were creating new sources of capital, adding to a stock of national capital. In the 1960s around 30 percent of Americans twenty-five and older had completed four years of high school or more; by 2000 this had increased to 80 percent.[27] This drive toward mass higher education exposed the realities of the inherent conflict over capital.

Pressure on companies to increase wages in line with occupational skills were already evident back in the 1950s and 1960s, but at the time rising costs were transferred to consumers via price hikes.[28] Growing international competition and inflationary pressures in the 1970s made further price hikes unsustainable without eating into corporate profits, creating the conditions for an economic civil war that would come to have profound implications for the future of the class structure.

On the one side are those whose claims to capital rests on their education and work experience—certified human capital. They are the bulk of the working and middle classes. Their income, wealth, and well-being depend on maintaining, if not increasing the market value of what they know (and who they know). On the other side are those whose claims to capital primarily derive from their ownership of businesses, equities, property, or land. It includes those in senior executive roles within many firms whose interests are closely aligned to those of shareholders.

In knowledge-intensive companies, a firm's assets shift from the ownership of physical assets such as land, factories, or machines, where property rights are clearly defined, to intangible knowledge-related assets, where property rights are less clear-cut.[29] Employers confront the prospect of a larger share of the profits going to a new generation of knowledge workers and companies losing control of corporate assets if ideas remain in the heads of employees at liberty to transfer allegiance to a competitor. If employees control the vital assets of the company because they are the key to innovation, the company risks giving them considerable bargaining power in salary negotiations.[30]

It follows that the more companies depend on the productivity of knowledge, the greater the challenge to their property rights over intangible assets, if they depend on extending "permission to think" to a growing proportion of the workforce. In such circumstances the task of business is to capture and control as much intellectual know-how as possible without undermining the organization's capacity to innovate and compete in global markets. In celebrating the age of human capital, its protagonists neglected the fact that "the loss of control over production violates the profit-making objectives of a firm."[31]

Faced with this threat to control and profitability, corporations created a series of strategies, including changes in the rules of the game based on a resurgent neoliberalism in the 1980s. The human capital equation was repackaged to conform to a new "gospel of wealth," giving priority to property rights relating to shareholders and the captains of industry rather than the majority of the workforce.[32] Tax cuts introduced by President Reagan in America and Prime Minister Thatcher in Britain in the 1980s signaled a return to nineteenth-century naked capitalism. Norton Garfinkle points to a shift from the contribution of ordinary workers to the exceptional entrepreneur, making sure that the most productive people were free to create wealth for the rest: "Government simply needed to get out of the way."[33]

We have described how company executives, with everything to gain by joining forces in the battle for shareholder value, engaged in various forms of productivity capture, from tax cuts to reducing the power of unions and offshoring high-skilled jobs. These include the use of technology to routinize what was once high-skilled work, by employing digital Taylorism, by converting knowledge work into working knowledge and turning it into corporate intellectual property. Once it is standardized and turned into algorithms, those parts of the job that can be routinized can then be transferred across the globe. At the same time, transnational corporations can source their talent from across the globe, typically at a much lower price than in countries like the United States and Britain, thereby cheapening the cost of educated workers in those countries.

Later we will expand on how elites exploited greater market power to undermine the capital claims of the rest of the workforce rather than knowledge workers using certified human capital to gain a larger share of company profit. The outcome of this struggle is transforming the market position of many of those in middle-class jobs, and rather than delivering economic opportunities and higher wages it has undermined them.[34] Many middle- and working-class families that have taken out loans to fund their educational and career aspirations have been left frustrated: the promise that an investment in education will result in good, well-paid jobs has not been fulfilled.

Orthodox theorists struggle to explain today's income inequalities in part due to a narrow conception of market power, which assumes that the only source of legitimate power is exercised by individuals in pursuit of self-interest within a context of market competition. In such circumstances people should be free to use individual abilities, networks, and financial resources to gain and maintain resources within the marketplace. Other forms of power over markets are viewed as disruptive distortions of market forces that infringe on individual economic freedom, reduce efficiency, or negatively impact economic growth. Neoliberal economists accuse trade unions of blocking economic efficiency because they operate as monopolies in the labor market, with the potential to increase pay above productivity.[35]

Therefore neoliberals see no need for restraint on the individual exploitation of market power, and they reject state interventions and collective trade union action as monopolistic. This leads to conceptual blindness and is ethically barren. The stark conclusion to be drawn from a revisionist history of human capital development is that it fares better under regulated markets because it's less exposed to a new version of the "great training robbery" instigated by business and industrial elites. In short, deregulated market competition ultimately freezes out the benefits of human capital investment for most workers and their families.

The Misconception of the Human Capital Problem

The orthodox approach views labor scarcity *as if* it is the fundamental economic problem and as offering an efficient and fair system of income distribution. This envisages an economy where there is a shortage (or scarcity) of people with higher-level skills. We have described how this is premised on a number of related ideas. First, education can be thought of as an economic investment, allowing people to acquire marketable skills to be traded for a higher income, given its scarcity value, as people will be paid what they are worth, reflected in differences in individual marginal productivity.

Second, there is an evolutionary process that begins with a largely illiterate workforce and moves through economic stages to arrive at a knowledge-based economy. This process increases the importance and value of skilled labor as it becomes the key to productivity, profits, and national prosperity.

Third, there will always be a premium attached to higher-level skills because technological innovation will drive up the demand for them. Economic history at least from the turn of the twentieth century is, from an orthodox view, characterized by skill biased technological change. Scarcity value of labor is linked to increasing technological complexity raising the demand for higher-educated workers or due to an increasing supply of skilled workers driving demand based on a version of Say's Law (endogenous growth theory).

Fourth, there are other scarcity factors on the supply side, where scarcity may result from a lack of investment in human capital (whether public or private); a lack of alignment between education and the changing needs of industry; or innate limits to the potential pool of ability on which companies can draw, especially in advanced, knowledge-driven economies. As the barriers to a college education have been lifted for a growing share of Americans, along with many others worldwide, there has been more emphasis on the quality of supply and whether it is of the right sort. There has also been extensive discussion of the best way to measure the value of human capital (credentials, cognitive skills, noncognitive skills, etc.) when more people have a college degree and when skill requirements become difficult to define.

There seems little doubt that the expansion of education has undermined a key dimension of labor scarcity, based on the idea of a limited pool of ability and talent available to nations. Our revisionist view of educational expansion suggests that the historical unfolding of human capability reflects the social barriers to learning opportunities that have since been removed for some, although not all, rather than innate limits to human capability. This highlights an altogether different approach to the skills or job mismatch in creating enough quality employment opportunities to meet the rapid increase in the numbers of people entering the world's labor markets with high levels of educational attainment.

The fundamental problem is not that there is a shortage of the relevant skills that employers demand but that there is a lack of good-quality jobs. The problem that needs to be addressed is not labor scarcity but job scarcity. This reflects the fact that individual prospects for the majority of the workforce have been reversed when compared to the heady days of Schultz's human capital revolution or Becker's "age of human capital."

The *as if* assumptions need to be rejected for the increasing competition for decent jobs in both developed and emerging economies has resulted in a narrowing of freedom, as people need to invest more time and effort jumping through more and higher hoops in order to stay in the competition. This is a manifestation of the "impossible pressures" put on people in today's global economy. This has narrowed rather than extended human freedom as predicted by the orthodox approach, given that "market liberalism makes demands on people that are simply not sustainable."[36] An urgent need therefore exists to present a radically different interpretation of human flourishing under conditions of economic and social transformation.

PART III

The New Human Capital Theory

9

Starting Principles

THIS CHAPTER PRESENTS an alternative theory of human capital. It rejects orthodox accounts based on *labor scarcity* and the idea that people are in a skills competition, played out in formal institutions of education and training, through which individuals acquire different "bundles of valuable 'human capital' that, due to its scarcity, generates a flow of income over the career path."[1] We will outline a different approach built on the starting premise that twenty-first-century economies are characterized by *job scarcity*, reflecting inherent capacity problems in creating enough good-quality jobs that match the skills and capabilities of the workforce.

First, we will consider job scarcity and some of its implications for the development of an alternative theory of human capital. Second, we look at why translating human behavior into capital is different from other forms of capital assets, and why the foundations of individual economic welfare under market capitalism are inherently insecure. Third, we present an alternative understanding of the self and why people seek to earn a living from their efforts, knowledge, and skills in different ways. Fourth, we recognize fundamental inequalities in opportunities to develop individual capabilities, which cannot be explained by individual level investments in human capital. Fifth, we highlight the socioeconomic foundations of human capital, rejecting the overarching model of neoliberal economics from which orthodox theory derives.

Job Scarcity

At the core of the *new* human capital is the view that job scarcity, characterized by a lack of decent job opportunities that meet the expectations of the workforce, offers a more promising and realistic foundation for public policy. This is not to deny that there are circumstances where labor scarcity, in the form

The Death of Human Capital? Phillip Brown, Hugh Lauder, and Sin Yi Cheung, Oxford University Press (2020).
© Oxford University Press. DOI: 10.1093/oso/9780190644307.001.0001

of skill shortages, may exist, but framing the analysis of human capital around job scarcity opens up new theoretical foundations that require us to reimagine individual opportunity, educational purpose, economic contribution, distributional justice, and role of the labor market.

In previous chapters we presented evidence showing that demand will not reflect supply when employers seek to exploit a more highly skilled workforce. While recent developments in orthodox theory have given more attention to changes in job tasks and the occupational structure, especially those associated with technological innovation, the theory remains locked into a model of skills competition—people rewarded according to investment in marketable skills—which invariably leads back to education and investment in human capital as the key policy solution.[2] Here the focus is on gaining a better understanding of the changing needs of industry, such as the ideal combination of cognitive and noncognitive skills, for which training can then be tailored.

Support for our alternative approach comes from the World Bank, a major player in promoting orthodox theory in developing countries under the Washington Consensus. The Bank was forced to pause for reflection in the aftermath of the 2008 financial crisis, when 22 million people lost their jobs in a single year. The Bank's *World Development Report* on Jobs challenged its own conventional wisdom that investing in skills leads to job creation, higher productivity, and rising labor income and found that high unemployment and skills mismatches are often attributed to shortcomings in education and the training systems, but "massive investments in training systems, as seen in many parts of the world, might show disappointing results as hoped-for job outcomes do not materialize."[3]

Adopting a jobs lens is a central part of the new human capital because "the idea that development happens through jobs sheds new light on the strategies, policies, and programs governments can pursue."[4] It also sheds new light on the labor market and the distribution of structural opportunities shaping patterns of social (im)mobility. Yet we are not simply presenting a jobs focus in opposition to a skills focus. It is not only changes in employment but also the supply of people seeking to capitalize on their skills and abilities that is transforming the competition for jobs. This requires a more integrated and contextual approach.

A jobs focus also looks beyond the idea of atomized individuals lined up within the marketplace, distinguished by their level of skills training, to highlight the relational quality of economic and social life. It involves taking account of the attitudes, behaviors, and capital of others. The translation process involved in "earning by doing" includes other actors (even when people are un-aware of them), such as others looking for jobs or competing for promotion. People have to negotiate a positional competition that highlights the double life we all lead; even if we could all do our best, we can't all be the best. While anyone can formally apply for any occupation, jobs competition is based on the duality of employability. Capitalizing on individual skills depends on con-vincing an employer one has what it takes to do the job, but also convincing them that one is able to do a better job than other job applicants.[5]

The more people there are applying for the same job, the more positional considerations there are beyond being suitably qualified or having the ability to do the job. This relative dimension of jobs competition reveals how educa-tion, experience, and individual achievements typically involve a social judg-ment that position students, interns, and employees, relative to others. The market value of individual knowledge and skills ultimately depends on what other people bring to the job market in the competition for whatever jobs are available at any given time.

It is this aspect of the new human capital that explains why equality of op-portunity is so important: because people are positioned differently in terms of being able to develop skills and get a good education. Class differences in educational performance and major inequalities in translating life experiences, skills, and educational achievements into jobs point to differences in market power that cannot be explained or addressed solely in terms of investments in education and training or differences in innate abilities. In competitive labor markets those from more privileged backgrounds have a far greater chance of getting a decent job compared to those from less privileged backgrounds, even with the same academic credentials.

This explains why some people have done everything expected of them but still can't find suitable employment. We will examine the meritocratic implications of this in the following chapter, on rethinking labor supply and the future of education, but for now it is sufficient to note that the relational character of the economy and the competition for positional advantage is central to understanding the work involved in translating skills into capital.[6]

A focus on job scarcity, rather than labor scarcity, also rejects Becker's claim that the labor market can be studied as a supply-side issue of matching skilled workers with occupational opportunities. A jobs lens brings into focus the struc-ture of occupational opportunities and the jobs people perform. The demand for different kinds of workers plays a major role in structuring the opportunities to translate learning into earning.[7] The labor market is an instrument both for matching people to jobs and for managing job scarcity that derives from inherent inequalities in the division of labor. Some jobs are judged to be better than others because of their intrinsic interest, higher remuneration, or greater social status. Such jobs are typically in short supply, and invariably there are more people wanting them than there are job openings. The best person for the job is rarely the only person for the job, which is why a lot of people are being rewarded or rejected for something other than their knowledge and skills.

There are periods or places where the expectations and aspirations of the present and future workforce are matched by suitable vacancies in the job market, but these circumstances are rarely found in an era of mass higher education. Today there is a significant mismatch between occupational aspirations and labor market realities. This suggests that the labor force comprises large numbers of people employed in jobs that they would rather not be doing or for which they are overqualified, if not unemployed. In such circumstances, job competitions are characterized by what is demanded by employers because firms compete for workers far less than workers compete for firms.[8] The potential for digital technologies to automate managerial and professional as well as more routine occupations underlines the importance of using a jobs lens.

The job scarcity model that informs the new human capital therefore points to major policy challenges on both sides of the labor market, but especially around issues of job creation, job design, skill usage, industrial policy, and income distribution, rather than simply skills upgrading. There are institutional features that structure the relationship between education, jobs, and wages in different national or firm contexts, explored in later chapters. The focus on jobs also leads to unavoidable issues of individual and social returns when contemplating the future of human capital. Using a job scarcity lens, we have a better way of understanding why some people struggle to earn a living despite being qualified, at the same time others with similar skill sets are paid much more.

The new human capital also presents a different approach to distributional justice. Within orthodox theory, opportunity and fairness are based on labor scarcity, whereby the differential value of individual skills and contribution is believed to reflect their value to employers and therefore is amenable to policy interventions aimed at narrowing income inequalities by giving more people access to marketable education and skills. But if the central issue is not labor scarcity but job scarcity, it is not only enduring inequalities in the development of human capabilities that need to be linked to a wider sense of educational purpose, but also questions of redistribution.

Humans as Capitalizing

The new human capital draws a distinction between *humans as capital* and *humans as capitalizing* on individual knowledge, skills, and other assets as a source of direct or indirect monetary rewards.[9] To become capital, all forms of assets involve a translation process, such as property into rents, but human capital has a distinct social, legal, and ethical character. It is misleading, as well as socially unacceptable, to treat humans as capital for the simple reason that human capital can't be bought or sold. As Lester Thurow points out, even self-imposed slavery is illegal, as workers cannot be sold in the marketplace but only hired.[10] They can, though, be exploited. This helps to explain why human capital is quite different from other forms of capital, such as financial capital, which can be used to buy goods, services, rentable property, or equities.[11]

But at the same time, market freedom rests on people's need to earn a living. Investing in individual human capital may increase the range and quality of jobs a person is qualified to apply for, but for the vast majority of the workforce who need to earn a living, the dull compulsion to capitalize through waged work is a key part of what it means to have market freedom. As captured in the famous lyrics of The Eagles' song "Hotel California," "you can check out any time you like, but you can never leave." People may have some choice over what jobs to apply for and employers to work for, but they have little choice about whether to work unless they are part of a small minority who are sufficiently wealthy to live economically free of the job market.

This is why we propose an account of human capital in the exchange or translation of individual actions into activities leading to productive work, within the wider definition of "contribution" that we shall discuss in Chapter 12. When defined as a catch-all, covering almost any kind of social or economic purpose or outcome, the concept of human capital loses much of its economic, political, and policy relevance.[12] Such a broad definition negates any tension between individual opportunity and income inequalities and denies the realities of market capitalism that demands that people take responsibility for their economic welfare. It also fails to acknowledge that individual capabilities extend beyond what is capitalized in waged work at any given time. It is an integral part of but does not define who we are. This presents a different understanding of the self and an individual's wider social and economic relations.

In the context of job scarcity, capitalizing on one's individual capabilities is limited to selling one's individual capacities for work when there may be many more people looking for employment than employers willing to hire them. Therefore our focus is on the way people develop, mobilize, and capitalize on individual capabilities within highly competitive markets. Equally, the lack of liquidity attached to human capital, as opposed to other forms of capital, makes the translation process an inevitably risky business. Qualifications and skills come without proprietary rights or labor market guarantees. They lack the property rights of owning land or buildings or having cash in the bank; people do not own human capital in the same way they own houses or automobiles. Investing in education and training is only a source of capital (immediate rather than long term) when put to work through employment for a wage.[13]

Human capital is an embodied rather than a liquid asset such as money that can be used to buy or sell with little impact on its value. It involves the application of our own labor rather than the direct exploitation of the labor of others. If an individual loses their job, they can capitalize on their human capabilities only by finding another source of employment. This lack of flexibility or freedom explains why people need some form of social security when suffering from ill health or job loss, as our acquired human skills cannot be traded for food or used to pay a mortgage without earning by doing.[14]

But what it takes to make a living wage can be organized in more or less humanizing ways. It can be institutionally or legally framed in ways that enhance or suppress the rights and powers of workers as opposed to employers, exposing conflicting interests at the heart of the means of production. This does not mean that some people cannot get rich by using their human capital, but this ability is likely to be limited to a few because it conflicts with the interests of firms that are asset-rich through property ownership of copyright, equities, buildings, and companies. Typically companies have more coordinating and buying power than individuals do to own and control the means of production. Even when human knowledge and skills become the lynchpin of economic productivity it cannot be assumed that human capital is more important than owning other forms of capital, such as equities or property, for reasons described earlier.

This also explains why the translation work required of individuals does not necessarily correspond to the productivity gains of employers or to national investments in education and training. How employers try to translate employee knowledge and skills into productive contribution and how this relates to workforce remuneration and company profits highlights long-standing issues of how employers try to translate employee potential into profitable activity. These competing claims to capital are at the heart of our alternative theory.

The Liberation of the Self

The new human capital breaks the link between Becker's *Homo economicus* and human capital development because those areas of life that do not fit neatly into his view of economic behavior are integral to our approach, giving weight to a broader range of capabilities and human motivations. Michel Foucault concludes that orthodox theory does not necessarily mean that all human behavior is reducible to economic behavior, but it provides a lens, or what Foucault calls a "grid of intelligibility," to identify which aspects of human behavior are worth focusing on, which by definition are intelligible only in economic terms.[15]

The new human capital uses a different lens and a different set of assumptions. It involves a wider conception of capabilities, exposing the narrow-mindedness of seeing individuals as *Homo economicus*, from which education is viewed as an investment in skills to be sold on the labor market and captured in a single measure, such as GDP per capita.[16] We retain a central focus on individuals rather than structures or systems, for the simple reason that the liberation of the self is key to human flourishing, economic innovation, and a shared prosperity, we reject the claim that individual self-interest and free-market competition are the source of freedom and economic prosperity.

We reject Becker's view of self-interest as a "cynical depreciation of human nature." Individuals do not come installed with "selfish genes" and "stable preferences." Studies of social and economic life show that people do not live on autopilot, driven by rational impulses to maximize their utility. Even in circumstances of extreme provocation, where people are constantly bombarded with aspirational images of material success and the celebration of self-made billionaires, few people turn into the Wolf on Wall Street.[17]

Redefining human capital involves a different understanding of, if not a new relationship with the self, opening a world of human possibilities when our understanding of labor supply is not limited to a hierarchy of more or less skilled people seeking to maximize their utility. When markets are treated as generative and individuals are treated as passively responding to market signals, there is little need to consider individual identities beyond the enterprising self.

Orthodox theorists may reject the idea of homogeneous labor, but their understanding of individual differences does not extend to ways of seeing the world and the meaning and value that people give to what they do beyond pecuniary gain. People have different goals as well as different means to achieve them. If the redefinition of human capital involves a different understanding of the self, it calls into question the zombie view of the workforce instilled with little more than different amounts of human capital with different capacities for investing, producing, or consuming.[18] When individuals seek to capitalize on abilities, skills, or knowledge, they engage in a meaningful activity, even when it involves meaningless work.

Therefore human beings cannot be treated as if they are capital, because a lot of individual behavior is not directed toward the capitalization of the self. People's capabilities and actions are not limited to what is rewarded in the labor market. Much of human behavior may have little or no direct economic value (and is valued for other reasons beyond monetary or psychic gain, although this is almost impossible to prove). In short, the opposition between self-interest and self-sacrifice or disinterest is false. In orthodox theory a fixed view of the self is assumed, so that everything people do is viewed as self-interested. But as John Dewey explains, "the moment we recognize that the self is not something ready-made, but something in continuous formation through choice of action," the problem of self-interest gets cleared up.[19]

When medical staff volunteered to help the victims of Ebola or Coronavirus, they risked their own lives in using their professional skills to help others. This is clearly an expression of their interests, but it is primarily related to their sense of identity and social purpose. This in no way suggests that people have no interest in making money, gaining power or celebrity status, but it does mean that the workforce, present and future, is constituted by people who are motived in different ways. And individuals typically have mixed motives. As Amartya Sen has suggested, people have different reasons to value.[20]

Therefore what people choose to package in terms of skills, knowledge, or personality to make themselves employable involves an ongoing narrative with the self.[21] Only some of what individuals learn is certified and packaged in individual employability, with the potential to be capitalized in the labor market. Indeed individual priorities change over the life course, and important gender differences and inequalities remain when trying to juggle the demands of working life.

Individual choices are not simply a response to market signals—a rational calculation—but also involve an "imaginative anticipation" of a projected future self.[22] People make educational and occupational judgments shaped by individual horizons of possibilities that reflect, but are not determined by, their individual biography with reference to family background, education, and wider social experiences.[23] In short, people make their own histories but not in circumstances of their own choosing.[24] These histories combine a sense of *being* (who we are) and *becoming* (what we anticipate or aspire to become), leading us to interpret the same market signals—which are themselves often mixed or confused—in different ways.

Here the self is not the sum total of multiple identities but is characterized by dispositional struggles between being and becoming that orient "thoughts, perceptions, expressions and actions."[25] This includes the way people define suitable employment that continues to be guided by widespread gender stereotyping of jobs leading women into veterinary medicine, nursing, and early childhood teaching, and men into construction, engineering, and computer science.[26] These dispositional foundations of the self define labor supply under the new human capital, going beyond narrowly defined skills or competences. They are also sensitive to the potential for inner conflict or state of anomie in the tussle between self-identity and the realities of making a living.

Recapturing the wider purpose of education is therefore a key part of the new human capital. Education is not like investments in factories (widgets or minds), and liberation should not be confused with a better-paying job or upward social mobility. It includes a focus on the development of individual capabilities that cannot be reduced to employability, along with a sense of the unfinished—the development of dynamic capabilities over an individual's lifetime. This stands in stark contrast to the idea of humans as having machine-like qualities, in which early investments are made in their creation, but which deteriorate with age to become largely worthless when they lose their economic value. As the life course becomes more fluid, people find themselves in a permanent state of becoming.

Here there is some overlap with Sen's work, although we reject his distinction between a human capital and human capabilities approach. Sen offers an important counterargument to Becker's *Homo economicus*, in seeing that people have "reasons to value" different things that often have little connection to pecuniary gain. His approach, along with that of others, most notably Martha Nussbaum, focuses on individual freedoms and "the 'capabilities' of persons to lead the kind of lives they value—and have reason to value."[27] This has much in common with our view that people are not like capital and equally rejects the view that the only thing worth studying is what contributes to individual worth in the market.

In seeking to develop an alternative to Becker's economic approach, Sen presents his "capabilities approach" as distinct from human capital, although he acknowledges that "in principle" the concept of human capital can be used to cover the full range of what people have "reason to value." Interestingly, he uses the example of education to argue for the distinction between human capital and human capabilities: "If education makes a person more efficient in commodity production, then this is clearly an enhancement of human capital." But he suggests that even with the same level of income, different people benefit from education in different ways, "in reading, communicating, arguing, in being able to choose in a more informed way, in being taken more seriously by others, and so on." This leads him to the key point: that "the benefits of education, thus, exceed its role as human capital in commodity production. The broader human-capability perspective would record—and value—these additional roles. The two perspectives are, thus, closely related but distinct."[28]

But this distinction holds only if we continue to follow economic conventions because human capital "is typically defined—by convention—primarily in terms of indirect value."[29] If, for instance, we reject the conventional economic distinctions between education as investment or consumption, as we will describe in the next chapter, there is no logical reason why a socioeconomic theory of human capital cannot incorporate a new model of the individual, in which the full range of individual capabilities are recognized and studied as the basis on which humans seek to capitalize in exchange for an income and a more fulfilling life. It is important not to bracket off economic aspects of life as human capital as opposed to human capabilities, as the relationship between the two is key to a different understanding of individual flourishing, educational purpose, and economic freedom. Seeing the connection between human capital and capabilities is central to our argument because a wider understanding of capability will be needed, given the uncertain future that confronts the younger generation. Human capital cannot be conceived narrowly.[30]

The Myth of Labor Scarcity and the Dim View of Intelligence

The massive increase in the numbers of people qualified for high-skilled jobs exposed Becker's dim view of innate intelligence as little more than a contemporary example of Plato's "noble lie."[31] In Plato's *Republic*, Glaucon tells

Socrates of the need for "just one royal lie" in order to preserve the Republic.[32] Citizens are to be told, "You are brothers, yet God has framed you differently. Some of you have the power of command, and in the composition of these he has mingled gold, wherefore also they have the greatest honor; others he has made of silver, to be auxiliaries; others again who are to be husbandmen and craftsmen he has composed of brass and iron; and the species will generally be preserved in the children. But as all are of the same original stock, a golden parent will sometimes have a silver son, or a silver parent a golden son."[33]

When Glaucon finished his tale, he asked Socrates, "Is there any possibility of making our citizens believe in it?" Socrates was not hopeful but believed that future generations could be convinced of its validity. The emphasis on labor scarcity has perpetuated the claim that investing in education has to confront the view that some humans are innately better made than others. Its legacy has been to create a deeply embedded cultural myth which continues to shape views about human capabilities in the twenty-first century, such as the myth of a "war for talent" and Becker's views on IQ and sociobiology.[34]

Yet educational expansion points to a different interpretation: the historical unfolding of human capability reflecting social barriers to learning opportunities rather than innate limits to human capability. Human beings enter the world able to develop basic capabilities; as Nussbaum suggests, we therefore need a way of talking about "innate powers that are either nurtured or not nurtured": "We now know that the development of basic capabilities is not hard-wired in the DNA: maternal nutrition and prenatal experience play a role in their unfolding and shaping. . . . Basic capabilities are the innate faculties of the person that make later development and training possible."[35]

We also know that there are significant social inequalities in individual chances to develop and capitalize on education and training, reflecting socioeconomic background, gender, ethnicity, and nationality. The context in which individuals are born therefore shapes both their life chances and what they come to value. Individuals develop dispositional powers to act (including the development and use of language, skills, abilities) based on a developing self and identity work through primary socialization in early childhood, secondary socialization in schools, peer groups, and neighborhoods, etc., and increasingly tertiary socialization through digital technologies and the internet that expose people to the wider world in ways not previously possible.

The new human capital is therefore premised on an altogether different approach to human capital development that recognizes the "plasticity of our natures."[36] This concurs with Adam Smith's view that differences in individual abilities reflect inequalities in the quality of work opportunities rather than the division of labor reflecting inequalities in innate capabilities.[37] This rejects the deficit view that focuses on what those from disadvantaged backgrounds or ethnic groups lack: credentials, incentives, internships, or employability skills.[38] It assumes that by giving them more of what the middle classes already have, these deficits can be reduced without disturbing the privileges of more advantaged classes because there is always more room at the top. It also leads to exaggerated claims about the efficacy of educational (supply-side) reforms, despite its limited impact on the pattern of occupational mobility.[39] Without addressing class, gender, and racial inequalities in opportunity, there is little prospect of addressing issues of equity or efficiency.

A policy conundrum posed by the new human capital confronting all societies, but especially the most economically developed, is how to accommodate almost universal potential capability in unequal societies. How to create enough quality employment opportunities to meet the rapid increase in the numbers of people entering local, national, and global labor markets with high levels of educational attainment? Challenging fundamental inequalities in access to education and inequalities in wider life chances is a key part of an alternative understanding of human capital.

The Socioeconomic Foundations of Human Capital

The new human capital rejects the orthodox economic distinction between the market and society. Individual freedom is a social relationship, not a market relationship, and markets do not exist outside of society.[40]

In *The Great Transformation*, Karl Polanyi explains that it was not until the late 1700s that the idea of free labor markets was even discussed and the "ideal of the self-regulation of economic life was utterly beyond the horizon of the age."[41] The change from regulated to self-regulated markets in Britain at the time involved the complete transformation of society, made possible by extensive state action forcing people to live by market rules.[42] Polanyi observes that while it is true that "no society can exist without a system of some kind which ensures order in the production and distribution of goods," this "does not imply the existence of separate economic institutions; normally, the economic order is merely a function of the social order. Neither under tribal nor under feudal nor under mercantile conditions was there . . . a separate economic system in society. Nineteenth-century society, in which economic activity was isolated and imputed to a distinctive economic motive, was a singular departure."[43]

When the self-regulated market imposes a strict separation between economy and society, human behavior is typically accounted for as economic behavior.[44] This reminds us that orthodox theory involves more than a recognition of the increasing importance of individual skills and work experience to rising productivity and economic growth; it also involves locating the individual at the heart of economic analysis. Areas of social life previously viewed as noneconomic were reinterpreted in economic terms. Orthodox theory transformed many areas of social activity, including education, marriage, crime, and healthcare, into economic behavior and suitable subjects for economic analysis.[45] Treating people like human capital, Polanyi argues, turned them into "fictitious commodities" because the imposition of market mechanisms subordinates the substance of society itself and the diversity of human behavior to the logic and laws of the market.[46]

Recognizing the social foundations of the new human capital, we propose a socioeconomic theory of human capital to replace Becker's economic approach. Our theory rejects the stark distinction between economy and society. We don't get up for work and walk to the economy! We may go off to work in specially designed buildings called "offices," "shops," or "factories," but these are part of the wider social structure that also includes schools, hospitals, and prisons. Human societies are the foundations for capital accumulation, consumption, and distribution. As Fred Block suggests, "Both the efficiency and the quantity of production depend increasingly on organizational variables—the specific ways in which human beings and technology are brought together. The traditional concept of capital makes it difficult to grasp that human beings and their networks of interrelations are the society's central productive force."[47]

Our theory also rejects the idea of a universal market civilization, wherein societies are organized on market principles and individuals share "stable preferences" consistent with *Homo economicus*. Reconnecting the link between economy and society breaks the spell of Becker's economic approach, as there is no justification to the claim that the development of human capital depends on free-market competition. The increasing role of human knowledge and skills in productive activity and economic growth sits comfortably with different models of the individual, with varieties of capitalism and socialism, and within Western, Asian, or African societies. There is no one best way or model of human capital, but how human capital is understood and institutionally arranged will have significant individual, educational, economic, and social implications.

Our socioeconomic approach views national differences in social institutions, cultures, and politics as quintessential to human society.[48] There is no magic formula in the way people are educated or trained that can be applied to all countries regardless of national context. Context matters, and without an understanding of how local or national institutions embrace (or otherwise) Schumpeter's "gale of creative destruction," we have no sense of history, the present, or the political priorities or choices for the future.

The new human capital represents a contextual approach to the study of human capital, rejecting the one-size-fits-all idea that market forces flatten societies in the image of Becker's universal economic approach.[49] It takes seriously national differences and varieties of capitalism to explain why similar levels of investment in education can lead to very different consequences in the labor market and to income inequality. Although global capitalism poses a challenge to national cultures, institutions, and models of work organization, it does not simply flatten them into the same market mold. A global convergence in manufacturing capacity and service delivery, driven by a quality-cost revolution, does not lead to a convergence in the way societies are organized or governed. There is no sense in which this presupposes a global convergence around Anglo-Saxon neoliberalism, including "the belief that prosperity drags liberal democracy in its wake"; as John Gray observes, this belief "is an article of faith, not a result of disciplined inquiry."[50]

Because the relationship between education, jobs, and incomes is historically contingent and socially constructed, the possibilities for narrowing inequalities and extending individual freedom are greater than orthodox theories of human capital allow. As we will argue, the way education, employment, and income distribution are organized does not correspond to an iron law of economic efficiency, jeopardized whenever governments attempt to regulate markets in ways that spread the benefits of economic activity. Policymakers are not limited to supply-side solutions, such as further investments in education and training as a means of extending individual opportunities or narrowing income inequalities by increasing the supply of skilled workers.

Our approach comes close to what Robert Merton described as a "middle-range" theory, involving the development of "logically interconnected conceptions which are limited and modest in scope, rather than all-embracing and grandiose." This does not signal a lack of ambition but rather a rejection of a universal approach based on "a master conceptual scheme from which it is hoped to derive a very large number of empirically observed uniformities of social behavior."[51] However, in rejecting the high level "as if" assumptions of orthodox human capital theory we have also given an account of the economic and social principles which guide our enquiry.

A socioeconomic theory of human capital also involves returning the disciplines of economics and sociology to their common roots in nineteenth-century political economy. The major thinkers of the age did not treat the economy and society as separate disciplinary domains but saw them as integral to an understanding of the key issues of the day, including the direction of industrial change, urbanization, poverty, and wealth creation. The marginalist revolution in economics that helped to shape Becker's economic approach transformed economics from a cross-disciplinary study of the nature and causes of the wealth of nations into a narrow and abstract study of rates of return measured by wage dispersion.[52] Equally, contemporary sociology has tended to overlook issues of economic productivity, given a primary concern with social inequalities, welfare issues, and cultural politics. All of these issues are worthy of attention, but in developing a new theory of human capital we require an interdisciplinary approach that includes economics, sociology, psychology, education, social policy, law, and politics.

Conclusion

The new human capital involves reimagining education, work, and the labor market for a different economic and social world. In the next three chapters we offer a reinterpretation of labor supply, demand, and returns.

Rethinking Labor Supply

DEVELOPING A NEW understanding of human capital challenges the very notion of labor supply. In orthodox terms, it implies a stock or reserve of something, such as the stock of industrial components or office supplies. This is consistent with a *banking* model of investments, deposits, and returns, in contrast to an individual *growth* model used to characterize the *new* human capital.[1] The redefinition of labor supply we outline in this chapter seeks to recapture a wider understanding of education and human capabilities, given long-standing objections to treating individuals as passive consumers of knowledge and as a way of developing individual freedom and rebuilding social cohesion at a time of profound social and economic change.

The relationship between individuals, education, and employment in an era of twentieth-century industrialism is no longer appropriate in an age of machine intelligence. What it means to be educated, along with what it means to be employable, changes in different economic and spatial contexts and in relation to different models of employment. In the next chapter we will examine how some experts are predicting that widespread automation and advances in machine intelligence will replace human labor. These changes signal a further shift away from a job-for-life model to nonstandard employment and self-service careers, including part-time, temporary, gig assignments, zero-hour contracts, crowdsourcing, and grassroots open-source innovation. These arrangements are forcing people to reinvent themselves occupationally if they want to earn a living and to invent new ways of creating a meaningful and worthwhile life beyond full employment.[2]

Significant numbers of future jobs will no doubt continue to be individually rewarding, but much of the discussion about the knowledge economy and

The Death of Human Capital? Phillip Brown, Hugh Lauder, and Sin Yi Cheung, Oxford University Press (2020).
© Oxford University Press. DOI: 10.1093/oso/9780190644307.001.0001

skill-biased technological change presents an overly optimistic view of work in which the abilities and skills of employees are fully utilized. Technological innovation does not lead to a straightforward ramping up of the overall demand for skilled labor, as we will show in the next chapter. There is no technical fix by which educational reforms are geared to keep pace with technological innovation. In reality the jobs of the future may not provide people with full employment in line with their everyday lives, cognitive development, or intrinsic satisfaction. Today many qualified workers are not in jobs that exploit their talents. This echoes Adam Smith's view of education as a form of compensation for waged work given that many jobs lack meaningful challenge.[3]

The relationship between work and nonwork has also blurred when the means of production includes a laptop, iPad, or smartphone that can be used for work or for entertainment. Less obvious boundaries between work and nonwork are brought into sharp relief by older workers with an average life expectancy of seventy-nine years (for Americans), but with little prospect of full retirement in their sixties because of inadequate pension provision.[4] These trends have added a significant layer of complexity to how people construct a viable and meaningful livelihood over a lifetime. They reopen long-standing questions about the division of labor and the productive self. The renowned historian E. P. Thompson suggests that people will need to "re-learn some of the arts of living lost in the industrial revolution."[5] Rethinking labor supply therefore is not simply a question of making people more employable for existing jobs; it is about educating people as part of a lifelong journey on which waged employment (as distinct from other forms of work) is only a part, and for many not necessarily the most interesting part of their lives, unless we find new ways of imagining the future of work.

This points to a more proactive view of individuals not limited to cost-effective investment decisions in education and the job market. It points to a different way of understanding the processes and content of formal education, one that encourages alternative ways of imagining and thinking because future generations will have to negotiate a labor market and social world with fewer role models that support them in their personal lives and in paid work. Against this background, supply needs to be redefined as building individual and social capabilities that give people permission to think and act in order to take control of their lives, just at a time we are heading in precisely the opposite direction.

The Bankruptcy of the Banking Model
of Labor Supply

Earlier chapters described the dominance of economic interests in education and their profound effect on what is learned and how it is learned. Yet despite education being viewed as an economic investment, what actually happens in schools, colleges, and universities, including teaching and assessment, received remarkably little attention from early orthodox theorists. This was due to an almost exclusive focus on statistical measures of how learning equals earning. It was also assumed that as rational economic agents, individuals and their families would draw on available market signals to decide how best to capitalize on their investments in education.

More recently, orthodox theorists have sought to develop a more precise link between different kinds of skills and their returns in the labor market. We've described how they have been forced to develop more elaborate models of changing skill requirements to explain why some people seem to be earning a lot more than others despite having similar levels of education.

But rather than consider a fundamental shift away from what can be characterized as a banking model of educational investment, new forms of regulatory practices have been imposed on education, aimed at sustaining the neoliberal opportunity bargain. The (un)intended policy consequence of these tightening banking regulations has been the imposition of a straightjacket on teaching and learning in the name of improving standards, increasing accountability, and delivering employable workers.

Within the banking model, value and values are almost exclusively defined in financial terms, as rates of return on investments. To realize this investment, education is reformed to meet the needs of industry. These needs are given priority over other educational activities, which are viewed as consumption and judged to have little effect on individual rates of return or economic growth.

Within this model, students are involved in what Paulo Freire describes as an "act of depositing," linked to the role of credentials as a currency of opportunity, rewarded to those who have made the most of their educational investment.[6] Students are required to memorize and repeat received facts and concepts in exchange for certified skills, indicating differences in levels of investment.[7] Students adopt a largely passive role, and the teacher or instructor deposits useful information with the expectation that it will pay dividends to those willing to make a personal investment in the banking process. Learning is compartmentalized into isolated silos called "disciplines," with little connection between them.[8]

The goal is to turn out productive employees able to read and interpret market signals and respond to changing job market conditions. Within the job market individuals take a more active role in maximizing their rates of return on investments, under the constant threat of holding underperforming assets. As the social theorist Tomas Lemke has noted, the enterprising self "promises manifold options and opportunities . . . but it also necessitates the permanent calculation and estimation of risks, thus establishing a fear of failure."[9]

When systems of education are viewed in banking terms, there is a major focus on accounting standards linked to measures of performance. This aspect of the banking model involves teachers assessing standardized tasks and assignments that require set answers within a given time frame. When countries experience a credential currency crisis they typically reform banking regulations, especially to strengthen testing systems. New banking regulations have resulted in an intensification of "payment by results," where it is not only the students who are judged by test results but also the teacher.[10] School administrators judge teachers according to their success in getting students through tests with higher grades, which inevitably increases incentives for staff to teach to the test. Even those brilliant teachers able to inspire creativity and critical thinking confront the tyranny of incessant assessment, evaluation, and grading.

The banking model is also consistent with the stock view of human capital, with the aim of having more stock (and of higher value) than competitor countries. The assumption is that economic performance depends on matching or beating other countries on key banking indicators such as math or literacy scores. But given that countries use different currencies, comparative testing regimes such as the OECD Program for International Student Assessment and the adult skills version, the Program for the International Assessment of Adult Competencies, have become a significant part of the banking model. The result is that many countries use international league tables to measure educational performance as a key indicator of national competitiveness.[11]

Finally, within the banking model, students are assigned different credit ratings and access to different educational accounts, reflecting a market competition based on perceived ability, effort, and parental choice. Social elites are at liberty to use their market power to access premier banking with a more personalized approach in the expectation they will grow their accounts in ways that are consistent with corporate benchmarks of educational, managerial, or professional talent. At the same time, ordinary account holders receive standard levels of educational provision, although these could have a different character for women compared to men and for those from different social classes. Those who fail to take advantage of market opportunities to make something of themselves through early acts of depositing are likely to find it difficult to meet the standards of creditworthiness imposed by teachers, professors, or employers.

In preparing the groundwork for an alternative understanding of labor supply and its relation to education, we highlight three aspects of the banking model that reinforce the need for a different approach: education as investment, education in testing times, and twenty-first-century foundational skills.

Education as Investment

It has always been difficult to distinguish what people view as educational consumption, offering apparently noneconomic benefits such as personal development, as opposed to investment. We've argued that the appeal of the orthodox account was in reinterpreting the purpose of education as the key to economic growth and prosperity. It was a public relations success changing the way individuals, families, firms, and governments thought about education as a source of prosperity, profit, and growth.[12]

Theodore Schultz speculated on a potential decline in the role of education as an investment in future income. He recognized that if education became universal it could lose much of its labor scarcity value, akin to what he saw as the universal availability of food and shelter in affluent societies. In such circumstances education would no longer be an investment as there would likely be a decline in the private rate of return, so education would need to invent a different raison d'être. He writes, "Whether the consumption component in education will ultimately dominate, in the sense that the investment component in education will diminish as these expenditures increase and a point will be reached where additional expenditures for education will be pure consumption . . . is an interesting speculation. This may come to pass, as it has in the case of food and shelter, but that eventually appears very remote presently in view of the prevailing investment value of education and the new demand for knowledge and skill inherent in the nature of our technical and economic progress."[13]

Today this is more than an interesting speculation, as the distinction between education as investment or consumption is untenable. Thinking of education as individual sense-making rather than simply moneymaking, or in terms of its societal value beyond what is utilized in the formal economy, is not consumption. Again, this reflects the fact that the boundaries between social and economic activities (social lives and working lives) are difficult to maintain. People may not capitalize on the time, money, and energy they put into their education (or training), but that education may still be personally worthwhile and socially beneficial. Intrinsic human satisfaction from hard work (mental or physical) is notoriously difficult to measure by rates of return but cannot easily be bracketed off as consumption.[14]

Education in Testing Times

In the United States and Britain the repeated testing of students is not about the individual progress that students make; these testing regimes don't give formal feedback to students at all. Rather they are designed as market indicators of whether teachers and educational institutions are responding to the disciplines of the market. For parents and students, graded test results are presented as an indicator of benchmarked performance and of how their investments are performing.

But it does not take much imagination to see that with such high-stakes testing, teachers have an incentive to drill students for the test. A study by RAND Education, funded by the US National Science Foundation, found that "changes included a narrowing of the curriculum and instruction toward tested topics," and teachers, seeking to get more students above the proficiency benchmark, reported focusing more on students near "the proficient cut-score."[15] Knowledge, understanding, and creativity take second place to the much narrower imperatives of getting students through tests.

Of course, advocates of testing tell us that these tests encompass knowledge and understanding, but what they really do is prepare students to take tests, which rewards those who conform to the banking rules of the game. The effects on students' orientation to learning are profound, leaving students entering the job market without the capabilities required by current and future generations. Sam Carr, a social psychologist who has examined the effects of high-stakes testing, shows how it leads to an emphasis on extrinsic motivation as the key driver of educational performance, when today's students would be better served by the development of self-determination in which intrinsic motivation allows students to "play, explore and engage in activities purely from the pleasure derived from doing so."[16] He cites extensive evidence that an education that emphasizes autonomy in learning based on intrinsic motivation is far more effective than the testing regimes that currently dominate education. If we want to give young adults an opportunity to exercise autonomy under difficult conditions, then clearly we need to draw upon their intrinsic motivation.

Alternatively, repeated testing will prepare students for little more than the routinized work of digital Taylorism, in which workers memorize computer routines and follow scripts and initiative is highly circumscribed. Here the banking model of education is consistent with a model of economic organization whereby human decisions are taken by people in power within firms or government organizations that determine the use of digital technologies. As Simon Head observes, although we are often talking about abstract and impersonal electronic and statistical entities, "all the system's rules and commands in fact have human origins in the superior expertise of the technical, managerial elite whose wisdom is baked into the system." In such circumstances, "the majority of employees are in danger of becoming little more than an appendage to the machine." This, according to Head "is what 'dumbing down' means in the early twenty-first century."[17]

Therefore testing regimes are not neutral, despite claims to the contrary, as they are key to socializing young people into the disciplines of the market. Here changes in banking regulations are linked to a more fine-grained, competency-based approach to the skills of the future.

Are Twenty-First-Century Skills the Answer?

The reform of education to meet the needs of employers is a key part of delivering value for money under the banking model. This is despite the fact that employer needs are notoriously difficult to define and subject to change at short notice. Just-in-time production may work in factories and offices, but it doesn't work in schools, colleges, or universities. Students do not come ready-made with a shelf-life (like a supply of components); instead people need to retrain and change occupational roles on a regular basis throughout their working lives. John Dewey warns against limiting education to narrowly defined occupational goals, as "nothing could be more absurd than to try to educate individuals with an eye to only one line of activity," or, in today's context to front-load educational expenditure on outdated assumptions that it's an adequate preparation for life.[18]

Nevertheless there have been numerous attempts to specify the skills that will be required in the context of rapid technological change and international competition. These typically highlight science, technology, engineering, and math, along with a focus on flexibility, adaptability, problem-solving, and life skills, in recognition of rapid changes in the workplace. An interesting example is Frank Levy and Richard Murnane's studies of the foundational skills that humans will need to compete with the robots of the future. They describe tackling problems that lack rule-based solutions, such as a doctor diagnosing an illness with strange symptoms, a plumber fixing a complicated plumbing problem in an old house, a lawyer writing a convincing legal brief, and a chef creating a new dish from ingredients that are fresh that morning.[19]

Foundational skills include solving unstructured problems, dealing with new information, and influencing others. These skills presuppose higher levels of literacy than those that might have been expected prior to the introduction of computer-based work. Some of what is captured by foundational skills is consistent with the alternative model of individual growth we outline later, premised on skills for life rather than simply for the labor market.

But a problem with much of the discussion about foundational skills is that individual adaptability, flexibility, and agility are not skills that are taught, they depend on social circumstances. It is, for example, much easier to be flexible or adaptable when you have market power or when you are playing a low-stakes rather than high-stakes game. Some of what is defined as skills, especially core skills, also relate to issues of individual character and social attitudes, which cannot be broken down into identifiable skills. When the primary goal of education is to meet the espoused needs of the economy, there is therefore a tendency to shoehorn everything a student learns into the banking concept of skills.

Humanizing Human Capital: From Banking to Individual Growth

The new human capital puts individual growth throughout life at the heart of labor supply, requiring a different understanding of both the purpose and the organization of education and the economy.[20] It is an education that enables people to make a living and to negotiate an increasingly complex and uncertain social world. This is achieved by enhancing human freedom as a means of shaping rather than simply responding to changing economic and social circumstances. It shares much in common with UNESCO's vision for a quality education, which "fosters creativity and knowledge, and ensures the acquisition of the foundational skills of literacy and numeracy as well as analytical, problem-solving and other high-level cognitive, interpersonal and social skills. It also develops the skills, values and attitudes that enable citizens to lead healthy and fulfilled lives, make informed decisions, and respond to local and global challenges through education for sustainable development . . . and global citizenship education."[21]

The new human capital recognizes that a quality education for all cannot be delivered based on the changing needs of industry but must be based on a wider understanding of educational purpose. This is because the role of education in delivering personal growth and its role in making people employable often diverge.[22] A growth model involves giving people access to knowledge and opportunities where there is no sharp distinction between conception and execution or vocational and academic, as the future economy will be grown as much from the bottom up as from the top down.[23]

First, an individual growth model of labor supply views education as a source of individual empowerment, making it distinct from the banking model as an active rather than passive approach to human agency. This is key to humanizing human capital. Second, given the uncertainty we can expect in the labor market and beyond, it makes little sense to maintain a front-loaded approach, as learning new knowledge and skills is a lifelong activity. Third, it rejects the investment view of learning, which encourages acquisition rather inquisitiveness. While people will continue to engage in formal learning as a way of enhancing their job prospects or staying relevant in a changing job market, there is a better balance between short-term acquisitive learning and longer-term inquisitive learning that can sustain a lifetime of individual interest and growth.

Fourth, it is socially and economically inclusive. This is where educational ideals confront the realities of competing economic interests and social inequalities. Individual growth and freedom are not the preserve of an elite, often privately educated, but part of the widespread "freeing of individual capacity." It encourages a closer relationship between the capitalization of human labor and social aims, giving people an opportunity to make a productive contribution through meaningful and satisfying work, not limited to waged work.[24] This may be a long way from existing realities, evident in consistent calls to narrow education to meet the needs of industry rather than meeting the wider needs of individuals and society. We will say more about this, but before doing so we need to elaborate on what a growth model of labor supply would involve.

An understanding of what it means to humanize human capital through the reform of education—not limited to test scores and rankings—can be gained by drawing on the four interrelated pillars of lifelong learning that support UNESCO's approach to a quality education, noted above. There is no blueprint for local, regional, or national systems of lifelong learning given differences in institutional context, cultural traditions, and economic circumstance, but UNESCO's approach does provide an understanding of the direction of travel. It also offers an innovative approach to measuring the value of education beyond rates of return.[25]

Learning to Know

Learning to know has become even more important in an age when the old certainties have become uncertain, along with growing concerns about "fake news." Learning to know is about acquiring a body of knowledge and maintaining a thirst for knowledge beyond the requirements of market exchange. It relates to knowledge and the tools needed for further knowledge development as a lifelong process to gain a better understanding of the world and other people.[26]

This rejects the idea of school knowledge as beyond debate and something received by students, incentivized by future economic benefits. It also stands in opposition to what Jean-François Lyotard describes as the changing nature of knowledge in an age of digital disruption. He points out that in a changing world of information and knowledge, "the status of knowledge is altered as . . . knowledge is and will be produced in order to be sold." Knowledge is also consumed in order to develop new products and services. In both cases, he argues, "the goal is exchange."[27] This focus on obtaining optimally efficient outcomes is consistent with the banking model, but the danger is that knowledge is viewed as no more than a commodity to be bought and sold, leaving people locked into the here and now, lacking the rational foundation for judging between competing knowledge claims. There is therefore a balance to be struck between knowledge acquisition motivated by exchange and the wider growth imperatives for individuals, communities, and societies.

Learning to know is based on useful knowledge and empowering knowledge in shaping how people come to understand their place in the world and providing them with the tools to make informed judgments.[28] Michael Young argues that "the opportunity provided by schools for pupils to move between their everyday concepts and the theoretical concepts that are located in school subjects lies at the heart of the purpose of schools." What distinguishes these different ways of knowing "is that a pupil's 'everyday concepts' limit them to their experience, whereas the theoretical concepts to which subject teaching gives students access enable them to reflect on and move beyond their existing experience."[29]

Instead of fragmented knowledge and skills, atomized into chunks that are tested, learning is framed in a more coherent and holistic way to enable people to understand the world and their place within it.[30] Here there is common ground with the idea of twenty-first-century foundational skills, noted earlier, when viewed as a problem-based approach to learning, aimed at developing self-directed study, and a broad range of life and work skills relating to creativity and innovation, problem-solving, information literacy, communication, and critical thinking.[31] But it is domain knowledge, not only skills, that enable students to address the *why* and what if questions discussed in this book, as well as the *how* questions.[32]

David Brookes writes, "Ultimately, what matters is not only how well you can collaborate in groups, but the quality of mind you bring to the group . . . based on the foundations of factual acquisition and cultural literacy."[33] Soft skills, he concludes, have to be taught alongside factual literacy because the stairway from information to knowledge to individual judgment has not changed: "The rules have to be learned before they can be played with and broken." In other words, learning to know provides the basic building materials for individual foundational skills.

This gives learners an opportunity to envisage different worlds as well as the possibilities of negotiating them differently. Wrestling with these counterintuitive ways of seeing the world requires imagination, the habits of systematic analysis, and creativity and critical thinking that constitute learning to know. It follows that such empowering knowledge needs to be available to all who seek it, as a matter of social justice. We cannot therefore view access to higher education as a matter of supply and demand, where oversupply of educated workers in seen as merely inefficient; there is too much at stake to allow the judgments of employers or politicians to determine who shall be educated.[34]

Learning to Do

We reject the standard distinction between *knowing* and *doing*, which has served as an educational and social distinction, separating those who know from those who do. Traditionally academic study is for those learning to know and is associated with higher education leading into managerial and professional roles, whereas vocational education and training is for the doers, whose focus is on technical skills required for craft, technical, and routine service occupations. Here there are similarities to Becker's distinction between general and specific training. And because general training is the route to top vocational prizes, craft and technical apprenticeship training continues to be treated as a second-class option compared to studying for a university degree.

A different understanding of supply rejects the distinction between academic knowledge and vocational skills as a way of organizing education and training for people destined to do different things within a stratified occupational structure. We should not make the mistake of believing that particular cognitive and character traits map directly onto differences in the world of work; they never did and certainly do not do so today.

The distinctions between knowing (academic) and doing (vocational) relate to cultural assumptions as well as social inequalities that have a long class, gender, and ethnic history, given further impetus by the rhetoric of the knowledge economy that assumed that high-level cognitive skills learned at university will be at a premium. The limitations of this divide are evident in changes to employer hiring practices, where increasing attention is given to individual competence and the skills required to get the job done, which typically involve interacting, communicating, and coordinating with other people. Indeed the distinction between science (hard skills) and culture (soft or core skills) makes little sense when those studying STEM subjects require core skills for adequate job performance and those in non-STEM fields increasingly require the analytical tools that have grown in importance in many fields, including human resource management, marketing, and sales-related jobs.

Our rejecting a sharp distinction between knowing and doing is based on the fact that they are both integral to all forms of work. Consider Richard Sennett's concept of craft, that it is about "the desire to do a job well and for its own sake." It is not limited to skilled manual labor but equally applies to computer programmers, doctors, artists, and parenting when it is practiced as a skilled craft. He elaborates this point by arguing that "every good craftsman conducts a dialogue between concrete practices and thinking; this dialogue evolves into sustaining habits, and these habits establish a rhythm between problem solving and problem finding."[35] This closely relates to the empowering aspects of learning to know.

We only have to consider the dexterous skills of a brain surgeon like Henry Marsh and the types of reasoning that he must engage in to see Sennett's point. Marsh describes an operation on a young woman, Melanie, to take out a tumor, in the following terms: "I showed [my assistant] how to make a single burr hole in the skull, [using] a wire saw called a Gigli after its inventor—a sort of glorified cheese wire which makes a much finer cut through bone than the power tools we usually use—to make a very small opening in the skull just above Melanie's right eye."[36] To remove the tumor Marsh and his team had to have knowledge of the brain's functioning so that they appreciated the risks involved, in this case blinding Melanie, which they had to assess based on past practice.

This quote from a leading brain surgeon exemplifies the connection between knowing and doing that rejects the idea of a narrow vocational training as distinct from general professional training. Here it is difficult to improve on Dewey's idea of a vocation or a calling as "an organizing principle for information and ideas; for knowledge and intellectual growth. It provides an axis which runs through an immense diversity of detail; it causes different experiences, facts, items of information to fall into order with one another."[37] A vocation in this sense is a way of uniting knowledge with practice.

Dewey makes a related point as new technologies can be used to reinforce the distinction between knowing and doing, when permission to think is limited to experts and managers in command roles, while others are expected to execute work tasks, distancing workers from their labor. Dewey writes:

> An education which acknowledges the full intellectual and social meaning of a vocation would include instruction in the historic background of present conditions; training in science to give intelligence and initiative in dealing with material and agencies of production; and study of economics, civics, and politics, to bring the future worker into touch with the problems of the day and the various methods proposed for its improvement. Above all, it would train power of readaptation to changing conditions so that future workers would not become blindly subject to a fate imposed upon them. This ideal has to contend not only with the inertia of existing educational traditions, but also with the opposition of those who are entrenched in command of the industrial machinery, and who realize that such an educational system if made general would threaten their ability to use others for their own ends.[38]

Learning to do is therefore indispensable to individual growth in developing the foundational skills to enable people to live a full life as well as make a living, and to do things out of the ordinary, but equally to do ordinary things that can have an extraordinary impact on the lives of others. Many jobs may not offer the deep learning that this presupposes, as the skills to execute the work can be quickly learned. But the education we are advocating is for life, not just for paid work. The key challenge is to reform existing models of education, training, and lifelong learning in ways that enable a much closer relationship between knowing and doing.

Learning to Be

This is the heart of the new human capital. It's not about making up people based on their ability to perform according to some metric or other, or as a unit of human capital. The banking model replaced the intrinsic enjoyment of learning with the extrinsic rewards of credentials and promise of higher wages. Instead the emphasis of the new human capital is on education for personal growth, nurturing a holistic relationship between knowing and doing, in which waged work will play more or less of a role in people's lives. Learning to be involves enhancing self-knowledge through continuing education and learning, aimed at developing more of the human and creative potential of all, in all its cultural, economic, and social richness. This is a far cry from *Homo economicus*, requiring a different set of values in the process of learning.

Personal integrity and conduct are integral to knowing and doing. Recent discussions point to the fact that those without a college education were more likely to vote for Donald Trump in the 2016 presidential election, and the same is true for the Brexit vote in the United Kingdom, but level of education is no guarantee of integrity or ethical ambition. A harsh lesson of the 2008 financial crisis, which left future generations of Americans and Europeans with huge national debts, is that when abilities and talents are divorced from what Thomas Jefferson called "virtue"—and what we prefer to call "ethical ambition"—greed and corruption undermine the very foundations of capitalism.[39]

This highlights the danger of any model of human capital that puts self-interest above integrity in getting ahead in life. Hence ethical ambition is a significant element of the character of labor supply.[40] If any further evidence is required, George Steiner reminds us of the grim fact that 20 percent of the officer corps who ran Hitler's death camps during World War II held PhDs at a time when only 2 to 3 percent of the German population had completed a university education. "How was it possible," he asks, "for Hitler's SS troops to carry copies of Goethe's poems in their back pockets as they went about their daily dark deeds?"[41]

In antiquity, Richard Sennett explains, there was a widely shared understanding of character as the ethical value people placed on their individual desires and relationships with others. We can see how today's workplaces are associated with a "corrosion" of character because they undermine "the

long-term aspects of our emotional experience. Character is expressed by loy-
alty and mutual commitment, or through the pursuit of long-term goals, or
by the practice of delayed gratification for the sake of a future end."When
constantly exposed to competing ideas about what to think and how to behave, "character concerns the personal traits which we value in ourselves and
for which we seek to be valued by others."[42]

Today learning to be involves combining a sense of past, present and future (this is more than, but includes, a sense of occupational career). It is this
that substitutes for the corrosion of character in the absence of stable, lifelong
employment. For individuals it is what connects learning and doing over the
life course.[43]

The point to emerge from this discussion is that knowledge and skills that
can be applied in paid and unpaid work require a set of characteristics and
values in relation to learning that extend well beyond the borders of the labor
market. The search for knowledge and practical applications, seeing the world
through new lenses, finding novel solutions to problems, patience when they
do not materialize instantly, and the value of doing a job well are all necessary.
Underlying these characteristics is the confidence to take risks and a willingness to learn new things. It is the development of these qualities that are too
frequently denied by high-stakes competition, repeated testing, and an acquisitive approach to learning.

Learning to Live and Work with Others

Learning to live and work with others is a fact of life. In the early years we
typically learn to live with others in families, gradually incorporating family
friends and the local neighborhood, followed by school, college, and the
workplace. But, as previously discussed, we can be politically or institutionally encouraged to see ourselves as selfish competitors in a dog-eat-dog world,
or we can recognize our interdependence as part of what is means to live in an
advanced civilization. What is taught and the way it is taught reflect what is
valued within the wider society.

In the new human capital, mutual recognition, dignity, and respect are
at the heart of living together and are reflected in the way we judge different
jobs, treat the less fortunate, and reward economic activity. They do not need
to be sacrifices to deliver a sustainable future economy or national economic
growth. But in an age of uncertainty, when many people are on the defensive
in seeking to protect what they have, let alone improve on what they've got,
it is not easy to create social generosity that recognizes the needs of strangers.

The importance of this challenge is difficult to overstate in a context of job scarcity, where the labor market is unable to deliver on the promise of education or deliver distributional justice. Learning to live together, even within the same society, let alone the wider world, will depend on changing the ways we think about both the poor and the wealthy, along with finding ways of bringing these worlds closer together in the interest of all. But how we live and work together can't simply be taught, because it is part of a lived experience.

Our understanding of emotional labor illustrates the point. Many jobs involve the exercise of emotional labor, requiring employees to manage their feelings in accordance with the organization's model of customer service, alongside the emotional demands of family and neighborhood life.[44] Managing emotions is central to the banking model of education. It is treated as a skill that needs to be learned, based on a rational calculation of effort for reward in the form of credentials in the hope that these can be exchanged in the job market. In an era of neoliberalism we have come to take it for granted that emotional labor is reduced to a forced civility, imposed by the demands of the market rather than spontaneous interaction based on mutual dignity and respect. Simon Head makes an important connection between equity and emotional labor. Good service, he suggests, is difficult to produce when the conditions for mutual understanding and respect are absent, as is commonly true of highly unequal economies such as America and Britain. In Scandinavian economies "a strong tradition of civic equality . . . gives employees and customers a shared language of courtesy and respect, so that their public selves can manage the transactions of everyday commerce without recourse to emotional labor," which amounts to forced civility.[45]

But it is also the case that mutual respect and tolerance of others depends on understanding.[46] At the micro level this requires a focus on collaborative skills or co-intelligence aimed at developing teamworking skills and co-creation. This reflects the fact that what makes us human is not only the ability to learn and use skills, but how we use our individual capabilities in combination with others. This is true of both the way we become competent employees and in the way we participate in the wider society. How we work with others is not only something we pick up on the job but requires practice, including interactions mediated through social media and other forms of digital technologies.

To make a life with others we need a common understanding based on a set of values that connect knowing and doing. Earlier we made the point that one of the key ways in which we can consider the possibility of other worlds and ways of doing things is by empowering knowledge. It is a way of lifting us out of the local and the particular; considering the recent political divisions over immigration, this is an important part of education for all citizens.

At the same time, our knowledge of how to make a life with others has become more complex as the new frontiers of genetics, robotics, machine intelligence, and environmental meltdown impinge on our lives. The world is changing too quickly for mutual understanding to be front-loaded in early childhood education. It is a lifelong process of learning and reflection, which is the essence of learning how to learn. Living with others requires a shared dialogue between concrete practices and thought, about problem finding and problem solving: it is about statecraft, a way of seeing shared problems and addressing them, knowing that there are always power dynamics and competing views that have to be negotiated.

With uncertainties surrounding advances in automation and artificial intelligence and the continuation of current trends in the global labor market, fundamental changes are affecting national politics, including the rise of right-wing authoritarian governments. In this context education and democracy take center stage. And here the news is mixed. Dewey, among many other philosophers, saw education as important to the fostering of democracy, in part through the mutual respect and tolerance that could be learned in school. How has it fared given the current inequalities in education and the advent of populist parties and national leaders?

Ben Ansell and Jane Gingrich have analyzed European data on attitudes to democracy, and while they find that higher education facilitates a positive view of democracy, they also note that this does not apply to those who are in jobs that do not match their qualifications; these employees are more likely to vote for radical or populist right parties, and the same is true of those who have not gone to university. But even among graduates there are differences between those who support redistribution, which must surely be central to addressing the inequalities and uncertainties we can expect, and those who do not. Ansell and Gingrich hypothesize that these differences are based on the type of work graduates engage in; those employed in the public sphere are more likely to favor redistribution, while those in the private sector do not. This tells us education seems to foster positive views of democracy, but it is not a bulwark against the types of policies that we will need to develop, including reducing inequalities in life chances through education and, as we shall argue in chapter 11, providing a basic income to ensure that all citizens have a decent standard of living.[47]

Human Capital Is Degraded by Inequality

The new human capital is premised on the proposition that it is not innate talent that is in short supply but suitable jobs and educational opportunities. Talents are widely distributed, and differences in attainment and performance need to take account of inequalities in social opportunity rather than simply innate differences. If societies are to use education and the labor market as the arbiters of social inequality in the allocation of people to different jobs offering differences in life chances, income, and individual satisfaction, then the selection process cannot be arbitrary but must be efficient as well as fair.[48] We've seen that improving the quality of the labor supply not only depends on making people more skilled; it also depends on giving people opportunities to grow over a lifetime, which crucially depends on access to quality education. Moreover, restructuring the future economy also depends on the social qualities of the workforce. As Dewey teaches, "Only diversity makes change and progress."[49] There are therefore good economic reasons for using education and training systems to break down the barriers that educate some to command and others to follow. There are also good social and economic reasons for downward social mobility from privileged families if it encourages the circulation of opportunities and rewards likely to bring with it fresh insights, innovation, and different ways of working. But at the same time as being efficient it must also be fair.[50]

We have outlined a growth model of education and lifelong learning aimed at creating the foundations for self-development for all. But any analysis of the new human capital has to be grounded within its socioeconomic context. This can be applied at a local, organizational, national, or international level, although it needs to be able to show how social structures and human action interact within different contexts. People cannot be categorized simply as more or less skilled or well qualified according to different levels of investment in education and training. They are positioned within stratified labor markets and education systems, which can be organized in different ways with different consequences for self-development and how individuals capitalize on their prior learning.

It is not enough to change what is taught and how things are taught; we must also transform the opportunity structure.[51] It has been shown that education credentials and jobs are positional goods. Investing in more skills or getting a college degree is an individual attainment relative to the performance of others in an explicit or implicit hierarchy of achievement.[52] Here education systems play a key role as they are designed to create a hierarchy of academic achievement, with students awarded different grades, qualifying them to compete for different kinds of employment, in a context where there are rarely enough of the good jobs that people want, at the same time as a growing supply of labor market entrants. Therefore a master's degree may add to a person's existing knowledge and allow them to record a high-level credential on their curriculum vitae, but it may not give them an added advantage in the job market. As we've explained, labor market success depends on the employability of others.[53]

If people are judged in comparison to others, leading to different opportunities to capitalize within the labor market, we need to address social inequalities based on social class background, gender, ethnicity, and nationality. Class differences in educational performance and major inequalities in translating educational achievements into jobs point to differences in market power that cannot be explained or addressed solely in terms of investments in education and training.[54]

In competitive labor markets those from more privileged backgrounds have a far better chance of getting a good job compared to those from less privileged backgrounds, even with the same academic credentials. This is partly due to the "artificial aristocracy," who use their wealth and influence to maintain their privileges without virtue or talent.[55] Challenging fundamental inequalities in access to a high-quality education and inequalities in wider life chances is a key part of an alternative model of human capital.

Currently one of the main ways of increasing opportunities and intergenerational social mobility is by extending access to a college or university education. Using contextual information, including social background, in university admissions may help but is unlikely to significantly reduce inequalities in the labor supply because "more means different" as new sources of distinction emerge within the education system and the labor market. We've seen how national and global league tables are one way in which elite universities seek to distinguish themselves from the rest, and middle-ranking universities from the run of the mill. In a context of rapid employment growth, where the number of skilled jobs is increasing, these positional inequalities are less pronounced because new job opportunities are being created. But when there are increasing numbers of well-qualified people seeking to capitalize when there are not enough good jobs, it reinforces existing inequalities, resulting in a massive waste of talent.

Reforming education and training systems are necessary to narrow inequalities in individual life chances, including moves to equalize educational resources. These inequalities must also be addressed to maximize intergenerational social mobility. But we must not lose sight of a model of individual growth that does not necessarily depend on individual occupational advancement.

Rethinking Meritocracy

A growth model of human capital recognizes the opportunity gap in the relationship between origins and destinations, based on social class, gender, ethnicity, or race inequalities as a major target for policy intervention. But opportunity cannot be limited to an equal chance to be unequal. Although there is an urgent need to reform educational systems and the labor market in the direction of a level playing field, doing so cannot fully compensate for family inequalities that give students and job seekers differential access to financial resources, cultural assets, and social networks that advantage those from more privileged backgrounds. The education system and labor market do not reflect the distribution of human capabilities but differences in individual (and family) capacities to compete. Even a reformed system of education is a relatively poor way of assessing ability, given that it measures a narrow part of what constitutes human capability. Given the "plasticity of our natures," we never know what each of us is truly capable of, and therefore we should not conflate individual capability with examination performance.[56]

In conjunction with increasing opportunities for all to compete for prizes we also need to focus on equality of outcome: the development of "threshold" capabilities that will shape individual functioning, including "capitalizing" aspects of the self.[57] A basic threshold of education is at the heart of inclusive growth rather than a banking model of human capital. This rejects the idea that individual entitlements should be commensurate with their investments in human capital, where merit is assumed to be warranted by performance. It equally rejects the idea of equality of opportunity, if this means having an implausibly equal chance of being unequal, because the odds of educational success are stacked against those from less advantaged backgrounds.

Martha Nussbaum asserts that all human beings ought to be supported to reach a certain threshold level of capability. She defines equality of opportunity by the extent to which the educational system enables everyone to live a successful adult life. This should not be reduced to "coerced functioning" measured by a narrow range of competences. "So the attitudes towards people's basic capabilities is not a meritocratic one—more innately skilled people get better treatment—but, if anything, the opposite: those who need more help to get above the threshold get more help."[58] This does not mean that everyone has to get there at the same time or in the same way, but it does shift the focus in terms of what is taught, how it is taught, and how it is resourced.

Education systems can be reformed to institutionally encourage individual opportunity and learning through the development of "active habits involving thought, invention, and initiative in applying capacities to new aims."[59] But the threshold of capabilities is dynamic, not set in stone; the educational threshold appropriate in 1970s America is obviously different from the threshold appropriate for all in 2020. Equally, what is achievable in emerging economies may not be the same as in developed economies but should be guided by the principles of a quality education for all consistent with the individual growth model. In developed economies the threshold for education could be set in ways that end the sharp distinctions between graduates and nongraduates and rejecting a "user pays" models of college or university tuition fees, justified under the banking model of education.

Colleges and universities should be as diverse as possible in terms of social class, gender, and ethnicity. This requires experimenting with selection to the most prestigious universities based on the recognition that students from working-class backgrounds may not have the grades of their more privileged counterparts but once admitted may achieve to the same, or even higher level.

Conclusion

This chapter offers a different way of thinking about labor supply. An individual's human capital is defined as a relationship between the self and work, as well as a social and economic relationship with others. Not all of who we are or what we do is capitalized. People have choices in terms of how to manage this relationship in living to work or working to live. We've argued that focusing on investments in education or rates of return reveals precious little about the quality of the labor supply (rather than the sum of individual skills) or what people actually do for a living.

The social quality of the workforce (adaptability, trust, cooperation) is as important as the technical quality of individual skills. Knowing the numbers of people qualified at different levels is a useful indicator, but it tells us little about the development, character, and quality of labor supply. Here the stock of human capital is replaced by a flow of dynamic capability—highlighting the individual and combined capacity for learning and productive activity in rapidly changing contexts. The value of human capital and its relationship to work, productivity, and economic growth are not fixed in time or place, requiring a new competition policy based on job scarcity.

Rethinking Labor Demand

HAVING DESCRIBED AN alternative view of labor supply, we now turn to questions of labor demand at the heart of the new human capital. We want to challenge Gary Becker and his way of looking at labor markets, where the main focus is on labor scarcity and a skills competition, in which individuals, firms, and nations compete on differential investments in education and training.[1] We also challenge David Autor's claim that "the issue is not that middle-class workers are doomed by automation and technology, but instead that human capital investment must be at the heart of any long-term strategy for producing skills that are complemented by rather than substituted for by technological change."[2]

The extent to which people can capitalize on education, training, and work experience depends on both the composition of the workforce (supply) and the demand for workers. How we understand the future of work will therefore have a profound impact on the fate of human capital. It is changes in the occupational structure rather than investments in education and training that shape the demand for professionals or managers. In this chapter we will argue that the new human capital rejects the view that demand issues can be resolved through a combination of technological and educational solutions. Rather a jobs lens is required to shed new light on changes in the occupational structure, transforming the way people capitalize on their education, along with the distribution of individual life chances.

Reinstating the labor market at the heart of human capital analysis reveals an endemic capacity problem of how to create enough jobs, of sufficient quality, to meet the occupational and wage expectations of the workforce. The expansion of higher education has not been matched by a commensurate rise in the demand for skilled occupations, although the extent of this mismatch varies from country to country.[3] This requires an understanding of

The Death of Human Capital? Phillip Brown, Hugh Lauder, and Sin Yi Cheung, Oxford University Press (2020).
© Oxford University Press. DOI: 10.1093/oso/9780190644307.001.0001

job scarcity and the problems it poses to individuals seeking to capitalize on their knowledge and skill. It also presents a problem to governments seeking to identify policy reforms to maintain a meaningful relationship between learning and earning. Here governments have a key role to play in addressing the market failures of recent decades. Active state action is required in response to job scarcity and the wider economic challenges confronting both developed and emerging economies. But for reasons we describe, distributional issues around learning, working, and earning can't be fully resolved by active labor market policies.

Labor Demand and the Future of Work

In rethinking what we mean by labor demand and how it shapes the way individuals capitalize on job opportunities, we need to return to first principles.[4] When thinking about labor demand, typically measured by level of workforce skills or earnings, it is easy to forget that we are talking about what people actually do for a living. In agrarian societies labor was largely focused on material survival, but in mature economies there is a complex division of labor geared toward meeting basic needs and also delivering an extraordinary array of goods and services.

If we consider economics to be the study of the provision of the material well-being of society which requires workers to specialise rather than doing everything for themselves, then productivity is dependent on the social institutions that can best enable that material well-being. How to organise the division of labour has been a matter of ongoing debate since Adam Smith's *The Wealth of Nations*.

However, this social division of labor found in all human societies does not neatly map onto models of employment, as represented in orthodox theory. Some of the activities that may contribute to labor productivity, economic growth, or human flourishing remain unrecognized or undervalued precisely because they are not judged to have economic value—they stand outside wage competition and the price mechanism. It is only when social activities get bundled and formalized in labor contracts that they are judged to constitute part of labor demand because they are defined to have market value. This has been so taken for granted that orthodox theory is based on a standard model of full-time employment that characterized the second half of the twentieth century, at least for male workers. The exception is self-employment, where the relationship between learning and earning is shrouded in the magic dust of entrepreneurial enterprise.

In orthodox approaches, labor demand remains closely related to those activities comprising the formal economy, defined as people who are economically active. In developed economies this seems to be a relatively straightforward accounting process as people are either employed, unemployed, or outside of the job market (economically inactive). But a great deal of work is not underwritten by standard contracts of employment, especially in emerging economies; as the World Bank has acknowledged, jobs can be defined in different ways:

> Worldwide, more than 3 billion people have jobs, but the nature of their jobs varies greatly. Some 1.65 billion have regular wages or salaries. Another 1.5 billion work in farming and small household enterprises, or in casual or seasonal day labor. The majority of workers in the poorest countries are engaged in these types of work, outside the scope of an employer-employee relationship. Another 200 million people, a disproportionate share of them youth, are unemployed and actively looking for work. Almost 2 billion working-age adults are neither working nor looking for work; the majority of these are women, and an unknown number are eager to have a job.[5]

There has also been growth in nonstandard employment in developed economies.[6] In 2015 the OECD published a report on inequality and the labor market, documenting the proportion of jobs that constituted nonstandard work and arguing that such work is one of the major causes of income polarization. This group includes those on temporary or zero-hours contracts, part-time employees, and the self-employed. Overall those engaged in nonstandard work receive lower incomes and compose a growing proportion of a nation's labor force. Approximately 40 percent of workers in Germany and the United Kingdom were found to be in nonstandard forms of work, while in the Netherlands the proportion is 60 percent.[7]

The International Labor Organization calculated that approximately 30 percent of American workers were in nonstandard jobs in 2015.[8] At the same time over 30 percent of working-age Americans, almost 38 million men and 57 million women, appear in employment statistics under the label "not in the labor force." Another 7 million American workers are formally registered as unemployed.[9] Combining these figures with the predicted growth in the number of people working in the variously labeled "on-demand," "platform," or "gig" economy compounds problems associated with the standard supply-demand model of orthodox theory. When we add to these data women's unpaid and unrecognized work in reproductive and informal educational work, which underpins the economy, it is clear that we need a different way of thinking about demand.

In contemplating the future of labor demand, we not only need to consider what activities in everyday life are viewed as having economic value and are part of established official definitions of employer demand; we also need to consider the prospects for future labor demand. Here we begin by considering the "double movement" of technological innovation to challenge the way skill biased technological change theorists draw distinctions between routine and nonroutine jobs, and between jobs that are skill-replacing and those that are complementary to new technology. These distinctions do not adequately capture the underlying business processes involved. They ignore the history of economic innovation, where creative destruction is followed by the destruction of the creative. In other words, productivity depends on knowledge innovation and its rapid diffusion, codification, and standardization in a bid to increase efficiency and profit margins.[10]

New Technologies and the Counterrevolutions of Innovation and Standardization

In orthodox theory, technological change is of great importance because it is assumed to drive the demand for high skills in the limitless progression toward a high-wage workforce. This is consistent with the idea of a "fourth industrial revolution" that is predicted to accelerate the demand for high skills, at the same time as automating lower-level jobs.[11] Klaus Schwab, who heads up the World Economic Forum, envisages a technological future resulting in many new positions and professions being created: "For this reason, scarcity of a skilled workforce rather the availability of capital is more likely to be the crippling limit to innovation, competitiveness and growth."[12]

We've described this way of seeing the economic world in terms of Goldin and Katz's race between education and technology, where the central problem is whether the education system can keep up with the blistering pace of technological change. But there is a very different way of understanding the relationship between education and technology that offers an alternative interpretation, raising fundamental questions about the future demand for high-skilled or knowledge workers, and whether earning will match learning.

The importance attached to technological change has a relatively long economic history because it was identified as the major source of productivity and economic growth. It also helped to distance economics from the taunt of being the "dismal science" in the late nineteenth century. But in presenting the "simple answer" of technological change, Daniel Bell recognized that it begged a complex question.[13] The complexity stems from the fact that technological change is a catch-all for the best methods, techniques, and organizational practices that contribute to productivity. This, as Bell observes, can mean many different things: "It can be a machine to forge car engines replacing old hand-casting methods. It can be a physical technique, such as building a ramp to move stones up a pyramid. It can be a simple sociological technique such as a rough division of labor in the construction of a shoe or a sophisticated technique of industrial engineering such as time-and-motion studies."[14]

The orthodox response is to claim that there has been a fundamental change in the way technology is used, where productivity now relies on the widespread use of knowledge workers. Bell and other luminaries beyond the economics profession followed this line of argument, including the management guru Peter Drucker. In Drucker's account, the economic utility of knowledge shifted from a period of industrial capitalism, when knowledge was applied to the organization of work, such as in the creation of the Fordist production line, to today's high-tech digital economy. The creation of new knowledge defines the economy because it is the source of productivity and competitive advantage. Not surprisingly this has led the protagonists of skill biased technological change theory to investigate the scale of technological unemployment along with the kinds of jobs most likely to be affected by automation, robotics, and artificial intelligence.

We've seen that a major focus has been on identifying skills that are complementary to new technology rather than being replaced by it.[15] Skill biased technological change theorists assume that routine work will be automated, so the search is on to identify the knowledge and skills that cannot be replicated by machines. But while there is nothing new about manufacturing jobs being replaced by new technologies, we have reached the stage where companies such as Adidas can make shoes in Germany untouched by human hands. Manufacturing production in China has increased by 70 percent since 1996, but the workforce has declined by 25 percent, which means there are 30 million fewer Chinese workers in manufacturing.[16]

Such trends have led skill-bias theorists to look to unstructured problem-solving and working with new information as work that robots cannot do. They assume that these skills require high levels of education, which is why Autor stresses a need for greater investment in human capital. But this will do little to address the basic problem of job scarcity. In *Dancing with Robots*, Frank Levy and Richard Murnane explain that the demand for key functional skills, as they call them, flatlined in the first decade of the twenty-first century.[17] Paul Beaudry and his colleagues have shown that those now entering the labor market find a decline in high-skill jobs. The policy strategy of simply advocating more education to satisfy the demand for these skills is flawed.

The Double Movements of Technological Revolutions

Two employment revolutions have been linked to productive innovation since the late nineteenth century. Both are characterized by a double movement of knowledge innovation based on scientific discovery and technological innovation, such as the development of machine tools, electronic devices, and computers, followed by a process of codification and standardization. Although this is typically downplayed or ignored in accounts of technology and economic development, Jay Tate reminds us that "industrial revolutions are revolutions in standardization."[18]

The formative period for the first employment revolution dates back to the 1700s, at a time when much of the new technological know-how remained in the heads of British engineers and skilled workers. Various attempts by French, German, and American entrepreneurs and governments to acquire this knowledge led to various forms of legislation in Britain to restrict skilled workers and machinery from leaving the country through legal means, such as the Tools Act in 1785. Ha-Joon Chang observes that during this period there was a fierce:

> technological arms race . . . using recruitment schemes, machine smuggling and industrial espionage. But by the end of the century, the nature of the game had changed fundamentally with the increasing importance of "disembodied" knowledge—that is, knowledge that can be separated from the workers and the machines that used to hold them. The development of science meant that a lot of—although not all—knowledge could be written down in a (scientific) language that could be understood by anyone with appropriate training. An engineer who understood the principles of physics and mechanics could reproduce a machine simply by looking at the technical drawings. Similarly, if a chemical formula could be acquired, medicines could be easily reproduced by trained chemists.[19]

It was this process of disembodied knowledge that led to the explosion in scientific knowledge production, which in turn led to the rising demand for formal education and training. It is perhaps not surprising that it also led to a widespread view that "what has now become decisive for society is the new centrality of theoretical knowledge, the primacy of theory over empiricism, and the codification of knowledge into abstract systems of symbols that can be translated into many different and varied circumstances. Every society now lives by innovation and growth."[20]

Disembodied scientific knowledge clearly contributed to a significant increase in demand for knowledge workers, but this is only the first part of the double movement.[21] Even by the early twentieth century advances in scientific knowledge in physics, chemistry, and mechanical and electrical engineering were limited in terms of their impact on employment until they were harnessed to the technologies of *mechanical Taylorism,* characterized by the Fordist production line. The knowledge of craft workers was captured by engineers, then codified and redesigned in the shape of the moving assembly line. While this stripped craft workers of much of their knowledge and the opportunity to ply their trade, it created thousands of mass-production jobs that needed little formal training yet commanded relatively high wages, at least in key industries such as the automotive sector.

It also led to the vast expansion of office bureaucracy (which was mirrored in the public sector). New kinds of administrative jobs were created, including managerial occupations to oversee the production process, along with new jobs in sales, marketing, and finance as payment by installment grew in popularity. There were also more opportunities for employment in personnel departments to manage the wages and careers of the white-collar workforce. It was this growth in middle-class occupations that contributed to the idea of skill-biased technological change, but this ignores the realities of today's double movement.

The second great employment revolution began in the 1970s and continues today with advances in digital technologies. In the first stage of this double movement there has been an extraordinary increase in computing power, captured in Moore's Law, which predicts a doubling in computing capacity every eighteen months. This has given rise to new job opportunities—for computer programmers, software engineers, data analysts, and experts in cybersecurity—consistent with skill-bias theory, but it is also characterized by a second movement driven by the search for greater organizational control and for firms to profit from advances in technological capabilities. It's not simply the changing character of knowledge that needs to be understood but the power relations shaping how knowledge is defined, controlled, owned, and appropriated for profitable purposes.

Today the second movement remains in its infancy and can be characterized by digital Taylorism and the advent of AI.[22] Advances in communication technologies, including the capacity for digital processing and internet capability, have created the realistic possibility of developing global standards that reduce technical complexity and diversity. A building-block or Lego approach using platform architectures and reusable IT components is seen by many companies as a more efficient way of making their organizations more adaptable to change, to be applied to systems, processes, and people.[23] The same processes that enabled cars, computers, and televisions to be broken down into their component parts, manufactured by companies around the world and then configured according to customer specifications, are being applied to jobs in the service sector that do not depend on face-to-face interactions with customers. The upshot is that these jobs can be easily automated or exported to where they can be done most cheaply.

Terms such as "financial services factory" and "industrialization of services" are used to describe the transformation of the service sector. Accenture Consulting is a proponent of "the concept of industrialization—breaking down processes and products into constituent components that can be recombined in a tailored, automated fashion—to non-manufacturing settings."[24] Rather than sparking a new wave of office employment this new movement has seen office work being standardized, digitalized, modularized, and automated.

The manager of a Western technology company in Bangalore described to us how the source codes, akin to the secret formula for Coca-Cola, were retained within computer networks controlled by the head office in America, preventing employees from developing on-the-job knowledge and skills: "The presence of digital Taylorism can't be overstated because it is happening everywhere. All your call center jobs or your business processing that happens, it's typically Taylorism in a more digitalized world, because there are only five or six things you have to answer and they're on your system and you don't customize anything. . . . This is true of all kinds of jobs today in India. . . . Much of the work is very much like an assembly line." The head of operations for a mobile technology company who had recently moved to restructure global operations for a well-known household appliances company told us, "We need fewer fighter pilots and more drone operatives."[25]

New technologies have increased the potential to translate knowledge work into working knowledge, no longer limited to routine jobs. The separation between *conception* (thinking) and *execution* (doing) that characterized mechanical Taylorism is now being applied to technical, managerial, and professional occupations. This "new industrialism," as Simon Head calls it, is pushing out from its old heartland in manufacturing to the service economy and has also "pushed upward in the occupational hierarchy to include much of the professional and administrative middle class: physicians as well as call-center agents; teachers, academics and publishers as well as 'associates' at Walmart and Amazon; bank loan officers and middle managers as well as fast food workers."[26]

The rise of digital Taylorism has far-reaching implications for labor demand because it highlights changes in the way managerial and professional work is organized, rather than simply whether digital technologies will result in large-scale job loss. It is often thought that professional work is immune to the algorithms of software developers because of the need for judgment, flair, and complex evaluation. However, in the legal profession, for example, e-discovery software can scrutinize millions of pages of court evidence with much greater speed and with a higher level of accuracy than expensive lawyers.

What often goes unrecognized in debates about the impact of new technologies, especially of the skill-bias variety, is that the central issue is not simply whether smart machines can automate or even enhance the skills associated with a specific occupational task or role, but the transformation of the whole labor process when applied to the factory or the office.[27] Caroline Hanley uses the example of the automation of white-collar work at General Electric, which dates back to the 1950s, to challenge theories of SBTC. She correctly rejects the assumption that "new technologies are external stimuli that reshape labor demand rather than tools designed to change an existing division of labor, and that skill and productivity are objective metrics rather than workplace social constructs."[28]

Equally, we shouldn't be surprised by the latest revolution in standardization because if knowledge is the new source of wealth, then it is of little use to companies if it is locked in the heads of employees who can sell it for a higher salary to a competing firm. From a firm's perspective, the benefits of new technologies are limited unless the same practices, software, and systems are aligned across national or global operations.

It would, however, be an oversimplification to assume that the rise of digital Taylorism leads to a general deskilling of the workforce. Digital Taylorism offers firms new ways of segmenting their workforce:[29]

- **Developer roles.** The top echelons of the workforce are given permission to think and viewed as essential to take the business forward. They typically include staff involved in executive functions, along with those identified as talented researchers, managers, and professionals. They are highly qualified, are expected to work on complex and international engagements, and typically are recruited from elite universities.
- **Demonstrator roles.** These are assigned to implement or execute existing knowledge, procedures, or management techniques. They include consultants, managers, teachers, nurses, and technicians using knowledge delivered through digital software. Although demonstrator roles include well-qualified people, they are often below the talent radar in middle-level jobs, where much of the focus is on soft skills to ensure effective communication with colleagues and customers.
- **Drone roles.** These roles are typically less skilled and offer little discretion to employees, although a good level of literacy, numeracy, and teamwork skills are often required. Much of the work is digitally controlled and includes back-office functions such as data-entry jobs and customer contact in call centers, where virtually everything is prescribed or scripted in software packages. Many of these jobs are highly mobile as they can be standardized and digitalized. They are also roles at immediate risk of automation given advances in machine intelligence, voice recognition, and data harvesting.

This double movement in technological innovation is closely related to the changing relationship between work and place, with major implications for the future of labor demand. At the macro level the relationship between work and place has been transformed by globalization, at the same time there are changes at the micro level offering the potential for new models of bottom-up economic activity, although much of this activity will not deliver a living wage.

Technology and Globalization

At the macro level a radical separation between work and place has been driven by globalization, enabled by digital technologies. Across the developed world, globalization was seen by the pundits of borderless free trade to hold out the tantalizing prospect of the West doing more of the world's thinking, leading to a significant expansion in the demand for a knowledge-intense workforce. This was believed to strengthen the human capital mission of schools, colleges, and universities, as constraints on the demand for knowledge workers would be lifted due to an increase in the global demand for America's and Europe's knowledge workers.[30] In reality, the scale at which jobs are open to global competition remains a subject of some controversy, especially following America's use of punitive trade barriers to protect industries such as steel, but what has become clear is that skills are no barrier to international competition.[31] The increase in the global supply of high-skilled workers has resulted in a major shift in the organization of knowledge work, but not in the way predicted by orthodox theorists.

The idea of the West thinking for the world has confronted an exponential increase in the numbers of other nations with an educated workforce, competing on price as well as quality. We have noted the dramatic changes in the expansion of education since the 1990s, including China's commitment to become an innovation economy driven by an expansion of higher education. This expansion led Chinese to outnumber American college graduates by a ratio of over three to one. Similar trends, although less spectacular, are evident in other countries as university enrollments around the world have experienced rapid growth.

In conjunction with other state-led initiatives accelerating the pace of economic growth, some emerging economies have leapfrogged decades of incremental changes in technologies and business practices. Rapid advances in mobile and internet communications, knowledge diffusion, and the benchmarking of global quality standards have all contributed to a process of disruptive innovation.[32]

Globalization has given transnational companies much greater control, offering the flexibility to create sophisticated value chains across established borders and boundaries. Many aspects of production, design, and research are located around the globe, wherever comparable skills are available at lower costs. This includes widespread use of offshoring beyond back-office jobs already established in the 1970s and 1980s.[33] Globalization also initiated the global integration of human resources strategies. No longer was it necessary to base product market strategies on the idea that anything of quality would require paying high wages to high-skilled workers, invariably found in high-cost economies. Consequently many of the things that companies at the turn of the century thought could be done only in the West could be done in other parts of the world often at a cheaper price.

This has had a major impact on high-skilled workers in America and Britain. It has led tech corporations on the West Coast of America, such as

Apple, to use global value chains that include offshoring high-skilled work to Asia, given significant price differentials. Apple's partnership with Foxconn, for example, extends well beyond manufacturing and includes a business group involved in high-quality engineering services. There are also significant differences in operating margins: in 2012 Apple achieved 33 percent, compared to Foxconn's 3 percent. Little wonder that Foxconn is notorious for driving down wage costs, given such operating margins being imposed by leading tech corporations.[34]

Gerald Davis examined the decline in employment in what he calls the vanishing American corporation, despite rising stock market valuations. In 2015 Facebook had 1.35 billion users but only 9,199 employees and was valued at one quarter of a trillion dollars; Twitter had 288 million users and 3,638 employees; and Apple had a relatively large direct workforce of 56,000 employees. But when compared with the corporate giants of the past, these are small numbers; for example, in 1982 Exxon had 173,000 workers, although by 2012 this had declined to 77,000. Many of today's leading firms are making large profits with a small direct workforce, while offshoring non-core business to take advantage of international labor arbitrage.[35]

The radical separation between work and place resulting from globalization is driven not only by Western companies looking for new markets and greater profits; Chinese and Indian companies are operating a high-value, low-cost model in an attempt to compete for global market share.[36] Emerging nations have extended their ambitions from attracting foreign direct investment from European or North American companies to becoming innovation economies, building knowledge infrastructures, research universities, and technical capabilities linked to home-grown companies, including state-owned enterprises, with the aim of competing for profits in international markets. This has increased the competition for skills, exposing college-educated Americans and Europeans to the same cost pressures as less-skilled workers in manufacturing in the 1970s and 1980s.

The orthodox response is to argue that this is a temporary phenomenon while wages converge.[37] But differences in labor costs between developed and emerging economies are narrowing far more slowly than might be predicted, apart from a few hot spots in China and India. Over the coming decades companies will still have considerable scope to extract value from international webs of people, processes, and suppliers based on a reverse auction, where quality is maintained while labor costs decline, reflecting a trend toward a significant high-skilled but relatively low-wage workforce in America and Europe. Moreover, when companies decide to repatriate parts of their value chains to high-cost locations in America or Europe, it is likely to be associated with investment in automation, as in the case of Adidas's new manufacturing facilities in Germany.

The interplay between globalization, state deregulation, and technological innovation fundamentally alters the parameters by which business is conducted, resulting in the greater spatial and vertical stratification of skilled work, making it more difficult to match the skill requirements of transnational companies with national models of human capital development. When considered alongside the flexibility companies now have in deciding where to think and where to produce around the world, it poses a major challenge of how to create more of the work associated with a middle-class lifestyle not only in Western economies but around the world.

A Street-Level Revolution?

If the global separation of work and place is transforming labor demand in developed as well as emerging economies, technological innovations are also bringing the means of production closer to home, with the potential to transform the way we think about demand as separate from the supply of potential workers. It is not only where work will be done within the global economy (or the wage rates that different kinds of work will command) that requires a different understanding of labor demand, but also how the wage-labor model is constructed.[38]

The shift toward more flexible contracts of employment since the late 1970s has been further facilitated by new technologies requiring people to capitalize on their knowledge and skills within more precarious models of economic participation.[39] There has been a lot of discussion about online digital platforms with the potential to disrupt many areas of employment in a diverse range of business activities, including travel, accommodation, retail, banking, education and training, and software development. Some of the most high-profile examples are Uber, Airbnb, Upwork, Profinder, and Freelancer, along with online retailers such as Ali Baba and Amazon.

Such platforms offer a quick and cost-effective way of linking supply and demand; as Klaus Schwab argues, "This enables the effective use of under-utilized assets—namely those belonging to people who had previously never thought of themselves as suppliers (i.e. a seat in their car, a spare bedroom in their home, a commercial link between a retailer and manufacturer, or the time and skill to provide a service like delivery, home repair or administrative tasks)."[40]

This on-demand economy connects the plug-and-play or job-ready model of employment to flexible or nonexistent labor contracts, where market power is in the hands of the platform impresarios. Yet, according to Jeremy Rifkin, Paul Mason, and others, these models also revolutionize the productive economy, and therefore our understanding of labor demand. Rifkin believes the transformation of the workplace is part of a more profound shift, wherein producing additional products and services have "zero" marginal cost.[41] This means that the profits typically made by those involved in delivering a college course, publishing a book, or making products are, in principle, eliminated because of the declining cost of communicating, manufacturing, and selling. He suggests that over a third of the human race are already producing their own information on relatively cheap smartphones and computers which they can share via video, audio, and text at near zero marginal cost.[42]

Rifkin is not alone in arguing that the declining costs of the means of production, driven by advances in machine intelligence, robotics, and advanced analytics, hold out the prospect of "liberating" hundreds of millions of people from work in the market economy in the next twenty to thirty years.[43] Such a radical transformation of the occupational structure would render redundant the market distinction between labor supply and demand, between employers and employees, and between sellers and consumers, leading to a rapid growth in what Rifkin calls "prosumers," who will "be able to produce, consume, and share their own goods and services with one another on the Collaborative Commons at diminishing marginal costs approaching zero, bringing to the fore new ways of organizing economic life beyond the traditional capitalist market model."[44]

However, much needs to change beyond the technical limits of production for individuals to achieve greater economic freedom in the way they capitalize on their individual and collective capabilities. Large corporations are spending millions, if not billions of dollars on cloud-based facilities, harvesting big data, and buying out start-ups that threaten the value of their intellectual property. At the same time, they are driving down the wages of workers employed through their digital platforms. Until their power is diminished, there is little prospect of the individual freedoms that Rifkin and others have pointed to. But this discussion does raise some intriguing questions about the future relationship between learning and earning. It shows that they have been artificially conjoined in modern constructions of employment, often for the purposes of distributing economic surplus rather than for individual well-being.

Tomorrow's World Today

We do not need to wait for driverless taxis, digital journalists, or robo-lecturers to understand how the labor market already poses a fundamental challenge to the prospects for individual human capital. There is already a major capacity problem with little prospect that future productivity improvements will create more jobs than they destroy. However, many of the jobs that will remain in demand are ones where productivity, on conventional measures cannot be easily improved. We only need to look around us to see that millions of people are involved in meeting the basic needs of social life, such as caring, nurturing, feeding, transporting, selling, and protecting. Many of these jobs are not going to disappear anytime soon from developed or developing economies. Even if the way job tasks are organized changes over the next decade, it is unlikely to have a significant impact on the 5.27 million American workers needed in health care support occupations, where the fastest growing occupational category is home health aides in response to an aging population; a further 3.6 million are needed in protective service occupations such as firefighters and security guards; 12.9 million people involved in food preparation and related activities; 16.2 million in sales-related occupations' and over 10 million in transporting people and things around the United States.[45] Many of these jobs are vital to a civilized society, and many of them are going to be very difficult to automate in a cost-effective way, even if public opinion and government regulation do not stand in the way of automation.

Technology is not destiny. Its applications need to be understood in terms of the history, culture, and politics that intervene in the social shaping of technology and work organization. Despite the presence of technological substitutes for labor, the extension of automation to some areas of the service economy will be uneven because machines cannot replace the work of a Mozart quartet or, for that matter, high-quality teachers and medical workers.[46] This also applies to jobs that may be relatively easy to automate but where there are good social reasons for not doing so. Nespresso technology could replace all baristas because it provides a consistent cup of coffee without the variation that is inevitable in barista-brewed coffee.[47] Baristas need to take into account the appropriate pressure and temperature for particular coffee beans; the Nespresso machine takes the complexity out of the equation. Why, then, do we have so many baristas? Not because baristas are cheaper than Nespresso technology although Italian-designed coffee technology is expensive. Rather the answer is related to the cultural assumptions about the sociability of cafés.[48]

Those cultural assumptions explain why people working in cafés will be included in over 50 million job openings the US Bureau of Labor Statistics predicts

Table 11.1 Employment and wages of occupations with the largest numeric projected growth in jobs, 2012 and projected 2022 (numbers in thousands)

Rank	Occupation	Employment		Projected change, 2022		Median annual wage, May 2012	Typical education needed for entry
		2012	2022	Number	Percent		
—	Total, all occupations	145,355.8	160,983.7	15,628.0	10.8%	$34,750	—
1	Personal care aides	1,190.6	1,771.4	580.8	48.8	19,910	Less than high school
2	Registered nurses	2,711.5	3,238.4	526.8	19.4	65,470	Associate's degree
3	Retail salespersons	4,447.0	4,881.7	434.7	9.8	21,110	Less than high school
4	Home health aides	875.1	1,299.3	424.2	48.5	20,820	Less than high school
5	Combined food preparation and serving workers, including fast food	2,969.3	3,391.2	421.9	14.2	18,260	Less than high school
6	Nursing assistants	1,479.8	1,792.0	312.2	21.1	24,420	Postsecondary nondegree award
7	Secretaries and administrative assistants, except legal, medical, and executive	2,324.4	2,632.3	307.8	13.2	32,410	High school diploma or equivalent
8	Customer service representatives	2,362.8	2,661.4	298.7	12.6	30,580	High school diploma or equivalent
9	Janitors and cleaners, except maids and housekeeping cleaners	2,324.0	2,604.0	280.0	12.0	22,320	Less than high school
10	Construction laborers	1,071.1	1,331.0	259.8	24.3	29,990	Less than high school

Source: Bureau of Labor Statistics https://www.bls.gov/opub/mlr/2013/article/occupational-employment-projections-to-2022.htm

between 2012 and 2022. Of these, more than two-thirds (67 percent) will come from replacement needs as existing workers shift jobs or retire, rather than new jobs resulting from technological innovation and economic growth. And two-thirds (65 percent) of all job openings in 2020 require no more than a high school diploma—the same proportion as the two-thirds (105 million) of American workers in the overall economy who do not require a college education.[49] Some of the jobs with the fastest growth such as statisticians and software developers, do require a bachelor's degree or higher, but their numbers are small when compared to the jobs most Americans will seek to capitalize on their education, training, and experience.[50]

According to official figures, the picture in the European Union shares common features to the United States, as most job opportunities are expected to come from replacement demand rather than expanding employment opportunities. Of the 114 million job openings predicted between 2012 and 2025, fewer than 10 percent will be new jobs.[51] There is no anticipated decline in elementary occupations but a further loss of skilled manual occupations. Researchers predict little change in intermediate white-collar occupations despite a significant decline in clerical jobs due to the impact of digital technologies. Like the American data, the European case offers little evidence of a "hollowing out" of middle-skill jobs.[52] There is a significant difference, however, in the demand for higher-level skills across the European Union, as over two-fifths of jobs will be high skilled. But a closer look at the evidence also reveals increasing overqualification as "the trend over time is towards more people with high skills working in low-skilled jobs."[53]

This picture of the America and European workforce is in stark contrast to the view that a combination of technological innovation and educational reform will sustain the orthodox theory of learning and earning. Our alternative account of labor demand explains why job scarcity lies at the heart of the new human capital and why there is a major role for governments in job creation and economic development.

Industrial Policy to Raise the Demand for Good-Quality Jobs

The orthodox account asserts that labor markets need to be flexible to allow market forces to match supply with demand. It follows that the state has no role in constructing demand, epitomized by Becker's claim that the "best industrial policy is none at all" because business knows best, given its understanding of market conditions. But in today's economy many of the assumptions about labor demand no longer hold for the reasons we have described, including the fact that companies have found new ways of sourcing high skills at lower cost and elites have found ways of capturing the benefits of productive growth.

This means that industrial policy should not conflate national with corporate economic interests, even if they converge in certain circumstances. As we've seen, the result is a shift toward what Joseph Stiglitz calls a "rent-seeking society" and James Galbraith "the predatory state." But the power to extract private gain at the expense of society is not due to a lack of state involvement. The deregulation of markets and the privatization of public services are industrial strategies; as Britain's former prime minister Margret Thatcher reminded us, the resurgence of free-market competition involved being "in and against the state." Therefore the appropriate question is not *how much* but *what kind* of state involvement.[54]

While the private sector remains key to job creation, the new human capital calls for a more nuanced and balanced approach to industrial policy that cannot be limited to increasing economic growth or raising productivity independent of societal welfare, including opportunities for individuals to capitalize on knowledge, skills, and experience. Industrial policy is based on societal interests and develops ways of engaging private-sector companies in meeting nationally defined goals around decent work, etc. In a context of job scarcity it is especially important to recognize the interests of employees as well as employers, to find ways to increase real wages, reduce the numbers of working poor, and to build social cohesion through a shared prosperity. A clearly defined industrial strategy offers guidance for the coordination of activities involving different stakeholders, including employers.

At the heart of industrial policy is a commitment to reconnect the linkages between effort, skill, jobs, contribution, and rewards. This is why Ken Warwick's definition of industrial policy is an advance on other approaches, for he defines it as "any type of intervention or government policy that attempts to improve the business environment or to alter the structure of economic activity toward sectors, technologies or tasks that are expected to offer better prospects for economic growth or societal welfare than would occur in the absence of such intervention."[55] When there are severe constraints on public spending it is even more important to have a strategic vision of economic and social goals to inform national priorities and industrial strategy.

To achieve a new coalition between state and society requires a new breed of civil servants and policymakers who, as we were told in Singapore many years ago, are "smarter than the smartest captains of industry."[56] We need people who can create a clearly defined industrial strategy, aimed at delivering economic growth as if people matter. Such a strategy would seek to encourage companies to link technological innovation to enhancing job quality rather than use technologies to dumb down the workforce in a race to the bottom of wages, conditions, and career prospects.

Industrial policy cannot be gender-blind. Raising the demand for jobs will entail investment strategies that take women's work into account. In an analysis of several OECD countries, the Women's Budget Group has shown that an investment of 2 percent of GDP in the care sector doubles the number of jobs compared to the same investment in the construction sector. Of course this should not be an either/or choice, but what this calculation shows is that we need to carefully consider how the demand for work performed by women, across all jobs, can be raised.[57] Here we should see the public sector as a major employer able to determine job quality for a significant category of employees.

In Nordic countries a career structure has been created for early childhood educators, which includes their professional education and offers a living wage for their work. We know that early childhood education can make a significant difference to a person's life chances, so as a social contribution the creation of such career structures will be significant in terms of providing a foundation for future generations, while also providing opportunities for women to enter meaningful paid work. This is an example of where the state as an employer of first resort can enable social investment through education and the labor market for mothers of young children.[58] State-funded procurement is another place where issues of inclusion can be allied to sound economic policy, given that many private companies depend on public spending.

In contrast to orthodox economics, which assumes a set of principles for the creation of efficient markets, successful economic policy is as much art as science in the rebalancing of interests in favor of society rather than powerful economic interests. Industrial policy requires wide political support since the short terms of electoral cycles do not give policy initiatives time to breathe. A cursory look at industrial policy in the United States, China, South Korea, Singapore, Germany, and Brazil shows that these countries have adopted radically different approaches, in which successes have to be seen alongside failures.[59]

A senior executive for the Brazilian State development bank, which finances new industrial initiatives told us it took ten years to learn how to make good investments. We raise the example of Brazil on purpose because of its recent economic troubles, which reminds us that industrial policy alone does not guarantee economic success. While industrial policies can provide research and financial support for sunrise industries and help industries transition from one market strategy to another, especially when technology has fundamentally changed the nature of the market, they need to be realigned to a radically different approach to labor supply and to the redistribution of income and wealth.[60]

Conclusion

Regardless of how we interpret these trends and official projections, it is difficult to avoid the conclusion that there is a serious capacity problem at the heart of the labor market. The thrust of technological change shows little evidence of a new jobs engine, especially at the upper end of the job market. If anything, the mismatch between supply and demand is likely to grow, although this will be disguised by the fact that employers will ask for higher-qualified workers just because they see an advantage to getting high-skilled labor to do relatively low-skilled work. The capacity problem is not therefore limited to the unemployment figures, as quality jobs can be replaced by insecure and low-wage work without appearing so in official reports. The capacity problem is therefore one of job quality as well as overall employment numbers.[61] These pressures within the labor market may fuel a street-level revolution, harnessing new technologies to develop new ways of using and capitalizing on individual and common knowledge. But it is unlikely to provide a viable source of livelihood for most Americans and Europeans who find themselves in a more intense competition for more secure forms of employment.

Yet while issues of job creation, job quality, and job satisfaction remain central to individual welfare and well-being, it is the opportunity for individual growth in and through the multiple workplaces and the digital labor market that also defines the new human capital. In standard models of employment the focus is on training people for the job and in the job. When people's experience of work is shallow rather than having a job for life, the capabilities and empowerment of individuals is key, requiring a different model of learning and earning.[62] This exposes the fact that much of the focus on jobs derives from issues of earning rather than learning. This ultimately helps us to understand why loosening the relationship between learning and earning is the foundation for individual economic freedom.

12

Rethinking Economic Returns

HOW WE VIEW rates of return and their relationship to economic efficiency and fairness depends in many ways on how we understand the relationship between education, jobs, and income. We've described how orthodox models of wage distribution are based on three assumptions. The first is that people largely get what they deserve because differences in private rates of return reflect differences in individual marginal productivity (which reflect different levels of human capital investment). In short, equity is viewed as an externality of market efficiency. The second is that the value of human capital within the economy will continue to increase over time. The returns to human capital offer more people the chance to capitalize on further investments in education and training as employers come to demand a larger proportion of high-skilled workers. The third assumption is that if the education system is organized to win the race against technological change, income inequalities will decline over time, given that people are rewarded for what they contribute. In short, a market model is the best way of increasing private and public rates of return.

What is at stake when challenging these assumptions is nothing less than the distributional foundations of society. In defending the current model of labor scarcity David Autor is well aware that the future of automation could undermine the current model of income distribution in market societies: "If machines were in fact to make human labor superfluous, we would have vast aggregate wealth but a serious challenge in determining who owns it and how to share it."[1] Although we agree on the need to be cautious about exaggerated claims that paid work will be replaced by robots, an issue to which we will return in the final chapter, we cannot avoid distributional questions given the existing realities of job scarcity along with current levels of income inequalities, which, if left unchecked, will contribute to widespread alienation and social

The Death of Human Capital? Phillip Brown, Hugh Lauder, and Sin Yi Cheung, Oxford University Press (2020).
© Oxford University Press. DOI: 10.1093/oso/9780190644307.001.0001

instability.[2] Even if everyone could find employment, major problems of (re) distribution remain, reflected in current levels of income inequalities.

However, there is little prospect of returning to a standard model of full employment or of delivering equity or efficiency through further investment in education and training. Investing in human capital cannot be relied on to increase or equalize rates of return. Job scarcity points to a shortage of good jobs and differences in bargaining power rather than the idea of labor scarcity based on the presumption that wages reflect a scarcity of skills, knowledge, talents, or abilities. Today it is widely acknowledged that the benefits of economic growth are not automatically spread by market competition. There is no prospect of a spontaneous division of labor, whereby innate capabilities would match occupational roles.[3] The evidence we have presented shows that the opportunity bargain struck by neoliberal governments in which those that were prepared to invest in education would be duly rewarded is now dead. We therefore need a new accounting system.

A New Model of Human Capital Accounting

A different model of human capital accounting is required if life chances are to be improved, prosperity shared, and quality of life enhanced for all. There has been an overreliance on the price mechanism, in part because it is easier to measure and avoids the indivisible social processes that contribute to self-fulfillment, productive contribution, and wage inequalities. But "if our metrics of performance are flawed, so too may be the inferences that we draw."[4] We've shown how, paradoxically, even when we apply a rates-of-return analysis, learning isn't earning for many people. This provides some helpful political arithmetic in support of the new human capital, yet reducing the complex relationship between learning and earning to a simple measure of income differentials and inequalities tells us precious little about the quality of individual and collective life.

What is measured typically comes to define what counts. We cannot, then, ignore the relationship between purpose and measurement. A market society is different from a society with markets. In the latter there is a need to define social goals and then work out how markets should be organized to deliver them rather than assume that the market is society. As Amartya Sen insists, "The acknowledgement of the role of human qualities in promoting and sustaining economic growth . . . tells us nothing about why economic growth is sought in the first place. If, instead, the focus is, ultimately, on the expansion of human freedom to live the kind of lives that people have reason to value, then the role of economic growth . . . has to be integrated into the more fundamental understanding [of how] to lead more worthwhile and more free lives."[5]

Rethinking economic returns and how they are understood is part of a wider debate about the limitations of existing economic indicators, such as gross domestic product and per capita income, in developing new measures of everyday life that reject the arithmetic of neoliberalism. The United Nations' Human Development Index, work by Joseph Stiglitz, Amartya Sen, and Jean-Paul Fitoussi as part of the Commission on the Measurement of Economic Performance and Social Progress, and several other initiatives are dedicated to developing new measures aimed at shifting the emphasis "from measuring economic production to measuring people's well-being."[6]

Consistent with this ambition to create a wider accounting system that extends beyond measures of market activities to include sustainable well-being, the social rates of return can't be captured by economic growth based on GDP data because there is a big gap between these figures and individual well-being. The same applies to income data used to measure private rates of return. The analysis presented in this book supports the view that a different metrics "should not just measure average levels of well-being within a given community, and how they change over time, but also document the diversity of people's experiences and the linkages across various dimensions of people's lives," including individual living standards and learning opportunities throughout the life course.[7]

Beyond Private Rates of Return

An alternative accounting system rejects the distinction between private and social rates of return on which so much contemporary economic and public policy is based. Challenging the orthodox accounting system based on rates of return is a way of extending what counts in rethinking the relationship between learning and earning, but also has redistributional implications.

Private Rates of Return and Social Contribution

In orthodox accounting models, returns are measured by the amount of money earned by different categories of workers, assumed to be a return on their individual productivity. Problems associated with using income data as a measure of individual productivity have already been discussed; the relationship between individual income and social contribution is equally problematic. A financial trader with an income of $400,000 plus bonuses earns way more than the nursing assistant earning $28,000 for looking after the trader's grandfather. But there is no discussion of how their work contributes to the wider society (or economy) because wage differences are assumed to reflect what is valued in the market, given a vague assumption that the more someone earns, the more they are contributing to national general prosperity and economic growth.

The focus on skills and wages is therefore divorced from everyday realities of what people do for a living as part of the societal division of labor. In previous chapters we highlighted the fact that most people work with fellow employees to create or deliver goods and services for the benefit of others. A lot of these jobs may not command much bargaining power in the labor market but play a central role in the functioning of a civilized society.

This matters because Western economies are characterized by a weak relationship between market wages and social contribution. We seem to be able to put a price on things perceived to have worth in the market, but this does not align with social worth because it's claimed that they are more difficult to evaluate. We have already shown how certain roles, such as cooking, cleaning, and childcare, have traditionally been discounted as women's work and devoid of economic value.

Women also make up a considerable number of the two-thirds of Americans in jobs that do not require more than a high school education; therefore a different accounting system is required that includes greater recognition of the social contribution made by people who add to the quality of life of others. Just because, in countries like Britain and America, these jobs do not require more than a high school education does not mean that they are any less important to the economy or wider society or that the people doing these jobs lack skills; it simply means that these workers are less likely to be paid a high wage or to be able to afford a four-year college education. It is often jobs, not people, that lack skills.

Myth of the Self-Made Individual

What is private about the private rates of return is that wages or payments for labor time are paid to individuals. But they are not private in the sense that wages do not simply reflect difference in individual abilities, educational investments, or personal achievements. Lester Thurow observes, "The creation of human capital is by its nature a social, and not an individual, process. Human skills only grow if one generation teaches the next what it has learned so that the second generation can devote itself to expanding existing knowledge and acquiring new skills rather than to rediscovering and relearning what the previous generation has already mastered. Self-education is inherently limited."[8]

What makes us human is not only the ability to learn and use skills but also how we use our individual capabilities in combination with others. This is true of both the way we become competent employees and the way we participate in the wider society. Indeed the more technologically advanced societies become, the more we depend on other people to ensure that we can open work files located in the cloud, ensure that our smartphones remain smart, and ensure that our (soon to appear) driverless automobiles do not crash. These high-tech aspects of our social dependence are relatively insignificant compared to the people who provide food, water, energy, medical care, and education services that enable us, as individuals, the time to train and the opportunity to capitalize on our skills and abilities.

In short, the private rates of return include a significant social dividend, especially for those most successful at capitalizing within the labor market. As the German economist Friedrich List noted in the late nineteenth century, "The present state of nations is the result of the accumulation of all the discoveries, inventions, improvements and perfections and exertions of all the generations that have lived before us: they form the intellectual capital of the present human race."[9]

Therefore, in a different accounting system, human capital needs to balance individual merits and achievements with the fact that without society we create nothing. In a world with large numbers of college-educated people, for instance, established measures of the stock of national human capital are less important than the institutional capacity to support innovation, civic engagement, co-creation, and a shared sense of economic purpose. This involves people being educated differently if there is to be an improvement in the quality of life in a context of rapid economic change.

Private Rates of Return and the Distribution of Talents

We have argued that the current distribution of incomes in America and Britain reflects positional inequalities in the structure of job opportunities rather than the distribution of innate and trained talent. Here it is worth returning to Adam Smith's view of how individuals come to perform different roles within the division of labor. In *The Wealth of Nations* Smith explains how differences in natural ability, talent, and character are used to justify occupational inequalities consistent with Plato's "noble lie," which we discussed in chapter 8.[10] Smith describes how over time the positional advantages of the philosopher in comparison to the street porter are translated into a gift of nature. However, these individual differences are not the cause of the division of labor but an effect of it.

People get to where they are in life not simply through their own abilities and efforts but because of their relative standing and role within the division of labor. Despite the development of national education systems, they have had relatively limited success in equalizing the life chances of family members occupying different positions in the occupational structure. In other words, those who fill the best jobs should not necessarily be venerated for being the most talented and gifted members of society on which the rest of the population depend, for others may have similar skills and capability but not land a good job.

The constraints imposed by the division of labor under capitalism continue to mean that many people finish up in jobs that do not reflect their capabilities due to labor market rationing. It is often forgotten that those who get what are widely seen as the best jobs enjoy privileged opportunities to capitalize on their knowledge, skills, and know-how over others who may be perfectly capable of fulfilling the same roles. John Kenneth Galbraith points to the danger of assuming "that all work—physical, mental, artistic, or managerial—is essentially the same. . . . To the economists it has seemed a harmless and, indeed an indispensable simplification."[11] But all work is not the same; there are hidden inequalities in the quality of working life given that some people earn money doing things they enjoy, while others do things they find self-alienating, but both are accounted for in the same way with a paycheck at the end of the day, week, month, or project.[12]

Differences in individual contribution need to be recognized and rewarded, at the same time rejecting the narrow view of what counts in orthodox economics. Aspiration and ambition, as well as opportunity, are integral to the new human capital, but they are not equated solely with higher earnings. The new human capital includes being engaged in forms of work that offer greater prospects of intrinsic satisfaction, job security, or what can be termed "deep" employment, offering extended learning opportunities within the same organization, rather than "shallow" work episodes associated with gig or on-demand jobs. Money, then, need not be the primary motivation for entering a better job; interesting work or learning opportunities can also be a source of motivation and satisfaction. Moreover, in a context of job scarcity those fortunate enough to get highly paid jobs can expect to pay a higher social dividend (tax rate). This is in line with innovative approaches to job sharing, collective ownership, and not-for-profit organizational models.

Social Rate of Return as a Social Dividend

In the new accounting system we are proposing there is no sharp distinction between economic and noneconomic benefits in recognition of the societal foundations of the economy and the refocusing of economic goals to explicitly include the quality of social life. Under this accounting model *social returns* include the scale of income inequalities. If societies create economic growth but much of the productivity is captured for the benefit of a few rather than the majority, the result is a low social rate of return when defined in terms of the quality of life. The more the benefits of economic activities and growth are shared, the higher the rate of social returns. This is key to establishing a new relationship between learning and earning.

Orthodox theory treats the social or public rate of return as an *externality* or as *social profitability* resulting from investment in education. The OECD recognizes so called noneconomic benefits, but these are typically treated as secondary to issues of productivity and economic growth. They include lower crime, better healthcare, more social cohesion, and more informed and effective citizens.[13] These are not secondary but primary considerations, which directly impact quality of life.

In the new human capital the relationship between private and public rates of returns is turned on its head, given that investment in education is not the primary cause of economic development but a consequence of it. Society is not frozen or detached while individuals develop productive capabilities through education, leading to positive (or negative) externalities, such as contributing to national economic growth or higher levels of civic participation.

Education should not be viewed as an economic investment in individuals who in aggregate terms deliver externalities in the wider society. It is society that puts the "human" in human capital.[14] Our starting point for understanding the social rate of return—as for private rates of return—is the social division of labor, which both shapes and is shaped by the productive and distributional foundations of economic life.[15] The role of education in contributing to social rates of return depends on how it interacts with or complements other institutions that shape learning, earning, and the quality of life.[16]

Learning and Earning: From Returns to Thresholds

The quality of a nation's human capital depends on a new relationship between learning and earning wherein thresholds of lifelong learning are aligned to income thresholds that provide the foundations for individual growth and improve the quality of life for all. Positive attempts have been made to create a lifelong learning index building on the four pillars outlined in the Delors Report, *Learning: The Treasure Within*. Although our growth model extends its original formulation, the various attempts to develop a wide-ranging index to include aspects of learning beyond measures of employability, skill gaps and skills mismatch, or rates of return is a step in the right direction. The Canadian Composite Learning Index brought together statistical indicators to capture learning in the home, school, workplace, and wider community.[17] The Europe Lifelong Learning Index is another attempt to capture aspects of the four pillars in different learning environments based on a "cradle to grave" approach.[18] Johnny Sung and Simon Freebody have linked the four pillars to data from the OECD Program for the International Assessment of Adult Competencies to develop a comparative framework showing that Scandinavian countries perform better than most other developed countries given their inclusive and more egalitarian approach.[19]

Although there are significant challenges in finding adequate measures, we ultimately need a human capital index that measures the proportion of people who achieve lifelong learning and income thresholds consistent with a growth model of human capital. This will require individual-level data on both subjective and objective measures of learning, living, and earning. Advances in real-time labor market information and online career portals, such as MySkillsFuture in Singapore, offer new sources of data that could be incorporated into a new human capital index.[20]

It is the progressive potential for discretionary learning (not limited to capitalizing in the labor market or to learning in formal contexts) that informs our approach to distributional reform, especially in a context of technological change, job scarcity, and egregious income inequalities. For discretionary learning to be achieved we need to rethink the distributional foundations that give proper consideration to the conditions of people's lives. To achieve the liberation of learning from the tyranny of earning, issues of economic insecurity and income inequalities need to be addressed by establishing income thresholds, giving a decent standard of living to all. If economic freedom is freedom from the economic, including the liberation of learning, then we need to move in the direction of a basic income guarantee, in part to redress the balance of economic power, which has been increasingly concentrated in the hands of a few, forcing other people to do whatever is required of them to make a living.

This focus on greater equality of condition rather than simply market opportunities to compete for unequal prizes is consistent with the original definition of the American Dream by James Truslow Adams. In 1931 he conceived America as a land in which life should be better and richer and fuller for everyone, with opportunity for each according to ability or achievement.[21] In the same year, R. H. Tawney, the English economic historian and ethical socialist, wrote that equality was more than a question of economic prizes being open to all; it should offer the potential for all to develop their skills and abilities and to live meaningful lives. "It implies," he wrote, "the existence, not merely of opportunities to ascend, but of a high level of general culture, and a strong sense of a conviction that civilization is not the business of an elite alone, but a common enterprise which is the concern of all. And individual happiness does not only require that [people] should be free to rise to new positions of comfort and distinction; it also requires that they should be able to lead a life of dignity and culture, whether they rise or not."[22]

Linking the new human capital to policies aimed at reducing inequalities in income and wealth is not simply to come down on the side of fairness instead of efficiency. They are not zero-sum. There is not an inevitable trade-off between the two; reducing economic insecurity and giving people a decent standard of living is a source of productive capability and innovation. Comparative evidence shows that societies with better scores on quality of life indicators tend to be more equal, at the same time that lower levels of inequality at the upper end of the income parade do not appear to jeopardize national economic competitiveness.[23]

Jacob Holm and colleagues found that discretionary learning is key to organizational and societal innovation because it depends on the tacit knowledge and experience-based learning of employees and citizens. This is most likely to be found in countries with models of income distribution and labor market policies that simultaneously promote job mobility, life-long learning, and income security.[24] Such policies that support what have been variously called "flexible security," "flexicurity," "participation income," or "basic income," which we will consider shortly, are also of wider significance; we've described how the same technologies that enable productivity capture through the control of source codes, big data, etc. can also facilitate a bottom-up surge in economic activity that does not conform to standard models of employment and have already become a feature of the working lives of millions of people.

Juha Järvinen is part of the Finnish experiment offering a basic income to the unemployed. When he was asked what the unconditional basic income had done for him, he showed a journalist his workshop. "Inside is film-making equipment, a blackboard on which is scrawled plans for an artist's version of Airbnb, and an entire little room where he makes shaman drums that sell for up to €900. All this while helping to bring up six children. All those free euros have driven him to work harder than ever."[25] It is likely that on the basis of his industry, Järvinen will find a job or will have the opportunity to develop his own business. But this is a much more positive experience when people have a degree of financial security rather than being forced to take any job to survive.[26] In this respect the introduction of an income threshold for all is a form of social investment to make the labor market work for everyone.

A Basic Income Threshold?

There has been renewed interest in the idea of a basic income or national guaranteed income, intended to give every person in a society an income beginning at a certain age, usually eighteen, without any conditions attached to it and for an unlimited time. It is an idea with a long history, going back to Thomas Paine, who in 1795 advocated a citizen's dividend for all American citizens as compensation for "loss of his or her natural inheritance, by the introduction of the system of landed property."[27] It has been advocated by writers on both left and right of the political spectrum as a way to enhance economic freedom and restricting the role of the state in people's lives.

Renewed interest in a basic income threshold reflects growing concerns about the impact of digital technologies on jobs. But even if the machines don't turn out to be quite as smart or job-ready as some people are claiming, serious consideration still needs to be given to issues of redistribution to fund economic security for all. Aside from inequalities in income and wealth, labor markets no longer provide all workers with a living wage. In many countries low-paid workers cannot survive without either top-up incomes provided by the state or having multiple jobs. The introduction of a basic income has the potential to increase the minimum wage employers will offer, since no one would need to work for poverty wages. This would help to redress the current imbalance of power between the workforce and economic, business, and social elites.[28] We have also noted that the formal labor market of paid work does not take into account significant contributions to society, including the social reproductive work relating to young children and family care work. A basic income threshold would go some way to addressing these injustices.

A basic income was implemented in Alaska in 1999, using oil and gas revenues to fund an income for almost all residents. There have also been numerous pilot studies in Brazil, Canada, Finland, India, Kenya, and the Netherlands. In Scotland there are trials in four areas, including Glasgow and Edinburgh, to assess the viability of a universal basic income, along with its social and economic implications.[29] Hillary Clinton considered the idea of "Alaska for America" in her 2016 election campaign but decided it was too costly. However, after her election defeat to Donald Trump she reflected, "I wonder now whether we should have thrown caution to the wind and embraced 'Alaska for America' as a long-term goal and figured out the details later."[30]

One of the appealing aspects of an unconditional basic income is less complicated rules and bureaucratic procedures than those currently used to determine who is deserving of social benefits. There would be no role for the state in means-testing individuals and families, a point that attracted neoliberal thinkers like Milton Friedman. It would remove the stigma and intrusive bureaucracy suffered by claimants. The stress that social security claimants often experience, so vividly portrayed in Ken Loach's award-winning film, *I Daniel Blake,* would be a thing of the past.

Calculations suggest that the savings to the state from abolishing the various forms of social security would go some way to paying for an unconditional basic income. But here things start to get more complex, as there are many different experiments under way that use different funding models. Michalis Nikiforos, Marshall Steinbaum, and Gennaro Zezza at the Roosevelt Institute in New York City have modeled the macroeconomic effects of a universal basic income.[31] Their findings support the view that the shift toward a basic income is beneficial rather than economically ruinous. They argue that the US economy could withstand large increases in federal spending and would stimulate higher economic growth due to cash transfers putting more money in the hands of the less affluent, leading to an increase in aggregate demand.

They model the implications of three proposals for household tax rates, assuming the full costs are met through taxation rather than increased government debt. Proposal 1 Is a basic child allowance of $250 a month for all children under sixteen; Proposal 2 is a small basic income of $500 a month for all adults, and under Proposal 3 the basic income is increased to $1,000 a month for all adults.

While the tax implications of a child allowance would be modest, an unconditional $1,000 a month for all Americans would require a significant redistribution of resources even if it can be shown to be beneficial to the overall economy. Moreover if people were given $1,000 a month they would still need to capitalize in the labor market to achieve a decent standard of living (see Table 12.1).

Given these cost implications, we recommend an incremental approach that would include the introduction of a universal child allowance, contributing to the achievement of a learning threshold for school-age pupils and students, as discussed in chapter 10.[32] It does not immediately follow that all forms of social security should be provided by a universal basic income at the level of a living wage.[33] Nevertheless it would remove most of the transaction costs relating to the administration of social security at the same time as taking the bureaucratic stress away from vulnerable people.

It seems inevitable that the clamor for a fairer and more efficient model of (re)distribution will continue to increase, in much the same way that the welfare or social state was built in the twentieth century based on the gradual extension of social rights to include education, healthcare, retirement, and social security.[34] At the same time there are legitimate objections to the introduction of a basic income: the cost of replacing all forms of social security with a basic income, the social need for work, and the pathologies of human behavior if people get something for nothing.

Table 12.1 Change in the average tax rate by income bracket in the fully tax-funded scenarios

	Proposal 1 ("child allowance")	Proposal 2 ($500/month/ adult)	Proposal 3 ($1,000/month/ adult)
Lowest Quintile	0%	0%	0%
Second Quintile	0%	0%	0%
Middle Quintile	0%	0%	11%
Fourth Quintile	0%	5%	12%
81st to 90th Percentile	2%	11%	21%
91st to 95th Percentile	2%	13%	23%
96th to 99th Percentile	3%	16%	30%
Top 1 Percent	4%	26%	35%

One concern that we share is that a universal basic income could leave people socially isolated, unlike paid work, which gives people social connections that they might not have otherwise. Research shows that even when jobs are low paid, such as in supermarkets, work creates meaning and purpose in people's lives.[35] And this is important. Equally, for many low-paid workers the main concern is keeping them and their families above destitution.

This has led to skepticism by some on the liberal left that a universal basic income will fail to deliver the promise of greater economic freedom because the threshold will be set to ensure material survival but no more. As such it is viewed as a strategy to buy quiescence. A further objection is that if people get something for nothing they will lose a sense of purpose and a sense of what is to be valued. While such a view is consistent with *Homo economicus*, it is not supported by the arguments developed in this book, especially when we consider the large numbers of informal caregivers in society whose lives would be changed for the better by a universal basic income.

Also unresolved is how to link a basic income threshold to a new relationship between earning and learning. There is more to the quality of life than a basic level of economic security, and there is a danger that a basic income will be used to buy off the socially disadvantaged rather than develop the individual growth potential of all. Current experiments aimed at assessing the merits (or otherwise) of a basic income threshold need to be extended to include lifelong learning thresholds that provide the foundations for individual growth throughout the life course. A guaranteed basic income could be linked to learning credits and the funding of higher and adult education, which encourage both social and economic participation.[36]

Experiments linking learning and earning thresholds need to consider alternatives to the "user pays" model of higher education funding, supported by orthodox accounts of private rates of return, which claimed to result in a significant premium for those with a bachelor's degree. When we look at the disaggregated data we have presented and then consider the uncertainties that young people now confront in the labor market, the justification for charging fees on the basis of a graduate premium is feeble. For the majority, there is a high risk involved in individual investments in post–compulsory education that has been ignored by policymakers.[37] We have already referred to the high levels of debt students in the United States and England are accruing.

We owe it to future generations to provide a fair system of education funding, not only for those in higher education but for all. Unfortunately in some countries the institutional basis for lifelong learning has been decimated as the focus has been on first-chance education. In England, further education colleges, the equivalent of community colleges in the United States, have paid a high price for austerity while British universities have thrived. Yet it has been in further education colleges that lifelong learning was provided. Singapore has glimpsed what the future holds and through the MySkillsFuture initiative has offered each citizen $500 Singapore dollars—to be increased over time—to spend on formal learning activities. These are straws in the wind, but they point to a new relationship between earning and learning. Equally, many countries across Europe have rejected a "user pays" approach to the funding of higher education, in part because it saddles people with high levels of personal debt and works to the disadvantage of those least able to pay or translate learning into earning for reasons that have little to do with individual talent and ability. As a matter of principle, it seems clear that we now need to provide free (or low-cost) higher and lifelong education to all those who want to avail themselves of it.

Fiscal Revolution?

The distributional questions of who does what and who gets what can no longer be ignored. If market competition cannot provide a fair and efficient foundation for twenty-first-century economies, the role of government becomes more strategically important in both job creation and the distribution of income and wealth. We've argued that governments are key stakeholders in investing in the workforce and connecting people to employment opportunities. This view rejects the artificial separation between state and market in orthodox theory that has obscured the foundations of production and distribution of income and wealth. In the new human capital the relationship between state and market is not viewed as a zero-sum game with one or the other gaining the commanding heights. Rather, as we've seen, the aim of public policy is to reimagine the links between learning and earning (and the related link between justice and efficiency) in building the socioeconomic foundations aimed at improving the quality of life for all. A key role for government is therefore managing distributional disputes, for, as Thomas Piketty warns, "At the heart of every major political upheaval lies a fiscal revolution."[38]

The developed economies are richer beyond the wildest dreams of Adam Smith or Alfred Marshall. Today the problem is less one of wealth creation than wealth distribution, although sustainable economic growth remains a key national goal. While acknowledging the value of ad hoc experiments with new models of a guaranteed minimum wage or basic income, there has been far less political appetite to redress the runaway incomes of top earners. Although it is fair to say that virtually no one believes that top salaries are justified, governments have been reluctant to increase the top rates of income tax, which would be a good indicator of whether a fiscal revolution was under way. Denmark has the highest rate of personal income tax, but it was cut from 60 percent, and America and Britain have also cut the top rate of tax. The threshold at which people pay the top rate is also important; it is a little over average wages in Denmark, but approximately four times average wages in Britain and eight times the average in the United States.[39] Almost without exception these tax reforms are heading in the wrong direction as the focus remains on increasing incentives to push people into waged employment.

In rethinking returns and their relationship to a productive and just economy, we cannot ignore the issue of unproductive wealth, which has led to the transfer of resources from the poor and middle classes to the wealthiest in society. Such transfers have served to undermine the skills and efforts of the vast majority, who depend on capitalizing within the labor market as their only source of income. Despite all that's said about human capital in recent decades, it is often undervalued, epitomized in the relationship between wealth and income. Stark inequalities in the distribution of wealth also demonstrates that we have not entered an age of human capital, understood by Becker as the most important form of capital. The richest sixty-two people on the planet have the same wealth as the 3.6 billion people who make up the poorest of the world's population despite major global investment in education.[40]

Firms such as Microsoft, Apple, and Google, to name a few, have made extraordinary profits primarily because the cost of technological innovations in product development are funded with public money. Mariana Mazzucato explains why the "genius" of Steve Jobs rested on a myth about the origins of Apple's success. Jobs gave inspiring speeches about "pursuing what you love," "staying foolish," and the ability to be a bit "crazy," but Mazzucato explains that while these are important characteristics, "without the massive amount of public investment behind the computer and Internet revolutions, such attributes might have led only to the invention of a new toy—not to cutting-edge revolutionary products like the iPad and iPhone which have changed the way that people work and communicate."[41]

Unmoved by concerns about their exploitation of this social dividend, the fifty largest US companies had until recently $1.4 trillion in offshore tax havens, close to the GDP of Canada and more than the GDP of Russia or Mexico. Although corporate tax cuts offered by the Trump Administration has resulted in the repatriation of some of this money. Moreover, despite making $4 trillion in profits between 2008 and 2014, for every dollar these companies paid in corporate taxes they received $27 in federal loans, loan guarantees, and bailouts.[42] Oxfam estimates that tax avoidance by leading US companies costs America $111 billion each year and a further $100 billion every year in poorer countries, preventing crucial investment in education, healthcare, infrastructure, and initiatives aimed at poverty reduction.[43] Automation will potentially lead to the further transfer of assets from the majority of the workforce to company executives and shareholders, removing their only potential form of capital attached to individual skills. Without a redistribution of income and wealth, this amounts to human capital asset stripping. This underlines the urgent need to rebalance the distribution of economic rewards and calls for a new bargain that values human capital over the gospel of wealth as the social dividend that underscores both private and public rates of return needs to be accounted for.

When people are working to make ends meet or to pay off tuition loans and mortgage debt, it is demoralizing to think of people living off inherited wealth or rent, benefiting from hikes in property prices that result in some people never being able to afford their own homes, at the time that others have watched their properties soar in value due to luck rather than individual merit.[44] Many in the middle classes, especially in cities including London, New York, and Beijing, have earned more from property than from wages, a situation fueled by changes in inheritance tax, lax policing of corporate tax, and individual wealth management.[45] All of this has distributional implications for the new human capital, which recommends the progressive taxation of property, inheritance, and wealth, which are passive in the sense that they do not directly relate to individual effort or skills.[46]

Conclusion

This chapter has argued for a fundamental revaluation of how the productive dividend is to be shared. If there is little prospect of narrowing income inequalities or upgrading the quality of life for all through existing supply-side policies, the new human capital requires a wide-ranging policy response to address inequalities of condition alongside inequalities of opportunity. This is why the question of returns (economic prizes) is so important: we need a new narrative and public policy agenda aimed at spreading the benefits of economic activity to enable human flourishing across society. It requires a redefinition of economic purpose linked to reimagining both earning and learning and the relationship between them.

A key insight is that what is capitalized by individuals and firms rests on a social dividend that needs to be built into the distributional foundations of the new human capital. It shares the widely held view that the competition for economic prizes should be constructed so that every individual has an equal chance to win. But in subscribing to equal opportunity it leaves unanswered two fundamental questions: how to distribute work in a context of job scarcity and how to distribute economic prizes.[47]

This chapter has sought an alternative approach to the relationship between efficiency and fairness. The new human capital takes its starting point as the study of the division of labor. This includes a wider understanding of education purpose, productive contribution, and the quality of life, showing that the possibilities for narrowing inequalities and extending individual freedom are greater than orthodox theories of human capital allow. The division of labor reflects a scarcity of jobs rather than a scarcity of labor or innate talent. Firms are not bound to organize their workforce to reflect a scarcity of innate talent. There is no iron law of economic necessity or technological imperative that impels us into a world of divisive inequalities. Today's inequalities do not reflect economic necessity for the ultimate good of all. There are important national differences in the relationship between education, jobs, and incomes, showing that societies have more degrees of freedom than is often assumed. Economic prosperity is not inevitably sacrificed by attempts to govern the market in ways that spread the benefits of economic activity. Policymakers are not limited to supply-side solutions, such as further investments in education and training as a means of narrowing income inequalities by increasing the supply of skilled workers. So what are the prospects for the future?

13

Conclusion

A RACE AGAINST TIME

We shall honour those who can teach us how to pluck
the hour and the day virtuously and well, the delightful
people who are capable of taking direct enjoyment in
things. . . . But beware! The time for all this is not yet.
For at least another hundred years we must pretend to
ourselves and to every one that fair is foul and foul is
fair; for foul is useful and fair is not. Avarice and usury
and precaution must be our gods for a little longer still.
For only they can lead us out of the tunnel of economic
necessity into daylight.

—JOHN MAYNARD KEYNES,
Economic Possibilities for Our Grandchildren (1930)

THIS BOOK ARGUES that orthodox human capital theory is an impediment to the advancement of individual freedom and to the creation of a
more inclusive and economically viable future.[1] Our conclusion is based
on mounting research evidence showing that, for many, learning isn't
earning. It also rests on our contention that historical possibilities exist to
improve the quality of individual and social life through the transformation of economic means.[2] We need a new way of thinking about human
capital.

The book describes how human labor and its relationship to capital
appeared in various strands of eighteenth- and nineteenth-century political
economy, to later become one of the most enduring economic theories of
our age. The appeal of orthodox theory stems from the fact that it offers
something to everyone. For individuals it is the chance for economic prosperity, interesting employment, and social mobility; for employers it offers

The Death of Human Capital? Phillip Brown, Hugh Lauder, and Sin Yi Cheung, Oxford University Press (2020).
© Oxford University Press. DOI: 10.1093/oso/9780190644307.001.0001

access to a better-trained workforce; and politicians and policymakers can present education as the missing link between economic efficiency and social justice.

The idea that everyone could become a capitalist by investing in education and training as human capital was also politically appealing. Through such investments employers would pay higher incomes to educated workers, leading to a greater share of profits going to those who invested in their human capital, ending the age-old struggle between the interests of bosses and those of workers.

We have come a long way from an economy characterized by mass ranks of routine manual workers trudging through factory gates. The rise of the middle classes associated with the growth in professional, managerial, and technician jobs is testimony to the transformation of developed economies over the past century, alongside more recent developments, including the rapid rise of the economies of China and India. But what we described as a "happy accident" in twentieth-century America was wrongly presented as a universal theory of economic behavior and future prosperity: the human capital story is not the one characterized by Theodore Schultz. If the historical legacy of orthodox theory reveals anything, it is that the conflict over capital has been redefined but not resolved.

The contrasting models of human capital presented in this book point in opposing directions. The choice is between a resurgent neoliberalism consistent with orthodox theory and a different way of thinking about efficiency and social justice premised on the *new* human capital. Here human beings are not classed as capital or wealth but are the purpose for which wealth exists. It does not assume that all human behavior is reducible to economic behavior, or that Americans, let alone the rest of the world, have stable preferences or are motivated by rational self-interest.[3] It is extraordinary that an economic theory with "human" in its title has so little to say about what makes us human or about differences in human aspirations, motivations, and identities.

The new human capital theory rejects the idea of treating humans as capital as the route to individual freedom via investment in education. It is the extent to which people are forced to develop and sell themselves in order to make a living that defines individual freedom, at a time when the labor market is failing to deliver efficiency or justice. It signals a shift in economic priorities, from making people fit for existing economic arrangements to making existing economic arrangements fit for human purposes.[4]

Future Prospects

The new human capital therefore confronts a race against time, signaled by the mismatch between today's economic possibilities and social realities. In Keynes's famous essay *Economic Possibilities for Our Grandchildren*, he described the "economic problem" as creating material abundance, achievable by 2030. But even in such a world he envisaged everyone needing some form of work to find contentment, though he thought that no more than three-hour shifts or a fifteen-hour week would suffice. Some people, such as those currently locked out of the labor market or on zero-hours contracts, already face a struggle to achieve this, while for many others this seems like a remote possibility given long working hours. Despite our labor-saving technologies, new technologies have resulted in widening inequalities between the working rich and the working poor.

On this point Keynes underestimated how "technological unemployment"—defined as the discovery of new techniques of economizing on labor outrunning the pace at which we can find new uses for labor—would create new inequalities in the distribution of work rather than simply lead to a re-duction in employment numbers.[5] Inequality in access to waged work is one of the three social inequalities that need to be addressed under the new human capital, the others being inequalities in life chances (capitalizing on individual skills) and wage and wealth inequalities (and their relationship to productivity, profits, and social contribution).

These inequalities remain important because reducing working hours to leave more time for the "art of life" still depends on the act of making a living. This is why the new human capital retains the idea of individuals capitalizing on their knowledge and skills and supports initiatives leading to an active basic income for all. It registers a fundamental difference between the own-ership of capital and capitalizing on human labor. Human capital has no sep-arate existence beyond embodied labor, which can be sold to someone else. It is inflexible in the sense that it can't be converted in the same way people can sell shares in one company and move them to firms with better financial prospects with the click of a mouse. Equities don't get ill or old, even if they can decline in monetary value. Notwithstanding that people can change jobs to get higher wages, this is an altogether different proposition to buying and selling equities or owning property, and it also depends on the availability of suitable job openings. It is the inherent insecurity of labor under capitalism that explains why individuals cannot be fully responsible for their economic welfare and why a community or societal approach provides the wherewithal for people to live dignified, meaningful, and active lives.

Whatever label we want to give to the early decades of the twenty-first century—knowledge economy, digital economy, second machine age, fourth industrial revolution—money will remain the dominant form of exchange, and how much money people have will shape their quality of life. Most people who are not independently wealthy rely on finding a job given that it's the source of any semblance of economic freedom. Without waged employment people are unable to pay their way in the world and have little prospect of maintaining their living standard. Here orthodox theory has obscured changes in the structure of the labor market at a time when many workers have been exposed to the full force of market competition, stripped to little more than their human capital as welfare safety nets have been removed, giving people little choice other than to invest in more and more education in the hope of market salvation.

A standard error in orthodox theory is to assume that the job market will continue to absorb the energies and talents of the workforce. This relates to the idea of labor scarcity and the view of technology outpacing education. Alignment problems leading to a mismatch between the products of education and the requirements of industry are not uncommon, but what we confront today is a major capacity problem, described as job scarcity rather than labor scarcity. This raises questions that go well beyond educational reform to issues of (re)distribution of both work and wages. We argue that today's labor market can't deliver a shared prosperity and is distorting the distribution of income. It does not reward the skills, talents, and contribution of the majority.

Job scarcity is where technology, organizational restructuring, and the global division of labor undermine the economic capacity to produce suitable job opportunities, especially for a more educated workforce. This is due not only to technological unemployment in respect to job numbers, but also to "technological underemployment," where jobs do not use the skills of the workforce, as distinct from "temporal underemployment," where people are not provided with viable working hours.

This fact reveals a further limitation of Keynes's account of the economic problem to be solved. It is not only one of productivity in pursuit of material abundance but includes the accumulation of surplus value, never equally shared. We've witnessed how much of the benefit from rising productivity has been captured by top managers and shareholders rather than labor. In other words, making profits is much more important than creating abundance to the "purposeful money-makers" who are supposed to lead us out of the tunnel of economic necessity.

Alongside questions of efficiency, productivity, and sustainability, the economic problem centers on income inequalities and the distribution of profits. Why would business elites and the wealthy concede to a different model of social and economic organization when they are able to own and consume the benefits of the human capital of others? Indeed Keynes's "economic problem" has been turned on its head. Orthodox ideas are not retained simply to ensure efficiency but also for the purposes of maintaining current patterns of income inequalities.[6]

We've seen how the conflict over the definition, creation, and distribution of capital has been exploited by elites able to use their greater market power to capture much of the benefit of productive labor. At the same time, they leave the majority of the workforce exposed to unequal market forces, on the false promise of individual economic freedom, with people in control of their own destinies, depending on a willingness to invest in their human capital.

This is why Marxist economists distinguish between the forces of production relating to the technological possibilities to raise productivity and the social relations of production, which include issues of ownership, profits, and the relationship between capital and labor. This conflict over capital poses a fundamental challenge to the new human capital, as its prospects depend on rebalancing the power relations between capital and labor.[7]

Impossible Pressures of Market Freedom

Today's economy reflects the "impossible pressures" that are being imposed on workers around the world. Rather than extend economic freedoms it creates relentless pressures on people, hitting especially hard those who have little market power to capitalize on qualifications, experience, or social networks in the job market. It is also keenly felt in contexts of market uncertainty and job insecurity, as household bills and credit cards are typically paid on a monthly basis.

The unreasonable demands made on people to make a living wage or sustain a middle-class lifestyle involve leaving people to individually cope with the dramatic fluctuations in economic circumstances, including declining salaries and irregular waged work. It is a situation that Karl Polanyi argued is both morally wrong and deeply unrealistic. But in such circumstances people will mobilize to protect themselves from such contingencies, heightening the intense scramble for individual advantage in the competition for credentials and jobs. They are equally likely to feel rising levels of institutional disappointment when they have done everything asked of them but still find themselves not earning despite learning.[8]

In many countries, young people have taken to the streets in protest. There are many reasons for these demonstrations; among them are the greed, corruption, and inequalities of corporate capitalism. Concerns about an uncertain, if not bleak future confronting young people gave rise to the movement Juventud Sin Futuro (Youth without Future) in Spain, reflecting a fundamental breakdown between educational achievement and occupational opportunities.[9]

The hidden injuries of class have become the open wounds of economic conflict in the latest stage of capitalist development. But despite moral outrage, the sharp end of the conflict over capital is evident in the rise in mental illness, stress levels, homelessness, and dependency on food banks, which are the visible and hidden injuries within the middle as well as working classes. The electoral success of Donald Trump in America and the Brexit vote to leave the European Union in the United Kingdom are expressions of the impossible pressures imposed on people by the free market, as they realize that trying to get a better education or update their training, even if feasible, is unlikely to work.

Keeping the Bargain Alive

A key question is how much improvement is possible under existing arrangements.[10] Orthodox theorists maintain a commitment to upgrading the skills and productivity of the workforce. However, this book has shown that neoliberal models of human capital are part of the problem rather than offering a viable solution to "so much want" amid "so much wealth."[11] Yet there is nothing automatic about a shift away from orthodox human capital as it is ultimately a matter of political contestation. It is the battleground over which our understanding of human capital will be fought in the coming years, if not decades.

Unsurprisingly there are powerful vested interests mobilized to deny the human capital crisis and to extol the virtues of market capitalism. The Trump Administration has a partly build wall along the border with Mexico to restrict numbers entering the United States and encouraged the creation of new jobs in neighbourhoods hit by deindustrialization, even though many of these jobs are associated with high rates of carbon emissions. We have seen how the failed promise of "learning equals earning" has been blamed on the education system, workers with the wrong skill sets, immigrant workers undercutting wages, and global free trade (previously hailed as key to advancing American and Western European economic interests). A policy of quantitative easing has also been applied to higher education, giving the appearance of widening opportunities, which has done little more than add to labor market congestion.

Turning to the education system to compensate for economic troubles is nothing new, but as E. F. Schumacher observes in his celebrated book *Small Is Beautiful*, "The problems of education are merely reflections of the deepest problems of our age."[12] This is something that governments, especially of neoliberal persuasions, find difficult, or are unwilling, to comprehend. There is a long procession of "education" presidents and prime ministers, but what we need are "jobs" presidents and prime ministers who acknowledge the limits of educational reform and the realities of the future of work and wage inequalities.[13]

We argued in chapter 8 that a growth model of education is crucial to the new human capital if people are to flourish. But growth will not be solely for the purpose of economic returns, which is what the long procession of presidents and prime ministers have assumed. But if education's relationship to the economy has been fractured, then the temptation will be for policymakers to agree with Bryan Caplan's view that the education system "is a waste of time and money."[14] We anticipate that there will be a major battle for the kind of education that we have outlined if it is to overcome the idea that education's sole purpose is to serve the current neoliberal economy. The prospects for the educational reforms we advocate therefore depend on how the core conflict between corporate elites and their political allies and the middle and working classes plays out.

Self, Opportunity, and Economic Freedom

The conflict over capital will therefore play a key role in shaping the prospects for the new human capital. This is not limited to addressing the greed of the top 1 percent, the rent-seeking behavior of elites, or ending the use of corporate tax havens that rob communities and nations of desperately needed tax dollars to pay for education, healthcare, social infrastructure, and ultimately a basic income threshold. The prospects of the new human capital will also depend on changing the narrative of human capital development, as the way we organize education, employment, and income distribution is a "visible expression of the scale of moral values which rules the minds of individuals, and it is impossible to alter institutions without altering that valuation."[15] This involves rejecting the overarching model of neoliberal economics from which orthodox human capital theory derives and which has served to obscure how people understand their self-worth, economic contribution, and relationship to the wider society. In reducing economics to self-interest, private rates of return, and "learning equals earnings" it leads into the trap of assuming that life's destiny is limited to getting a better-paid job and social mobility. It also reduces the workforce to a stock of human resources consisting of people who are more or less skilled, with the policy goal of making people more employable.

It requires reimagining individual, social, and economic purpose and how these are measured. It calls for renewed efforts to build opportunity, fairness, and productive contribution, reflecting the changing world in which we live. The new human capital is nothing less than a renewed individual bargain based on a different political economy. Without it current and future generations alike are going to struggle to live meaningful and worthwhile lives, with the potential of significant social unrest.[16]

This renewed individual bargain requires different policy priorities that address issues of job scarcity rather than labor scarcity. If the fundamental problem is one of labor scarcity, the question of human capital is treated as a private issue of finding suitable ways and means to invest in education and training to benefit from what is seen as the rising demand for skilled workers. It may also lead to policy initiatives to reform education to widen access to disadvantaged groups and to increase opportunities for upward social mobility, although such initiatives often amount to little more than trying to make those from working-class backgrounds behave like those from more privileged families.[17]

When viewed as a job scarcity issue, the private problems of getting a decent education, finding meaningful employment, and earning a living wage are not resolvable purely through individual abilities and efforts.[18] While there is a focus on equity issues of increasing educational opportunities and improving prospects for social mobility as a route to people living productive and meaningful lives, it also recognizes a systemic problem that is largely beyond the efforts of individuals to resolve.

A key public issue raised by job scarcity is that without a viable labor market the whole edifice of the neo-liberal market economy, along with its supporting narrative of individual freedom, opportunity, and prosperity, is under threat. Therefore the policy implications associated with this alternative approach includes the fact that fairness cannot be limited to initiatives aimed at improving educational standards or increasing intergenerational upward social mobility but must include the wider purposes of education beyond investment in human capital. Self-development should not be restricted to the imputed needs of industry; it should also address issues of (re)distribution of income and wealth. This is why we have drawn a distinction between a *banking* model of education and an individual *growth* model of lifelong learning. We have also argued for a new human capital index that includes the extent to which nations meet learning and earning thresholds across the life course.

Education will be central to a civilized future in which people of all ages have the possibility of thinking through how, individually and collectively, they can make a living and a good life when confronted with the labor market and environmental uncertainty and political turmoil that now surrounds us. Today's schoolchildren know this, which is why some demonstrate against climate change while a number of political elders, with a narrow instrumental view of education, see their protest as irrational and advise them to return to the classroom and study for their exams. But one thing is clear: education has a significant role to play in the development of democratic citizenship, but we have also been at pains to argue for the underlying conditions that are needed for education to be successful.

Central to these possibilities is a concern for the everyday conditions of people's lives rather than simply the opportunity to progress into something better. This is why the new human capital has to address both inequalities in condition as well as inequalities in opportunity. Here economic freedom is freedom from the economic, both in a subjective sense of self-development and in an objective sense of having meaningful opportunities and the material foundations for self-development, including access to education and work not wholly dependent on capitalizing within the job market.

This view of economic freedom does not lose sight of how people will make an economic contribution in the future, but it avoids treating humans as capital because it is only a part of what defines us as individuals and has been shown to be an inadequate measure of the quality of life. Whether new technologies are used to increase the skill content of a few or many jobs, rests on human decisions that are taken by people in power within organizations or governments that ultimately decide whether or how they are going to use these technologies. We've already mentioned Simon Head's description of how the system rules and algorithms involve human decisions, typically made by a technical, managerial elite whose preferred ways of doing things get "baked into the system, leading to a process of 'dumbing down' in the early twenty-first century."[19] In other words, the more the clever bits are baked into the system, the less people understand of the process. Where this narrowly conforms to the needs of industry the education system will continue to be organized on a banking model.

The fight to free people from an education that treats them as a stock of human resources at the disposal of employers is key to the shift toward the new human capital we are proposing. For when we view people as a stock of human resources it is easy to understand how the purpose of education gets reduced to an investment in a nation's or firm's economic resources, at the same time reducing everything that's important about individuals to what they can potentially sell on the job market.

In an age of machine learning, training humans to be smart machines is an education in technological servitude. If machines come to do more of the work done by humans, it is how we develop ourselves in a process of lifelong learning that offers the best chance of achieving productive well-being. Equally, how we organize ourselves socially—not limited to market competition—that is the real source of individual freedom. It is the quality of our social relations, along with the quality of our machines, that holds the key to inclusive well-being and a vibrant economy. Therefore permission to think needs to be extended to all rather than only the few.

In Keynes's vision of the "economic possibilities for our grandchildren" he was fully aware of the challenge involved in adjusting education to a new way of life, which requires future generations breaking the spell of Becker's *Homo economicus*—the acquisitive and purposive behavior associated with neoliberalism. "There is no country and no people," writes Keynes, "who can look forward to the age of leisure and of abundance without a dread," as doing so would require readjustments to the habits and instincts instilled over countless generations.[20] To think of ourselves as sources of capital is as much self- as socially imposed, driven by the dull compulsion to earn, compete, and consume within a system of market capitalism.

We anticipate that technological unemployment is likely to become more of a problem. The claim that new jobs will emerge as they've done in the past is barely reassuring to those who are unemployed, in temporal underemployment, or discouraged from entering the labor market. Such concerns raise issues about the distribution of employment leading to the need for new ways of defining, organizing, and rewarding work, as it is at the heart of capitalization in the new human capital.

It has been shown that a national economy is made up of a vast array of human needs as well as wants. Millions of people will continue to be involved in meeting the basics of social life: caring, nurturing, feeding, transporting, selling, and protecting. These involve jobs that are not going to disappear anytime soon, whether in developed or developing economies. Many of these jobs are vital to a civilized society, but they do not involve extensive education and training to perform. We've seen that nearly two-thirds of American job openings in 2020, for example, require no more than a high school diploma.

Orthodox theory obscures these economic and social realities because it ignores what people do for a living rather than what they earn from what they do. It flattens social contribution to a market relationship by treating income as a measure of individual contribution rather than an expression of market value, which may have little connection with individual marginal productivity, let alone social contribution. It flattens human activities into an equivalence of *worth*, standardized in the form of monetary income. It flattens all human endeavors in the creation of human capital, ignoring vastly different ways, and vastly different circumstances, in which people earn their daily bread, rice, or pasta. In these terms the hospital nurse is on par with the financial advisor helping wealthy individuals and companies to reduce their tax obligations by using offshore trusts. When all labor is flattened by the price mechanism, the labor involved in writing this book is accounted for in the same terms as for someone having to work on a factory production line.[21] Within the new human capital we've argued for a fairer balance between market value and social value. It is not at all clear why those doing the most interesting jobs and enjoying high social status are also paid relatively high salaries, while those having to do difficult jobs with little opportunity to use their individual capabilities receive little recognition and low wages.

The new human capital rejects the distinction between labor supply and demand in orthodox theory, with its focus on employment and wage distribution rather than the wider division of labor. The result is an analytical blindness that ignores much of the nonwaged work on which the visible economy depends. Thinking in terms of the social division of labor highlights essential human needs and wants within complex societies, which reinforce the fact that there is not a scarcity of work but a scarcity of waged employment. The artificial distinctions between work and employment expose inconsistencies, if not prejudice, often to the disadvantage of women, as much of their contribution is outside the formal definition of employment and therefore invisible.

Obvious examples are nurturing the young toward adulthood and caring for the old no longer able to contribute to the economy but still part of the economy—given that we have strict rules against euthanasia as opposed to the recycling of worn-out machines.

Locating the issue of job scarcity within an understanding of the social division of labor shifts our understanding of economic contribution measured by wage differentials. It challenges the inherent bias in connecting learning to earning, related to the idea of individual marginal productivity. It is not only a discredited justification for paying some people a lot more than everyone else; it also has the intended (or unintended) consequence of assuming that the poor receive little because they make little contribution, because they haven't invested in their human capital. When we take account of the wider division of labor we begin to see that the problem results from an analytical and political blindness, which cannot be resolved by the education system or the job market. This is why the new human capital points to a different model of (re)distribution that includes reducing income and wealth inequalities as a precondition for individual freedom.

We like to think that people deserve what they get and that differences in circumstances and opportunity reflect something other than arbitrary inequalities. This book presents a sobering assessment of the orthodox account of "learning equals earning" and offers a different way of understanding ourselves and the prospects for economic freedom. Ultimately it points toward a new mode of human existence within reach of the developed economies. This calls for a different narrative that connects with the disconnections in people's lives, their sense of disappointment, anomie, and unfairness. However, the distributional conflict revealed in this book, and at the very heart of capitalism, is yet to be resolved. Robert Solow, the Nobel Prize–winning economist, writing on Keynes's *Economic Possibilities for Our Grandchildren*, argued that where labor can be substituted for capital goods (technology), profits "will come over time to absorb an ever-increasing share of aggregate income." He then asks, "How will we live then?," and his answer is "For the grandchildren, or their grandchildren, to have a viable world, the ownership of capital will have to be democratized. If capital is the only source of income that matters, then everyone who matters—in other words, everyone—will need an adequate claim against capital." In other words, this is not just about taxing away wealth but about giving people a stake in society. He notes that it will take political imagination and ingenuity to address this question.[22]

History has taught us that the end of one era and the start of another is always contested and complex, that there is no clear line between them. But it is time we gave thought to how we will move into an era in which the divisions that characterize the present are addressed. Modern economies are complex systems that require complex answers. There is no silver bullet, and societies will need to take the basic strands of the new human capital and apply them in vastly different national contexts. Yet the complexities of modern social and economic life do not render public policy impossible. Collective capacity building is required to embrace the multifaceted realities of social and economic life, including the unintended consequences of purposive actions.

Although critical of the standard economic theory of human capital, we have taken considerable care to engage with orthodox theorists to give the reader a reasonable understanding of its main arguments and where they originate. Our purpose has been to highlight the need for economists, sociologists, psychologists, educationalists, social geographers, historians, technologists, and political scientists, among others, to recognize the mutual contribution all have to make. There are historical moments when the way we define the troubling times in which we live can have a profound impact on shaping the future of society. This is why the turf wars within the social sciences and the wider scientific community need to be put to one side in developing new approaches that hold out the prospect of offering future generations something better than today, measured by the quality of life, not the quantity of wealth.

These efforts need to focus on reducing inequalities to facilitate a more efficient, fairer, sustainable, and inclusive economic system, including changing the way we learn throughout life and the wider socioeconomic foundations of society. It's about living, producing, and rewarding people differently. The failure to address these challenges is signified by the death of human capital as we currently know it. But out of the ashes of the old will arise the prospect of a new human capital dedicated to transforming our understanding of the self, education, and the future economy.

Appendix

Data Sources in Chapters 4 and 5:

IPUMS USA 1970 Census 1% metro sample.
https://usa.ipums.org/usa/sampdesc.shtml#us1970c

IPUMS USA 1990 Census
https://usa.ipums.org/usa/sampdesc.shtml#us1990b

IPUMS USA 2010 American Community Survey
https://usa.ipums.org/usa/sampdesc.shtml#us1990b

Northern Ireland Statistics and Research Agency, Central Survey Unit, Office for National Statistics, Social Survey Division. (2015). *Quarterly Labour Force Survey, January - March*, 2009. [data collection]. *4ᵗʰEdition*. UK Data Service. SN: 6199, http://doi.org/10.5255/UKDA-SN-6199-3.

Office for National Statistics, Social Survey Division, Northern Ireland Statistics and Research Agency, Central Survey Unit. (2014). *Quarterly Labour Force Survey, April - June*, 2009. [data collection]. *3ʳᵈ Edition*. UK Data Service. SN: 6276, http://doi.org/10.5255/UKDA-SN-6276-2.

Northern Ireland Statistics and Research Agency, Central Survey Unit, Office for National Statistics, Social Survey Division. (2015). *Quarterly Labour Force Survey, July - September*, 2009. [data collection]. *4ᵗʰEdition*. UK Data Service. SN: 6334, http://doi.org/10.5255/UKDA-SN-6334-2.

Northern Ireland Statistics and Research Agency, Central Survey Unit, Office for National Statistics, Social Survey Division. (2015). *Quarterly Labour Force Survey, October - December*, 2009. [data collection]. *2ⁿᵈ Edition*. UK Data Service. SN: 6402, http://doi.org/10.5255/UKDA-SN-6402-2.

Northern Ireland Statistics and Research Agency, Central Survey Unit, Office for National Statistics, Social Survey Division. (2015). *Quarterly Labour Force Survey, January - March*, 2010. [data collection]. *3rd Edition*. UK Data Service. SN: 6457, http://doi.org/10.5255/UKDA-SN-6457-3.

Northern Ireland Statistics and Research Agency, Central Survey Unit, Office for National Statistics, Social Survey Division. (2015). *Quarterly Labour Force Survey, April - June*, 2010. [data collection]. *3rd Edition*. UK Data Service. SN: 6548, http://doi.org/10.5255/UKDA-SN-6548-2.

Office for National Statistics, Social Survey Division, Northern Ireland Statistics and Research Agency, Central Survey Unit. (2014). *Quarterly Labour Force Survey, July - September*, 2010. [data collection]. *2nd Edition*. UK Data Service. SN: 6632, http://doi.org/10.5255/UKDA-SN-6632-2.

Office for National Statistics, Social Survey Division, Northern Ireland Statistics and Research Agency, Central Survey Unit. (2014). *Quarterly Labour Force Survey, October - December*, 2010. [data collection]. *2nd Edition*. UK Data Service. SN: 6715, http://doi.org/10.5255/UKDA-SN-6715-2.

Northern Ireland Statistics and Research Agency, Central Survey Unit, Office for National Statistics, Social Survey Division. (2015). *Quarterly Labour Force Survey, January - March*, 2011. [data collection]. *4th Edition*. UK Data Service. SN: 6782, http://doi.org/10.5255/UKDA-SN-6782-4.

Office for National Statistics, Social Survey Division, Northern Ireland Statistics and Research Agency, Central Survey Unit. (2014). *Quarterly Labour Force Survey, April - June*, 2011. [data collection]. *2nd Edition*. UK Data Service. SN: 6851, http://doi.org/10.5255/UKDA-SN-6851-2.

Northern Ireland Statistics and Research Agency, Central Survey Unit, Office for National Statistics, Social Survey Division. (2019). *Quarterly Labour Force Survey, July - September*, 2011. [data collection]. *4th Edition*. UK Data Service. SN: 6906, http://doi.org/10.5255/UKDA-SN-6906-5.

Northern Ireland Statistics and Research Agency, Central Survey Unit, Office for National Statistics, Social Survey Division. (2019). *Quarterly Labour Force Survey, October - December*, 2011. [data collection]. *4th Edition*. UK Data Service. SN: 6975, http://doi.org/10.5255/UKDA-SN-6975-4.

Notes

CHAPTER 1

1. Theodore W. Schultz, "Investment in Human Capital," *American Economic Review* 51, no. 1 (1961): 1–17.

2. The scale of the mental health crisis in Britain is so great that then Prime Minister Theresa May recognized the significance of the problem. See UK Government, "Prime Minister Unveils Plans to Transform Mental Health Support," press release, January 9, 2017, https://www.gov.uk/government/news/prime-minister-unveils-plans-to-transform-mental-health-support.

3. Fahmida Rahman and Daniel Tomlinson, *Cross Countries: International Comparisons of Intergenerational Trends*, Resolution Foundation/Intergenerational Commission Report, February 2018, https://www.resolutionfoundation.org/app/uploads/2018/02/IC-international.pdf.

4. An immediate problem is that human capital has become part of public, political, and policy narratives. So rather than find an alternative that will have difficulty getting a public hearing, we redefine it in ways that fundamentally challenge what we call the "orthodox" theory of human capital and its links to neoliberal economics. There are different ways of defining and understanding concepts such are freedom, opportunity, and education that have competing implications for public policy, and the same is true of human capital theory. Treating human capital as a contested concept offers the best prospect of contributing to policy and scholarly debate.

5. Daron Acemoglu and David Autor, "What Does Human Capital Do?," NBER Working Paper No. 17820, Cambridge, MA, February 2012. They acknowledge their close relationship, referring to human capital theory as the canonical theory from which skill bias theory has departed in its core assumptions in pragmatic ways. In this book we will refer to both approaches as "orthodox" theories of human capital and highlight only specific aspects of skill-biased technological change (SBTC) as opposed to early orthodox theory, where appropriate.

   The early theorists, most notably Becker, are often described as "freshwater" economists from Chicago, meaning they take a pure, orthodox approach to human capital theory, in which their models are pitched at such a high level of abstraction that they seem barely related to the real world. These models are meant to depict the optimum market conditions for economic efficiency. Real-world conditions are then compared to this ideal, and when they are inevitably found wanting, policymakers are invited to draw the lesson that they need to bring their policies into line with the model.

Partha Dasgupta writes, "Markets come in so many varieties that it makes good sense to determine their ideal form and examine why and how actual markets differ from the ideal." He goes on to say, "Economists refer to departures from their ideal form as 'market failure.'" Partha Dasgupta, *Economics: A Very Short Introduction* (Oxford: Oxford University Press, 2007), 72. This is a classic statement in defense of orthodox economics, but while simple it hides a set of questionable assumptions that we shall challenge in this book. The most significant advances made by what are sometime called "saltwater" economists from the east and west coasts of the United States centers on SBTC, where theorists, including Daron Acemoglu, David Autor, Frank Levy, and Richard Murnane, take a more grounded view compared to Becker's economic approach. Becker's theory is founded on universal laws of market competition and the view that all behavior can be studied as economic behavior, captured by statistical modeling and quantitative measurements of years of schooling, academic attainment, and rates of return. (These are discussed in the next two chapters.)

6. David Autor, "Why Are There Still So Many Jobs? The History and Future of Workplace Automation," *Journal of Economic Perspectives* 29, no. 3 (2015): 28 clings to an orthodox view of labor scarcity rather than contemplating the wider consequences for economic change for the (re)distribution of income and wealth.

7. Whereas the question of labor demand has not been a pressing concern in orthodox theory—since it has assumed either that supply creates its own demand as employers seek to utilize the productive potential of more skilled workers or that technological innovation will simply raise the demand for high-skilled work—it is central to job scarcity.

8. Translation work is not a neutral process or one based on some measure of intelligence. It is informed by class, gender, and racial inequalities. We develop this point in part II.

9. See the discussion by Arne Kalleberg, *Precarious Lives* (Cambridge, UK: Polity Press, 2018).

10. We should emphasize that this book would not have been written without those upon whose shoulders we stand. There have been many critical analyses of human capital theory that have largely been ignored by orthodox economists and policy advisors, yet that have built the foundations for our work. We have in mind the work of Carnoy, Berg, Bowles and Gintis, Bourdieu, and Thurow, whose concept of a jobs competition we take forward in this book. Ingenuity has enabled orthodox economists to constantly update their theory in ways that have appeared relevant to changing circumstances. But they have now run out of road: it is the end of their research program.

11. We will discuss Thomas Piketty's account of supermanagers in a later chapter. See his *Capital in the Twenty-First Century* (Cambridge, MA: Belknap/Harvard University Press, 2014).

12. Amartya Sen, *Development as Freedom* (Oxford: Oxford University Press, 2001), 295.

CHAPTER 2

1. Robert Heilbroner, *Behind the Veil of Economics* (London: Penguin, 1989).

2. See B. F. Kiker, "The Historical Roots of the Concept of Human Capital," *Journal of Political Economy* 74, no. 5 (1966): 481–99.

3. See Alessandro Roncaglia, *The Wealth of Ideas: A History of Economic Thought* (Cambridge, UK: Cambridge University Press, 2005), 72; Kiker, "The Historical Roots," 482; William Petty, *The Economic Writings of Sir William Petty*, vol. 1 (1662), edited by Charles Henry Hull, 1899, Online Library of Liberty, http://oll. libertyfund.org/titles/petty-the-economic-writings-of-sir-william-petty-vol-1.

4. Petty, *The Economic Writings*. Petty viewed land and labor as interchangeable factors of production; "the most important Consideration in Political Oeconomies" was precisely "how to make a Par and Equation between Lands and Labour, so as to express the Value of any thing by either alone." See Roncaglia, *The Wealth of Ideas*, 73.

5. William Farr, "The Income and Property Tax," *Quarterly Journal of the Statistical Society* 16 (1853): 2.

6. John Locke, *Two Treatises of Government* (1823), Essay Two: "Concerning the True Original Extent and End of Civil Government," chapter 5: "Of Property," 122, http://socserv2.socsci.mcmaster.ca/econ/ugcm/3ll3/locke/government.pdf.

7. Locke, *Two Treatises*, 123.

8. See Max Weber, "Human Nature through a Capitalist Lens," in Jeremy Rifkin, *The Zero Marginal Costs Society* (New York: Palgrave Macmillan, 2014), 60–61.

9. Adam Smith, *The Wealth of Nations* (London: Dent, 1975), 5.

10. Adam Smith, *An Inquiry into the Nature and Causes of the Wealth of Nations*, edited by Edwin Cannan (Chicago: University of Chicago Press, 1976), book 1, chapter 10, part 1, p. 113.

11. Edwin Cannan's preface in Smith, *An Inquiry*, xi.

12. Smith, *An Inquiry*, 302–3. A more complete quotation is both interesting and damning: "The understandings of the great part of men are necessarily formed by their ordinary employments. The man whose life is spent in performing a few simple operations . . . has no occasion to exert his understanding, or to exercise his invention. . . . He naturally loses, therefore, the habit of such exertion, and generally becomes as stupid and ignorant as it is possible for a human creature to become. The torpor of his mind renders him, not only incapable of relishing or bearing a part in any rational conversation, but of conceiving any generous, noble, or tender sentiment, and consequently of forming any just judgement concerning many even of the ordinary duties of private life."

13. See the quotation from Smith.

14. This is diametrically opposed to Nassau Senior's *An Outline of the Science of Political Economy* (New York: Farrar and Rinehart, 1939). In Kiker's historical analysis of the concept of human capital he wrote that Senior "asserted that there is little difference between talking about the value of a slave and about the value of a free man. The principal difference is that the free man sells himself for a period of time and only to a certain extent, whereas the slave is sold for a lifetime" ("The Historical Roots," 486; see Senior, *An Outline*, 10).

15. See Sanchez Manning, "Britain's Colonial Shame: Slave-Owners Given Huge Payouts after Abolition," *Independent*, February 24, 2013, http://www.independent.co.uk/news/uk/home-news/britains-colonial-shame-slave-owners-given-huge-payouts-after-abolition-8508358.html. The comprehensive abolition of slavery in the United States was in 1843 and became the Thirteenth Amendment to the US Constitution in 1865. The British Abolition Act of 1833 included various exceptions that enabled the slave trade to continue. While this was the formal abolition of slavery in America and Britain, modern slavery is on the rise.

16. John Stuart Mill, *Principles of Political Economy with some of their Applications to Social Philosophy* (London: Longman, Green, 1848), book 1, chapter 3: "Of Unproductive Labour," I.3.9 footnote 3, http://www.econlib.org/library/Mill/mlP3.html. The full quotation is interesting in the context of this discussion, also in making the distinction between humans as capital (as under slavery, which Mill opposed) and as hired hands: "It seems to me, however, that the skill of an artisan (for instance) being both a desirable possession, and one of a certain durability (not to say productive even of national wealth), there is no better reason for refusing to it the title of wealth because it is attached to a man, than to a coalpit or manufactory because they are attached to a place. Besides, if the skill itself cannot be parted with to a purchaser, the use of it may; if it cannot be sold, it can be hired; and it may be, and is, sold outright in all countries whose laws permit that the man himself should be sold along with it. Its defect of transferability does not result from a natural but from a legal and moral obstacle."

17. As Daniel Bell notes, economics was called "the dismal science" because of the belief of the classical political economists that there were limits to capital accumulation and growth. Their pessimism was based on "the law of diminishing returns; the Malthusian principle in which an increase in real wages would simply lead to faster population growth and the dilution of that increase; and implicitly, an invariant state of technology." Daniel Bell, *The Coming of Post-Industrial Society* (New York: Basic Books, 1973), 190.

18. Adam Smith, *The Wealth of Nations* (Oxford: Clarendon Press, 1976), 111. Given that a country had all the capital necessary in relation to the business it could transact, "*the competition, everywhere, would be as great and consequently the* ordinary profit, as low as possible." For an interesting discussion of the historical sociology

of Adam Smith, see Giovanni Arrighi, *Adam Smith in Beijing* (New York: Verso, 2007). Arrighi claims that there is no inherent mechanism for overcoming the decline in economic growth resulting from a "stationary state." He writes, "Nowhere does Smith suggest that the invisible hand of the market acting on its own can get the economy unstuck from such a trap. If anything or anyone can, it is the visible hand of government through suitable changes in laws and institutions" (50).

19. See Sylvia Nasar, *Grand Pursuit: The Story of the People Who Made Modern Economics* (London: Fourth Estate, 2011), 51.

20. Nasar, *Grand Pursuit*, 51.

21. Nasar, *Grand Pursuit*, 65; A. B. Atkinson, *The Personal Distribution of Incomes* (London: Routledge Revivals, 1976), 36; Alfred Marshall, *Money, Credit and Commerce* (London: Macmillan, 1923), 262. See also Alfred Marshall's essay "The Future of the Working Class" given to an audience of "70 to 80 ladies" at the Reform Club of Cambridge, England, in *Memorials of Alfred Marshall*, edited by A. C. Pigou (London: Macmillan, 1925). Nasar has a good description of Marshall's belief that competitive markets would lift living standards for consumers and workers, an interpretation of market capitalism fundamentally different from that of Karl Marx and later Karl Polanyi (*Grand Pursuit*, 84). It also worth reflecting on Marshall's view of the role of women, who were largely invisible in public life at the time. Marshall was aware of the influence that J. S. Mill's wife, Harriet Taylor Mill, had on her husband's ideas, especially his essay "The Subjection of Women" (1869). Nasar suggests that, in seeing education as a weapon in the struggle against social injustice, Marshall "considered women society's principal change agent": "For Marshall, the existential problem for women and for the working classes was essentially the same: both lacked the opportunity to lead independent and fulfilling lives. Workers were condemned by low wages to lives of drudgery that prevented all but the most exceptional from fully developing their moral and creative faculties. Middle-class women were condemned by custom to ignorance and drudgery of a different sort" (*Grand Pursuit*, 62).

22. Marshall, *Money, Credit and Commerce*, 262; also in Atkinson, *The Personal Distribution*, 36.

23. See Richard Blandy, "Marshall on Human Capital: A Note," *Journal of Political Economy* 75, no. 6 (1967): 874. Marshall was also fully aware of the distinction between humans as capital, as in the slave trade, and humans capitalizing on their skills: "The first point to which we have to direct our attention is the fact that human agents of production are not bought and sold as machinery and other material agents of production are. The worker sells his work, but he himself remains his own property: those who bear the expenses of rearing and educating him receive but very little of the price that is paid for his services in later years." Alfred Marshall, *Principles of Economics* (1890), book 6, chapter 4, part 4, http://www.econlib.org/library/Marshall/marP46.html#Bk.VI,Ch.IV.

24. Kiker, "The Historical Roots," 481. But see Mark Blaug's introductory discussion "The Formation of Human Capital," in *An Introduction to the Economics of Education* (New York: Penguin, 1970); Blandy, "Marshall," 874–75.

25. Blandy, "Marshall," 874; Blaug, *An Introduction*, 2. Blaug goes onto to explain that Marshall was aware of Irving Fisher's wider view of capital "as simply any stock existing at a given instant that yields a stream of services over time, all flows of 'income' therefore being the product of some item of 'capital' whose value is calculated by capitalizing the income flow at an appropriate discount rate" (5). Although impressed with Fisher's "masterly argument," Marshall concluded that Fisher "seems to take too little account of the necessity for keeping realistic discussions in touch with the language of the market-place" (*Principles of Economics*, appendix E, note 2). Blaug concludes that "Marshall preferred the more conventional definition of his day which did not count the skills of the population as forming part of the capital stock or 'wealth' of an economy" (*An Introduction*, 5).

26. Theodore W. Schultz, "Investment in Human Capital," *American Economic Review* 51, no. 1 (1961): 1.

27. Phillip Brown and Stuart Tannock, "Education, Meritocracy and the Global War for Talent," *Journal of Education Policy* 24 (2009): 377–92.

28. Theodore Schultz, "Investment in Human Capital: Presidential Address to the American Economic Association," *American Economic Review* 51, no. 1 (March 1981): 3.

29. Blaug, *An Introduction*, 19.

30. Peter Blau and Otis Duncan, *The American Occupational Structure* (New York: John Wiley and Sons, 1967).

31. Blaug, *An Introduction*, 21. In redefining education as investment rather than consumption, he rejected John Maynard Keynes's widely held view at the time that the contrast between consumption and investment depends on who it is that makes the decision to purchase. Blaug explains that in Keynesian theory, education is treated as consumption rather than investment since expenditures on education are made by households or by the government acting on behalf of households out of taxes collected for them, whereas on-the-job training is clearly investment because it is an expenditure incurred by business enterprises (*An Introduction*, 17–18). For protagonists of human capital theory, this is an unhelpful definition because "the Keynesian view of education as consumption logically inhibits any consideration of the contribution of education to economic growth" (18). Blaug goes on to argue, "A good case can now be made for the view that educational expenditure does partake to a surprising degree of the nature of investment in enhanced future output. To the extent, the consequences of education in the sense of skills embodied in people may be viewed as human capital, which is not to say that people themselves are being treated as capital" (19).

32. "We can think of three classes of expenditure: expenditures that satisfy consumer preferences and in no way enhance the capabilities under discussion—these

represent pure consumption; expenditures that enhance capabilities and do not satisfy any preferences underlying consumption—these represent pure investment; and expenditures that have both effects" (Schultz, "Investment in Human Capital," 8).

33. Schultz, "Investment in Human Capital," 8. This was known as the labor theory of value, associated with Smith, Marx, and Marshall, the last of whom tried to navigate his way between classical political economy and the marginalists. Paul Mason argues, "Textbook economics is today built on marginalism's discoveries. But in the pursuit of maths over 'political economy,' the marginalists created a discipline which ignored the production process; reduced the psychology of the deal to a two-dimensional balance between pleasure and pain; saw no special role for labour; discounted the possibility of economic laws acting at a deep, unobservable level, independent of the rational will of human beings; and reduced all economic agents to traders, abstracting away from class and other power relationships." Paul Mason, *Postcapitalism: A Guide to Our Future* (London: Allen Lane, 2015), 162.

34. However, it is difficult to know what is being rewarded in generating a yield, and ultimately it's an ex post argument: we don't know whether it's an investment until there is a yield. This is particularly important in thinking about the changing relationship between education, jobs, and incomes, because orthodox human capital approaches can deal only with past returns and have no way of predicting future returns beyond extrapolating from past trends as they have no theory of the division of labor or the mechanisms of capitalist transformation.

35. Schultz acknowledged the "very helpful suggestions" he received from Milton Friedman.

36. Theodore Schultz, *Investing in Human Capital: The Role of Education and Research* (New York: Free Press, 1971), 10; Phillip Brown, Andy Green, and Hugh Lauder, *High Skills: Globalization, Competitiveness and Skill Formation* (Oxford: Oxford University Press, 2001), 13.

37. Andrew Gamble, *Hayek: The Iron Cage of Liberty* (Boulder, CO: Westview, 1996), 51. See also Lester C. Thurow, "A Do-It-Yourself Guide to Marginal Productivity," in *Generating Inequality: Mechanisms of Distribution in the U.S. Economy* (New York: Basic Books, 1975) and Simon Clarke, *Marx, Marginalism and Modern Sociology: From Adam Smith to Max Weber* (London: Palgrave Macmillan, 1985). There is an interesting discussion of the relationship between human capital and neoliberalism and "economization of the entire social field" in Michel Foucault's *The Birth of Biopolitics: Lectures at the College De France 1978–1979*, translated by Graham Burchill (London: Palgrave, 2008), 242.

38. Theodore W. Schultz, "The Value of the Ability to Deal with Disequilibria," *Journal of Economic Literature* 13, no. 3 (1975): 827–46.

39. Becker writes, "The combined assumptions of maximizing behaviour, market equilibrium, and stable preferences, used relentlessly and unflinchingly, form the heart of the economic approach as I see it." Gary S. Becker, *The Economic Approach to*

Human Behavior (Chicago: University of Chicago Press, 1976), 5. See also Gary S. Becker, "The Economic Way of Looking at Life," Nobel Lecture, December 9, 1992, https://www.nobelprize.org/uploads/2018/06/becker-lecture.pdf.

40. Gary S. Becker, *Human Capital: A Theoretical and Empirical Analysis with Special Reference to Education*, 3rd edition (Chicago: University of Chicago Press, 1993), 117.

41. Becker, *Human Capital,* 115–16.

42. Becker, *Human Capital,* 112–13.

43. Gary S. Becker, foreword in *The Oxford Handbook of Human Capital*, edited by Alan Burton-Jones and J. C. Spender (Oxford: Oxford University Press, 2011), xiiv.

44. Although he also recognized the law of diminishing returns of investing in the education of some people, such as older workers (see note 38 above).

45. See Ian Baptiste, "Educating Lone Wolves: Pedagogical Implications of Human Capital Theory," *Adult Education Quarterly* 51, no. 3 (2001): 191.

46. We had assumed that this phrase was attributable to Sean Hargreaves-Heap; however, after correspondence with him, its provenance remains uncertain.

47. Becker, *The Economic Approach*, 282. It should be said that Becker struggles with the concept of utility maximizing; by the time of his Nobel Prize acceptance speech he resorted to assuming only that individuals maximize their utility preferences, which rather begs the question of their pursuit of self-interest. See Geoffrey Hodgson, "On the Limits of Rational Choice," *Economic Thought* 1 (2012): 94–108, for a critique of utility maximization. Ian Baptiste writes that, "as utility-maximizing individuals, humans are incapable of engaging in activities other than those that maximize their benefits" ("Educating Lone Wolves," 191).

48. Becker asserts, "Everyone recognizes that the economic approach assumes maximizing behavior . . . be it the utility or wealth function of household, firm, union, or government bureau that is maximized" (*The Economic Approach*, 5). In his Nobel lecture he refines his ideas of rational choice, suggesting that "individuals maximize welfare as they conceive it, whether they be selfish, altruistic, loyal, spiteful, or masochistic" ("The Economic Way," 38).

49. See Becker, "The Economic Way," 46.

50. Becker, *The Economic Approach*, 5.

51. Becker, *The Economic Approach*, 5; Baptiste, "Educating Lone Wolves," 192.

52. Baptiste, "Educating Lone Wolves," 192.

53. Becker, *The Economic Approach*, 5; Baptiste, "Educating Lone Wolves," 192.

54. Becker, *The Economic Approach*, 5. We assume he would also include culture as well as structure. One aspect of this approach is that market congestion is invariably a short-term problem because people will adjust their expectations in line with market signals at the same time that employers will alter their business strategies to utilize the supply of skilled labor.

55. Baptiste, "Educating Lone Wolves," 191.

56. Milton Friedman, "The Methodology of Positive Economics," in *Essays in Positive Economics* (Chicago: Chicago University Press, 1953), 1–43, 41.

57. See Foucault, *The Birth of Biopolitics*.

58. Becker, *Human Capital*, 1964.

59. See Pedro Nuno Teixeira, "Gary Becker's Early Work on Human Capital—Collaborations and Distinctiveness," *Journal of Labor Economics* 3, no. 12 (2014): 3, https://izajole.springeropen.com/articles/10.1186/s40172-014-0012-2.

60. Jacob Mincer, "Investment in Human Capital and Personal Income Distribution," *Journal of Political Economy* 66 (August 1958): 287. This conformed to the idea of humans as expensive machines that wear out over time.

61. Gary Becker, "Investment in Human Capital: A Theoretical Analysis," Journal of Political Economy 70, no. 5, part 2 (1962): 9–49.

62. Becker, "The Economic Way."

63. This exchange is reported in Peter Fleming, *The Death of Homo Economicus* (London: Pluto Press, 2017), 181–82.

64. Mincer, "Investment in Human Capital," 298.

65. Becker, "The Economic Way," 43.

66. Melvin Reder, "Chicago Economics: Permanence and Change," *Journal of Economic Literature* 20 (1982): 13n20.

67. Gary Becker, "Human Capital Effort and the Sexual Division of Labour," in "Trends in Women's Work, Education and Family Building," *Journal of Labor Economics* 3, no. 1, part 2 (January 1985): S33–S58.

68. Becker, *The Economic Approach*, 20. See also Gary Becker, "Altruism, Egoism, and Genetic Fitness: Economics and Sociobiology," *Journal of Economic Literature* 14, no. 3 (September 1976): 817–26

69. For a recent attempt that engages with Becker's account from a feminist perspective, see Lynn Prince Cook and Jennifer Cook, "Productivity or Gender? The Impact of Domestic Tasks across the Wage Distribution," *Journal of Marriage and Family* 1 (2018): doi:10.1111/jomf.12467.

70. See David Deming, *The Growing Importance of Social Skills in the Labor Market* (Cambridge, MA: Harvard University and NBER, 2015) 34.

71. There are obviously alternative explanations, which we discuss in part II. For example, we can hypothesize that women may be more alert to the emotions and signals that are given out, especially in relation to men, because they are oppressed and need to read signals and emotions to survive. Such an explanation falls outside the *what if* assumptions of the theory and therefore are not considered by those working within the theory. But our analysis points to enduring patterns of sexual and racial discrimination that cannot be explained in terms of the troubles of individuals but rather highlight public issues of social structure.

72. Gary Becker, *The Economics of Discrimination* (Chicago, University of Chicago Press, 1957).

73. Becker, "The Economic Way," 39.

74. See Geoffrey M. Hodgson, "The Meaning of Methodological Individualism," *Journal of Economic Methodology* 14, no. 2 (2007): 211–26.

75. Theodore W. Schultz, "The Economics of Being Poor," Nobel Lecture, December 8, 1979, http://www.nobelprize.org/nobel_prizes/economic-sciences/laureates/1979/schultz-lecture.html.

76. Schultz, "The Economics of Being Poor." The full quotation reads: "Longer life spans provide additional incentives to acquire more education, as investments in future earnings. Parents invest more in their children. More on-the-job training becomes worthwhile. The additional health capital and the other forms of human capital tend to increase the productivity of workers. Longer lifespans result in more years participation in the labor force, and bring about a reduction in 'sick time.' Better health and vitality of workers in turn lead to more productivity per manhour at work."

77. D. Kapur et al., *The World Bank: Its First Half Century*, vol. 1: *History* (Washington, DC: Brookings Institution, 1997).

CHAPTER 3

1. See, for example, Daron Acemoglu and David Autor, "What Does Human Capital Do?," NBER Working Paper No. 17820, Cambridge, MA, February 2012. Margaret Blair calls human capital a "shorthand" term. Indeed the fact that it is difficult to pin down given the level of abstraction of Becker's universal theory or because it has been defined in different ways explains part of its appeal. See Margaret Blair, "An Economic Perspective on the Notion of 'Human Capital,'" in *The Oxford Handbook of Human Capital*, edited by Alan Burton-Jones and J. C. Spender (Oxford: Oxford University Press, 2011), 49.

2. Robert Reich, *The Work of Nations* (New York: Simon and Schuster, 1992); Phillip Brown and Hugh Lauder, *Capitalism and Social Progress* (London: Palgrave, 2001).

3. Karl Polanyi, *The Great Transformation* (Boston: Beacon Press, 1957), 73. For a detailed account of post–World War II economic nationalism, see Brown and Lauder, *Capitalism*.

4. Later market reforms of education were based on a user-pays model of funding, given the assumption that private rates of returns benefit individuals more than the wider society.

5. These calculations are taken from Philip Armstrong, Andrew Glyn, and John Harison, *Capitalism Since 1945* (Oxford: Basil Blackwell, 1991), 117.

6. Armstrong, Glyn, and Harrison, *Capitalism*, 167, 168.

7. These figures are taken from Angus Maddison, *Phases of Capitalist Development* (Oxford: Oxford University Press, 1982), 208.

8. See Brown and Lauder, *Capitalism*.

9. Federal Reserve History, "The Great Inflation, 1965–1982," https://www.federal-reservehistory.org/essays/great_inflation., accessed January 8, 2018.

10. The quote from Ronald Reagan is in M. Stephen Weatherford and Lorraine M. McDonald, "Ideology and Economic Policy," in *Looking Back at the Reagan Presidency*, edited by Larry Berman (Baltimore, MD: Johns Hopkins University Press, 1990), 125. The quote from Margaret Thatcher was reported in the *Sunday Times*, May 8, 1998. She went on to say, "But then it came. The face began to smile, the spirits began to lift, the pride returned." See Brown and Lauder, *Capitalism*.

11. These points are taken from the introduction to Hugh Lauder, Phillip Brown, Jo-Anne Dillabough, and A. H. Halsey, eds., *Education, Globalization and Social Change* (Oxford: Oxford University Press, 2006).

12. Brown and Lauder, *Capitalism*, 122.

13. Patricia Marchak, *The Integrated Circus: The Neo-Liberal and the Restructuring of Global Markets* (Montreal: McGill-Queen's University Press, 1990), quoted in in Brown and Lauder, *Capitalism*, 123.

14. They included the CEOs of Coca-Cola, Exxon, Hewlett-Packard, Bank of America, Fiat, Shell, Mitsubishi, and the Bank of Tokyo. See Brown and Lauder, *Capitalism*.

15. Leading educational sociologists in the early 1960s observed, "Education is a crucial type of investment for the exploitation of modern technology. This fact underlies recent educational development in all the major industrial societies. . . . Education attains unprecedented economic importance as a source of technological innovation." A. H. Halsey and Jean Floud, introduction in *Education Economy and Society*, edited by A. H. Halsey, J. Floud, and J. Anderson (New York: Free Press, 1961), 1.

16. Fritz Machlup, *The Production and Distribution of Knowledge in the United States* (Princeton, NJ: Princeton University Press, 1962). He identified five knowledge sectors: information technologies, mass media, education, research and development, and information services.

17. Peter F. Drucker, *Post-Capitalist Society* (Oxford: Butterworth-Heinemann, 1993), 36. In a similar vein Alvin Toffler argued that the role of labor shifted from the exploitation of muscle to mental power: "It is knowledge, not cheap labor; symbols, not raw materials, that embody and add value." Alvin Toffler, *Power Shift: Knowledge, Wealth and Violence at the Edge of the Twenty-First Century* (New York: Bantam, 1990) 82, quoted in Brown and Lauder, *Capitalism*, 118. Toffler was writing in the same year Schultz delivered his presidential address.

18. Daniel Bell, *The Coming of Post-Industrial Society: A Venture of Social Forecasting* (New York: Basic Books, 1973), 409.

19. Manuel Castells, *The Internet Galaxy* (Oxford: Oxford University Press, 2001), 1.

20. See Acemoglu and Autor, "What Does Human Capital Do?," for a discussion of the differences in approach. One way in which SBTC has changed is with respect to methodology. Its approach may be considered a form of pragmatic empiricism, in contrast to the strict empiricism of orthodox human capital theory. That said,

there is no methodological playbook for SBTC. To our knowledge no methodology paper has been written on the topic.

21. See Claudia Goldin and Lawrence Katz, *The Race between Education and
    Technology* (Boston: Harvard University Press, 2008).

22. Goldin and Katz, *The Race*, 292, 293. Likewise, Acemoglu and Autor argue,
    "Technological progress raises the demand for skill, and human capital investments
    slake that demand. When demand moves faster than does the supply of human cap-
    ital, inequality rises and vice-versa when supply outpaces demand" ("What Does
    Human Capital Do?," 2).

23. This approach provides an explanation for increasing income inequalities that
    significantly widened in both the United States and Britain in the 1980s. Based
    on a simple supply-and-demand framework, where there is an undersupply of
    skilled labor, the wages of those with a college education will rise; therefore an
    increase in the number of college graduates will result in a reduction in income
    inequalities because there will be greater market competition between college
    graduates.

24. See Paul M. Romer, "Endogenous Technological Change," *Journal of Political
    Economy* 98, no. 5, pt. 2 (1990): S71; Robert J. Barro, "Government Spending in
    a Simple Model of Endogenous Growth," *Quarterly Journal of Economics* 98, no. 5
    (1990): S103–S125.

25. Daron Acemoglu, "Technical Change, Inequality, and the Labor Market," *Journal
    of Economic Literature* 40 (2002): 12.

26. If endogenous growth depended on human capital investment, it also depended
    on knowledge innovation, exemplified by the success of Silicon Valley and Route
    126 in Massachusetts. Comparisons were frequently drawn between what were
    portrayed as the sclerotic economies of Germany and France, burdened with state
    regulations and controls, as opposed the neoliberal models of weak states and
    market individualism that were taking hold in the Anglo-Saxon economies. For the
    returns of human capital investment to be achieved, there needed to be a culture of
    enterprise together with incentives for individuals to maximize their utility, as by
    nature people will behave as entrepreneurs of the self when they are free to pursue
    their self-interest. In short, the rapid pace of innovation in knowledge economies
    placed increasing emphasis on governments to encourage entrepreneurship as a
    source of new investment, innovation, and jobs.

27. David Autor, Frank Levy, and Richard Murnane, "The Skill Content of Recent
    Technological Change: An Empirical Exploration," *Quarterly Journal of Economics*
    118, no. 4 (November 2003): 1279–333.

28. Their account has become known as the ALM model, after the names of the three
    authors, and is a modification of the original SBTC account. It can be argued that
    this approach to SBTC may represent a narrowing of the earlier, arresting conjec-
    ture that technology is, in general, skill biased, since technological development
    rewards only those with certain specific skills.

29. See Reich, *The Work*, quoted in Brown and Lauder, *Capitalism*, 118.

30. Drucker, *Post-Capitalist Society*, 7. Daniel Bell argued that knowledge, as opposed to labor in a Marxist sense, was the source of value. "When knowledge," he claimed, "becomes involved in some systematic form in the applied transformation of resources (through invention and design), then one can say that knowledge, not labour, is the source of value" (*The Rise*, 167–68).

31. Reich, *The Work*, 154. Reich was President Clinton's first labor secretary and has been a major opponent of neoliberal economics. However, he shared the view that the upside of the globalized economy was an almost unlimited supply of knowledge-intensive jobs and that investment in human capital offered the prospect of delivering prosperity and social justice.

32. Reich, *The Work*, 247.

33. Reich wrote, "Positive economic nationalism would seek to develop the capacities of the work forces of the Third World—not ... so that global companies can safely extract raw materials and sell products within them—but as a means of promoting indigenous development and thereby enhancing global wealth. To this end, the shift of high-volume, standardized production to Third World nations would be welcomed" (*The Work*, 314).

34. Richard Rosecrance, *The Rise of the Virtual State: Wealth and Power in the Coming Century* (New York: Basic Books, 1999), xi. Sometime later Thomas Friedman reported his surprise at the rapid advances that emerging economies such as India and China were making in competing for high-skilled, higher-value enterprise. However, he described this as a race to the top, posing little threat to the human capital agenda: "America, as a whole, will do fine in a flat world with free trade—provided it continues to churn out knowledge workers who are able to produce idea-based goods that can be sold globally and who are able to fill the knowledge jobs that will be created as we not only expand the global economy but connect all the knowledge pools in the world. There may be a limit to the number of good factory jobs in the world, but there is no limit to the number of idea-generating jobs in the world." Thomas Friedman, *The World Is Flat: A Brief History of the Globalized World in the 21st Century* (New York: Allan Lane, 2005), 230.

35. See, for example, John Chubb and Terry Moe, *A Lesson in School Reform from Great Britain* (Washington, DC: Brookings Institution, 1992). Here they extol the virtues of markets to "be allowed to work their wonders ... for everyone's benefit" (10–11).

36. National Commission on Excellence in Education, *A Nation at Risk* (Washington, DC: NCEE, 1983), 6, quoted in Brown and Lauder, *Capitalism*, 119.

37. National Commission on Education, *Learning to Succeed* (London: Heinemann, 1993), 33, quoted in Brown and Lauder, *Capitalism*, 119.

38. World Bank, *The East Asian Miracle: Economic Growth and Public Policy* (Oxford: Oxford University Press, 1993), figure 1, "Average Growth of GNP per Capita, 1965–90," p. 2.

39. World Bank, *The East Asian Miracle*, figure 1, "Average Growth of GNP per Capita, 1965–90," p. 10. The market-friendly approach is based on World Bank, *World Development Report: The Challenge of Development* (New York: Oxford University Press, 1991). See the critique by Robert Wade of this misinterpretation of East Asian policy: "Japan, the World Bank, and the Art of Paradigm Maintenance: *The East Asian Miracle* in Political Perspective," *New Left Review* 217 (1996): 3–36.

40. These figures are drawn from Phillip Brown, Hugh Lauder, and David Ashton, *The Global Auction: The Broken Promises of Education, Jobs and Incomes* (New York: Oxford University Press, 2011), figure 3.2, "Global Auction," p. 32.

41. American Presidency Project, https://www.presidency.ucsb.edu/documents/address-before-joint-session-the-congress-the-state-the-union-2. In the same speech he discussed investment in capital: "Yes, we are going to invest in America. This administration is determined to encourage the creation of capital, capital of all kinds: physical capital—everything from our farms and factories to our workshops and production lines, all that is needed to produce and deliver quality goods and quality services; intellectual capital—the source of ideas that spark tomorrow's products; and of course our human capital—the talented work force that we'll need to compete in the global market."

42. Reuters, "The 1992 Campaign: Excerpts from Clinton's Speech on Foreign Policy Leadership," *New York Times*, August 14, 1992, http://www.nytimes.com/1992/08/14/us/the-1992-campaign-excerpts-from-clinton-s-speech-on-foreign-policy-leadership.html?pagewanted=all.

43. "President Obama's Speech to the NAACP Centennial Convention," *US News and World Report*, July 17, 2009, https://www.usnews.com/news/obama/articles/2009/07/17/president-obamas-speech-to-the-naacp-centennial-convention. See also Arne Duncan, "Back to School: Enhancing US Education and Competitiveness," *Foreign Affairs* (November–December 2010): 65–74.

44. Tony Blair, "Leader's Speech, Blackpool, 1996," British Political Speech, http://www.britishpoliticalspeech.org/speech-archive.htm?speech=202. Although a famous slogan by Blair, it was actually borrowed from Bill Clinton: "Blair in His Own Words," *Independent*, September 27, 2006, http://www.independent.co.uk/news/uk/politics/blair-in-his-own-words-6231303.html.

45. We have witnessed the same thing in the context of higher education.

46. See the OECD's website, http://www.oecd.org/.

47. OECD, "How Does Educational Attainment Affect Participation in the Labour Market?," *Education at a Glance 2014: OECD Indicators*, 2014, http://www.oecd.org/edu/EAG2014-Indicator%20A5%20(eng).pdf, 102.

48. See, for example, Michaela Brockmann, Linda Clarke, and Christopher Winch, *Knowledge, Skills and Competence in the European Labour Market: What's in a Vocational Qualification?* (London: Routledge, 2011).

49. Eric A. Hanushek and Ludger Woessmann, *The Knowledge Capital of Nations: Education and the Economics of Growth* (Cambridge, MA: MIT Press, 2015), 27.

50. There have been many critiques of PISA's methodology. See, for example, Harry Torrance, "Globalising Empiricism: What, If Anything, Can Be Learned from International Comparisons of Educational Achievement?," in *Education, Globalisation and Social Change*, edited by Hugh Lauder, Phillip Brown, Jo-Anne Dillabough, and A. H. Halsey (Oxford: Oxford University Press, 2006).

51. See Diane Ravitch, "School 'Reform': A Failing Grade," *New York Review of Books*, September 20, 2011.

52. Hanushek and Woessmann, *The Knowledge Capital*, table 7.1, 164–65. See also OECD, "The High Cost of Low Educational Performance: The Long-Run Economic Impact of Improving PISA Outcomes, 2010, https://www.oecd.org/pisa/44417824.pdf.

CHAPTER 4

1. Evan Schoffer and John Meyer, "The Worldwide Expansion of Higher Education in the Twentieth Century," *American Sociological Review* 70, no. 6 (2005): 898–920; Martin Trow, "Reflections on the Transition from Elite to Mass to Universal Access: Forms and Phases of Higher Education in Modern Societies since WWII," in *International Handbook of Higher Education*, edited by James J. F. Forest and Philip G. Altbach (New York: Springer, 2007).

2. Claudia Goldin and Lawrence Katz, *The Race between Education and Technology* (Boston: Harvard University Press, 2008).

3. Eric A. Hanushek and Ludger Woessmann, *The Knowledge Capital of Nations: Education and the Economics of Growth* (Cambridge, MA: MIT Press, 2015).

4. See IPUMS USA https://usa.ipums.org/usa/sampdesc.shtml for a full data description of the Censuses and American Community Survey. The UK Quarterly Labor Force Survey (QLFS) collects data on employment and income on approx. 150,000 adults age 16 or above in 60,000 private households four times a year. To enure the sample size is adequate for statistical analysis after disaggregating by qualification level, age group and earning deciles, our analysis combined three years of the QLFS to construct a pooled sample of respondents aged 18-64 in 2009, 2010 and 2011 (N=41812). All samples were weighted using the income weight (piwt07). For further details on the LFS data series, see: beta.ukdataservice.ac.uk/datacatalogue/series/series?id=2000026. See also the Labour Force Survey User Guide: Volume 1: Background and Methodology. http://doc.ukdataservice.ac.uk/doc/3938/mrdoc/pdf/background.pdf. See Appendix for detailed data sources. See Appendix for full domentation of data source.

5. Goldin and Katz, *The Race*.

6. Thomas Piketty, *Capital in the Twenty-First Century* (Cambridge, MA: Belknap Press, 2014); Joseph Stiglitz, *The Price of Inequality* (New York: Norton, 2012); Anthony Atkinson, *Inequality: What Can Be Done?* (Cambridge, MA: Harvard University Press, 2015).

7. To do so raises fundamental questions about the idea of a universal law, for such a law seems more plausible where a notion of a graduate premium based on averages is used. The question of causation becomes much more problematic when data are disaggregated, and we need multiple causes to explain the range of returns when groups have the same education qualifications.

8. Income is in US dollars in 2009 and is inflation-adjusted using the consumer price index inflator provided by IPUMS-USA: https://cps.ipums.org/cps/cpi99.shtml.

9. Jan Pen, *Income Distribution: Facts, Theories and Policies* (New York: Praeger, 1971).

10. We must remember that changes in the graduate premium do not mean that graduate incomes are rising; they can also be the result of declining incomes suffered by those with a high school education.

11. https://www.epi.org/publication/the-top-10-charts-of-2014/, accessed January 10, 2018.

12. Authors' calculations using weighted data from IPUMS USA US Census 1970, 1990 1% metro sample, ACS 2010, ages 18–64.

13. College H (top 10 percent) are the only ones to sustain their incomes at 1970s levels. This is perhaps a little surprising given the rise in income inequalities since the 1970s. It is likely due to the privileged few with higher social class backgrounds who maintain their high earnings over time. Graduates in lower-income percentiles have all but experienced income stagnation. Rising income inequalities could also be explained by within-group differences in the top decile.

14. https://www.epi.org/blog/top-1-0-of-earners-see-wages-up-157-8-since-1979/.

15. In 1970 master's and PhD degrees were defined as five or more years of college education. About 4 percent of the sample achieved this level of qualification in 1970; this rate has risen to 10 percent in 2010. See IPUMS-USA for details: https://usa.ipums.org/usa-action/variables/EDUC#codes_section.

16. College Board. Student Debt Relief. https://www.studentdebtrelief.us/news/average-cost-of-college-2018/.

17. See Armstrong and Hamilton, *Paying for the Party: How College Maintains Inequality* (Harvard University Press, 2015); Suzanne Mettler *Degrees of Inequality: How the Politics of Higher Education Sabotaged the American Dream* (New York: Basic Books, 2014). See also Jon Marcus and Holly K. Hacker, "The Rich-Poor Divide on America's College Campuses Is Getting Wider, Fast," *Hechinger Report*, December 17, 2015, http://hechingerreport.org/the-socioeconomic-divide-on-americas-college-campuses-is-getting-wider-fast/.

18. Jacob Mincer, "Schooling, Experience, and Earnings, Human Behavior & Social Institutions. National Institute of Economic Research," NBER No. 2, New York, 1974. https://www.nber.org/books/minc74-1, accessed January 20, 2018.

19. Matt Dickson and Franz Buscha, "The Wage Returns to Education over the Life-Cycle: Heterogeneity and the Role of Experience," IZA Discussion Paper No. 9596, University of Bonn, 2015.

20. See Goldin and Katz, *The Race,* on how to reduce income inequalities, discussed in chapter 3.

21. It is important to note that the standard classification of occupations has changed over time, but we have tried to match the categories as closely as possible using the US Census Bureau crosswalks. See the occupation codes used here: IPUMS-USA, "Codes," https://usa.ipums.org/usa-action/variables/OCC#codes_section; for 1970: IPUMS-USA, "1970 Occupation Codes," https://usa.ipums.org/usa/volii/occ1970.shtml; for 1990: IPUMS-USA, "1990 Occupation Codes," https://usa.ipums.org/usa/volii/occ1990.shtml; for 2010: IPUMS-USA, "ACS [American Community Survey] Occupation Codes (OCC), 2000–2017," https://usa.ipums.org/usa/volii/occ_acs.shtml.

22. Corie Lok, "Science's 1%: How Income Inequality Is Getting Worse in Research," *Nature,* September 21, 2016, https://www.nature.com/news/science-s-1-how-income-inequality-is-getting-worse-in-research-1.20651.

23. See Peter Hall and David Soskice, eds. *Varieties of Capitalism: The Institutional Foundations of Comparative Advantage* (Oxford: Oxford University Press, 2001).

24. OECD (2016), Education at a Glance 2016: OECD Indicators, OECD Publishing, Paris, https://doi.org/10.1787/eag-2016-en. Figure A6.1.

25. Piketty, *Capital.*

26. Dickson and Buscha, "The Wage Returns."

27. Piketty, *Capital,* Figure 9.7, p. 323.

28. See the discussion by Kevin Murphy in his debate with Emanuel Saez in Kevin Murphy and Emanuel Saez, "Income and Wealth in America," in *Inequality and Economic Policy: Essays in Memory of Gary Becker,* edited by T. Church, C. Miller, and J. Taylor (Stanford, CA: Hoover Institution Press, 2015). Murphy says, "High skilled people are supplying more labor. They're working harder. They're working more hours. They're investing more in themselves. They're moving to places that demand more human capital. This, unlike growth in the number of individuals completing college, actually increases inequality."

29. Claudia Goldin and Lawrence F. Katz, "Gender Differences in Careers, Education, and Games: Transitions. Career and Family Life Cycles of the Educational Elite," *American Economic Review: Papers & Proceedings* 98, no. 2 (2008): 363–69.

30. Phillip Brown, Hugh Lauder, and David Ashton, *The Global Auction* (New York: Oxford University Press, 2011).

31. Will Abel, Reeca Burnham, and Matthew Corder, "Wages, Productivity and the Changing Composition of the UK Workforce," *Quarterly Bulletin*, April 8, 2016.

32. F. Pfeffer, "Persistent Inequality in Educational Attainment and Its Institutional Context," *European Sociological Review* 24, no. 5 (2008): 543–65; K. Shauman, "Are There Sex Differences in the Utilization of Educational Capital among College-Educated Workers?," *Social Science Research* 38 (2009): 535–71.

CHAPTER 5

1. Gary Becker, "The Age of Human Capital" in *Education in the Twenty-first Century*, edited by Edward P. Lazear (CA: Hoover Institute Press, Stanford University, 2002). See also Theodore W. Schultz, "Investment in Human Capital," *American Economic Review* 51, no. 1 (1961): 1–17. At the time Schultz originally presented his views on human capital, wages as a share of national income were rising and societies were becoming more equal in terms of income.

2. "Meritocracies and Intergeneration Mobility—Becker," *Becker-Posner Blog*, January 1, 2013, http://www.becker-posner-blog.com/2013/01/meritocracies-and-intergeneration-mobility-becker.html. See also Gary S. Becker, *The Economic Approach to Human Behavior* (Chicago: University of Chicago Press, 1976), 283.

3. See Thomas Piketty, *Capital in the Twenty-First Century* (Cambridge, MA: Harvard University Press, 2014).

4. The figure for Britain is taken from the TUC Touchstone Extras Series "Unfair to Middling" (London: Trades Union Congress, 2013).

5. Piketty, *Capital*.

6. https://www.epi.org/publication/raising-americas-pay/.

7. https://www.epi.org/publication/why-americas-workers-need-faster-wage-growth/.

8. See Piketty, *Capital*, Figure 6.1, "Capital-Labor Split in Britain," and Table 7.3, "Inequality of Total Income (Capital and Labor) across Time and Space."

9. US Bureau of Labor Statistics, "Estimating the US Labor Share," February 2017, https://www.bls.gov/opub/mlr/2017/article/estimating-the-us-labor-share.htm.

10. International Monetary Fund, *World Economic Outlook: Gaining Momentum?*, April 2017, 121, Figure 3.1. https://www.imf.org/en/Publications/WEO/Issues/2019/08/30/World-Economic-Outlook-April-2017-Gaining-Momentum-44510, accessed January 1, 2018.

11. Piketty, *Capital*, 302.

12. In the economies of Latin America and Asia we also see rising inequality between 1990 and 2010, although not to the same extent as in the United States and United Kingdom.

13. "Working for the Few: Political Capture and Economic Inequality, OXFAM Briefing Paper 178, Oxford, January 2014.

14. We will return to this issue in part III.

15. McKinsey Global Institute, "Playing to Win: The New Global Competition for Corporate Profits," 2015, https://www.mckinsey.com/~/media/McKinsey/Business%20Functions/Strategy%20and%20Corporate%20Finance/Our%20Insights/The%20new%20global%20competition%20for%20corporate%20profits/MGI%20Global%20Competition_Full%20Report_Sep%202015.ashx, accessed January 1, 2018.

16. Piketty, *Capital*, 331.

17. See Ed Michaels, Helen Handfield-Jones, and Beth Axelrod, *The War for Talent* (Boston: Harvard University Press, 2001); Phillip Brown, Hugh Lauder, and David Ashton, *The Global Auction: The Broken Promises of Education, Jobs and Incomes* (New York: Oxford University Press, 2011), chapter 6.

18. Graham Room points out that Piketty has no theory of how contemporary economies work and how therefore the wealthy have become wealthy and are likely to outstrip the earnings of workers. He notes that Piketty avoids mention of James Galbraith's argument that "much of this involves predatory looting of corporate and public wealth," which Room characterizes as "behavior that has less affinity with entrepreneurship than with Russian oligarchs and international criminals." Graham Room, "Capital in the Twenty-First Century," *Journal of European Social Policy* 25, no. 2 (2015): 242–48. Nor, as suggested in the main text, does Piketty develop an argument based on what is called the financialization of capitalism, which clearly has a role in explaining the global rise of the wealthy. See James K. Galbraith, *The Predator State* (New York: Free Press, 2009).

19. Galbraith, *The Predator State*; Joseph E. Stiglitz, *The Price of Inequality* (New York: Norton, 2012), xv.

20. Jose Gabriel Palma, "On the Discreet Charm of the (Rentier) Bourgeoisie: The Contradictory Nature of the Installation Period of a New Techno-Economic Paradigm," in *Techno-Economic Paradigms: Essays in Honor of Carlotta Perez*, edited by Wolfgang Dreschler, Rainer Kattel, and Erik Reinert (London: Anthem Press, 2011). Much corporate profit remains locked in offshore accounts to avoid national tax regulations.

21. See the next chapter.

22. Vikki Boliver, "How Fair Is Access to More Prestigious Universities?," *British Journal of Sociology* 64, no. 2 (2013): 344–64.

23. Jennie Brand and Yu Xie, "Who Benefits Most from College? Evidence for Negative Selection in Heterogeneous Economic Returns to Higher Education," *American Sociological Review* 75, no. 2 (2010): 273–302.

24. Richard Breen and John Goldthorpe, "Explaining Educational Educational Differentials: Towards a Formal Rational Action Theory," *Rationality and Society* 9, no. 3 (1997): 275–305.

25. Florencia Torche, "Is a College Degree Still the Great Equalizer? Intergenerational Mobility across Levels of Schooling in the United States," *American Journal of Sociology* 117, no. 3 (2011): 763–807.

26. Martin Carnoy, *Faded Dreams: The Politics and Economics of Race in America* (New York: Cambridge University Press, 1994).

27. Greg Duncan and Richard Murnane, eds., *Whither Opportunity? Rising Inequality, Schools and Children's Life Chances* (New York: Russell Sage Foundation, 2011).

28. In a democratic society it is important that students from all social backgrounds meet because it is a way that they can learn to understand each other; schools are increasingly unable to meet this democratic function. This is discussed in part III.

29. Stephen Raudenbush, Jean Marshall, and Emily Art, "Year-by-Year and Cumulative Impacts of Attending a High Mobility Elementary School on Children's Mathematics Achievement in Chicago," in Duncan and Murnane, *Whither Opportunity?* See also Ceri Brown, *Educational Binds of Poverty* (New York: Routledge, 2015).

30. Teresa Kroeger, Tanyell Cooke, and Elise Gould, "The Class of 2016," Economic Policy Institute, April, 21, 2016, Table 1, http://www.epi.org/publication/class-of-2016/#epi-toc-3.

31. Kroeger, Cooke, and Gould, "The Class."

32. Graduate employment and unemployment rates vary greatly in different countries. Geoff Maslen, "Wide variation in graduate employment rates globally," *University World News Global Edition*, January 18, 2019. https://www.universityworldnews.com/post.php?story=20190116181403880, accessed February 28, 2019.

33. Unemployment is also more cyclical than underemployment because the latter reflects structural changes in occupations and the labor market.

34. For current purposes we are using a narrow definition mainly focused on skills or education-based underemployment. For a wider definition see that used by the International Labor Organization, 2007. Ka Ho Mok and Alfred M. Wu "Higher education, changing labour market and social mobility in the era of massification in China", *Journal of Education and Work* 29, no. 1: 77–97.

35. Jaison Abel and Richard Deitz, "Underemployment in the Early Careers of College Graduates Following the Great Recession," Federal Reserve Bank of New York, Staff Report 749, September 2016. See also their earlier paper, Jaison Abel, Richard Deitz, and Yaqin Su, "Are Recent College Graduates Finding Good Jobs?," *Federal Reserve Bank of New York*, Current Issues in Economics and Finance 20, no. 1 (2014): 108.

36. Paul Beaudry, David Green, and Benjamin Sand, "The Declining Fortunes of the Young Since 2000," *American Economic Review* 104, no. 5 (2014): 381–86; Paul Beaudry, David Green, and Benjamin Sand, "The Great Reversal in the Demand for Skill and Cognitive Tasks," *Journal of Labor Economics* 34, no. S1, part 2 (2016): S199–S247.

37. Richard Vedder, "Is Underemployment of Recent College Grads a Serious Problem?," paper presented at The James G. Martin Center for Academic Renewal, Raleigh, North Carolina, October 7, 2016. Vedder and his associates conclude that about 52 percent of four-year college graduates are in jobs that match their skills, and 48 percent are overqualified. They also report that over 5 million college graduates are in jobs that require less than a high school education. See Richard Vedder, Christopher Denhart, and Jonathan Robe, "Why Are Recent College Graduates Underemployed?," Centre for College Affordability and Productivity, January 2013, https://files.eric.ed.gov/fulltext/ED539373.pdf.

38. UK Office for National Statistics, "Graduates in the UK Labour Market: Full Report," London, November 19, 2013; Robert E.Wright, "Is Graduate Underemployment Persistent? Evidence from the United Kingdom," IZA Discussion Paper No. 6177, Bonn, November 2011.

39. Kody Steffy, "Wilful versus Woeful Underemployment: Perceived Volition and Social Class Background among Overqualified College Graduates," *Work and Occupations* 44, no. 4 (2017): 467–511.

40. Michael Spence, "Job Market Signaling," *Quarterly Journal of Economics* 87, no. 3 (1973): 355–74.

41. Indeed many of the characteristics that Bowles and Gintis identified thirty years ago. See Sam Bowles and Herb Gintis, *Schooling in Capitalist America* (London: Routledge, 1976).

42. Arlie Hochschild, *The Managed Heart: Commercialization of Human Feeling* (Berkeley: University of California Press, 1983).

43. See Abel and Deitz, "Underemployment," for the United States. For the United Kingdom, see Kate Purcell, Peter Elias, Gabby Atfield, Heike Behle, R. Ellison, Daria Luchinskaya, Jane Snape, Lynne Conaghan, and Charoula Tzanakou, *Futuretrack Stage 4: Transitions into Employment, Further Study and Other Outcomes* (Manchester, UK: HECSU, 2012).

44. Thirty years ago, when only 10 percent of young people entered university, if twenty people applied for an office reception job, and only one person was a university graduate while the rest had high school diplomas, it was likely that the potential employer wondered why the university graduate had failed to find alternative employment. But when over 40 percent enter university, several job candidates are likely to be university graduates and the employer may well opt to hire one of them believing they will have better communication and organizational skills than high school graduates. Thurow writes, "Whenever statistical discrimination occurs, the linkages between individual characteristics and individual earnings is broken. The individual has the desired characteristics, but he cannot sell these characteristics since he has no way of demonstrating that he has the desired characteristics." Generating Inequality, 174.

Vedder, Denhart, and Robe offer the following example without relating it to statistical discrimination: "Suppose in 1970, a bar owner advertised for a bartender and received 15 applicants, most or all of whom had high school diplomas. He would most likely choose the bartender on criteria unrelated to educational credentials. Suppose today, another bar owner likewise advertises for a bartender, and also gets 15 applicants, but four have bachelor's degrees. The owner, to minimize time and resources devoted to interviewing a long line of applicants, might restrict interviews to the four holders of degrees, since it is likely a priori that these persons will on average be a little smarter, a little more reliable, etc., than the other applicants. Education, heretofore not much of a screening device, has become one in terms of hiring the most qualified person for jobs for which skill requirements are relatively modest and learned on the job quickly. The existence of an ample supply of college graduate bartenders has created a demand for them, sometimes explicitly stated in minimal education qualifications required for the job" ("Why Are," 8).

45. Ivar Berg, *Education and Jobs: The Great Training Robbery* (New York: Praeger, 1970), 186.

46. Ewart Keep and Ken Mayhew, "The Economic and Distributional Implications of Current Policies on Higher Education," *Oxford Review of Economic Policy* 20, no. 2 (2004): 299.

47. Thomas DiPrete and Claudia Buchmann, *The Rise of Women: The Growing Gender Gap in Education and What It Means for American Schools* (New York: Sage, 2013).

48. The Equality and Human Rights Commission, "Employers in the Dark Ages over Recruitment of Pregnant Women and New Mothers," February 19, 2018, https:// www.equalityhumanrights.com/en/our-work/news/employers-dark-ages-over-recruitment-pregnant-women-and-new-mothers.

49. Peter Blau and Otis Duncan, *The American Opportunity Structure* (New York: Free Press, 1967).

50. Higher Education Funding Council for England, "Differences in Employment Outcomes: Comparison of 2008–09 and 2010–11 First Degree Graduates," 2016, http://hdl.voced.edu.au/10707/421290.

51. Higher Education Funding Council for England, "Differences."

52. Wouter Zwysen and Simonetta Longhi, "Employment and Earning Differences in the Early Career of Ethnic Minority British Graduates: The Importance of University Career, Parental Background and Area Characteristics," *Journal of Ethnic and Migration Studies* 44, no. 1 (2018): 154–72.

53. Daniel Bell, *On the End of Ideology* (New York: Free Press, 1960), in which he cites the letter from Thomas Jefferson to John Adams, https://founders.archives. gov/documents/Adams/99-02-02-6198 in which he raises the idea of an artificial aristocracy.

54. International Monetary Fund, *World Economic Outlook*.

CHAPTER 6

1. Evan Schoffer and John Meyer, "The Worldwide Expansion of Higher Education in the Twentieth Century," *American Sociological Review* 70, no. 6 (2005): 898–920.

2. This piles on competitive pressures, which lead to unintended consequences such as undermining innovation and a decline in human creativity. This will be discussed in the final section of the book.

3. It also calls into question how society distributes income and puts money in people's pockets necessary to consume the products and services on which economic growth depends. These question will be addressed in the final section of

the book, but here we need to get a better sense of what has gone wrong when orthodox human capital theory is center stage in public policy.

4. But there is a crucial difference between *credential inflation* and *monetary inflation*, because credentials do not come with the same property rights as money as a form of exchange. On the £10 bank note is the statement "Bank of England: I promise to pay the bearer on demand the sum of Ten Pounds." On a $20 bill is the statement "This note is legal tender for all debts public and private," and if that is not enough, on the other side it says "In God we trust." Investments in human capital do not offer such security. There is no guarantee to pay the bearer of credentials with a job in the labor market, let alone one that matches their level of education.

5. Robert Frank and Philip J. Cook, *The Winner-Take-All Society. Why the Few at the Top Get So Much More Than the Rest of Us* (New York: Penguin Books, 1995).

6. Graeme Wearden, "Lure of City Money Too Strong for Young, Says Mervyn King," *The Guardian*, April 29, 2008. https://www.theguardian.com/business/2008/apr/29/executivesalaries.bankofenglandgovernor.

7. A decline in the value of credentials is inevitable unless it is matched by a rising demand for employees with corresponding skill sets, something that hasn't happened for reasons we will explain when we examine the future of work. Indeed while much has been made of the idea that knowledge is undiminished by its use, what some commentators fail to grasp is the other side of the equation: the market value of credentials (and human capital) depends on its scarcity value.

8. It could be argued that the devaluation of a college degree is a temporary phenomenon, caused by the 2008 Great Recession; that is what politicians hoped for, and many orthodox economic theories predict. In our view, there is no such comforting story to tell. The changes in graduate fortunes preceded the Great Recession and signal a fundamental structural change in the labor market.

9. Richard Vedder, Christopher Denhart, and Jonathan Robe, "Why Are Recent College Graduates Underemployed?," Centre for College Affordability and Productivity, January 2013, 8, https://files.eric.ed.gov/fulltext/ED539373.pdf.

10. Richard Vedder, Christopher Denhart, and Jonathan Robe, "Why Are Recent College Graduates Underemployed?."

11. Richard Vedder, Christopher Denhart, and Jonathan Robe, "Why Are Recent College Graduates Underemployed?."

12. This appears to be straightforward credential inflation, but some of the occupations they have chosen are problematic. Salespeople and bank clerks now have to operate computer systems, and this arguably requires new and different kinds of skill. Whether they match the knowledge and skills required of a four-year degree is another question, one that raises much more complex issues about how we are to judge the appropriateness of the knowledge and skills people have for the jobs they do. Many workers have sought to raise their wages and status by demanding degrees as a condition of entry in their specific occupation. Nursing, golf course management, and realty managers are examples. In such cases, it is more difficult to determine

how well their knowledge matches their work. What these cases point to is not the straightforward operation of demand and supply but a society in which the conventions for accessing employment have changed. Catherine Rampell, "Degree Inflation? Jobs That Newly Require B.A.'s," *The New York Times*, December 4, 2012. https://economix.blogs.nytimes.com/2012/12/04/degree-inflation-jobs-that-newly-require-b-a-s/.

13. Mike Brewer, Andy Dickerson, Lynn Gambin, Anne Green, Robert Joyce and Rob Wilson, *Poverty and Inequality in 2020: Impact of Changes in the Structure of Employment*, Joseph Rowntree Report, 2012. https://www.jrf.org.uk/report/impact-employment-changes-poverty-2020.

14. Randall Collins, *Four Sociological Traditions* (New York: Oxford University Press, 1994), 146.

15. Lewis Carroll, *Through the Looking-Glass and What Alice Found There*, chapter 2, "The Garden of Live Flowers," Project Gutenberg, http://www.gutenberg.org/files/12/12-h/12-h.htm#link2HCH0002.

16. See, for example, Fred Hirsch, *The Social Limits to Growth* (London: Routledge, 1976); Lester Thurow, *The Zero-Sum Society* (New York: Basic Books, 1980); Robert H. Frank, *The Darwin Economy* (Princeton, NJ: Princeton University Press, 2011).

17. Although it does not rule out the possibility that it could still be a by-product of wasteful competition.

18. Competition also depends on how people are positioned on the starting line. More competition can be created by reducing inequalities in educational opportunities, as President Lyndon Johnson's War on Poverty tried to do. But when competition is left to market forces it is reduced to the survival of the fittest, not simply in respect to academic ability but in terms of who has the deepest pockets or has the power to play by different rules.

19. For a discussion of "social congestion" and the related idea of the "opportunity trap," see Phillip Brown, "Education, Opportunity and the Prospects for Social Mobility," *British Journal of Sociology of Education* 34, nos. 5–6 (2013): 678–700. This extends the work of Fred Hirsch, *The Social Limits to Growth* (London: Routledge, 1976). See also Raymond Boudon, *The Unintended Consequences of Social Action* (London: Macmillan, 1982).

20. Here economic theory is socially blind, given its foundations in methodological individualism. For the purity of their modeling they consider that there is no such thing as society, although institutional economics has gone a long way to overcome the weaknesses of methodological individualism, a position that still bedevils human capital theory.

21. It is worth noting that human capital investment can lead to different outcomes at the same time, depending on whether we are talking about education or the job market. Despite egregious inequalities in educational provision, where some

children may get two or three times as much spent on their education, it may still result in a positive sum. Even if it does not narrow inequalities in life chances, the experience of a decent education can be individually empowering and socially beneficial, although research suggests that the best results are in educational systems where there is greater equality of opportunity.

22. The classic discussion of elite distinction is Pierre Bourdieu's *Distinction: A Social Critique of the Judgement of Taste* (New York: Routledge, 1984). See also Jean-Pascal Daloz, *The Sociology of Elite Distinction* (New York: Palgrave Macmillan, 2010).

23. For the distinction between rigging and ranking, see Phillip Brown, "The Globalization of Positional Competition?," *Sociology* 34, no. 4 (2000): 633–53.

24. When the median household income in the United States is under $55,775, a figure that has barely changed since 2005. "US Household Income," Department of Numbers, 2017, http://www.deptofnumbers.com/income/us/. See also Alia Wong, "When Private School Tuition Costs More Than College," *Atlantic*, November 21, 2014, https://www.theatlantic.com/education/archive/2014/11/when-private-school-tuition-costs-more-than-college/383003/.

25. College Board, "Trends in College Pricing 2016," 14, https://trends.collegeboard.org/sites/default/files/2016-trends-college-pricing-web_1.pdf.

26. Paul F. Compos, "The Real Reason College Tuition Costs So Much," New York Times, April 4, 2015, https://www.nytimes.com/2015/04/05/opinion/sunday/the-real-reason-college-tuition-costs-so-much.html?_r=0.

27. Zack Friedman, "Student Loan Debt in 2017: A $1.3 Trillion Crisis," *Forbes*, February 21, 2017, https://www.forbes.com/sites/zackfriedman/2017/02/21/student-loan-debt-statistics-2017/#8afd76c5daba.

28. Ben Chu, "The Charts That Show How Private School Fees Have Exploded over the Past 25 Years," *Independent*, May 10, 2016, http://www.independent.co.uk/news/uk/home-news/the-charts-that-shows-how-private-school-fees-have-exploded-a7023056.html. On the rising costs of a private education in Britain, also see Hugo Greenhalgh, "£180,000—13 Years of London Private School Fees," *Financial Times*, September 2, 2016, https://www.ft.com/content/80e317a4-6f74-11e6-9ac1-1055824ca907.

29. Lloyds Bank, "The Cost of Private Education Soars to £157,000," press release, August 28, 2016, http://www.lloydsbankinggroup.com/globalassets/documents/media/press-releases/lloyds-bank/2016/160828-cost-of-private-schooling_final.pdf.

30. "It is less likely to be the archetypal middle-class professional and more likely to be high-net-worth individuals, increasingly international. Many established independent schools like Eton and Harrow educate the children of some of China's wealthiest multimillionaires." Graeme Paton, "Middle-Classes 'Forced Out of Private Schools' as Fees Soar," *Telegraph*, July 6, 2014, http://www.telegraph.co.uk/education/educationnews/10947098/Middle-classes-forced-out-of-private-schools-as-fees-soar.html.

31. Gonzalo Vina, "UK Graduates Leave University with More Debt Than US Peers," *Financial Times*, April 28, 2016, https://www.ft.com/content/a1c27f38-0c86-11e6-b0f1-61f222853ff3.

32. Phillip Brown and Anthony Hesketh, *The Mismanagement of Talent* (Oxford: Oxford University Press, 2004); Phillip Brown, Sally Power, Gerbrand Tholen, and Annabelle Allouch, "Credentials, Talent and Cultural Capital: A Comparative Study of Educational Elites in England and France," *British Journal of Sociology of Education* 37, no. 2 (2016): 191–211.

33. Nikolas Rose, *Governing the Soul: The Shaping of the Private Self* (London: Free Association Books, 1999); Beverley Skeggs, *Class, Self, Culture* (London: Psychology Press, 2004). In order to understand the advantage of some groups over others we also need to understand the full range of capitals identified by Pierre Bourdieu, by which once the education rules have been rigged, some win and some lose. There is a clear economics to advantage and disadvantage in educational outcomes. Bourdieu's great insight was in showing that the interrelationship between economic, cultural, and social capitals can be translated into educational, credential, and labor market advantage.

34. Brown and Hesketh, *The Mismanagement*, 220.

35. Lauren Rivera, *Pedigree: How Elite Students Get Elite Jobs* (Princeton, NJ: Princeton University Press, 2015).

36. Karen Ho, *Liquidated: An Ethnography of Wall Street* (Durham, NC: Duke University Press, 2009).

37. C. Wright Mills, *The Power Elite* (New York: Oxford University Press, 1956), 141.

38. It could be argued that for such jobs "skill" is constructed as a form of social class. High-net-worth clients expect to be treated according to social class norms and also expect employees to have been educated at elite colleges.

39. Brown and Hesketh, *The Mismanagement*; Rivera, *Pedigree*; Ho, *Liquidated*.

40. David Kynaston and Francis Green, *Engines of Privilege: Britain's Private School Problem* (London: Bloomsbury, 2019).

41. Jane Kenway, Johannah Fahey, Debbie Epstein, Aaron Koh, Cameron McCarthy, and Fazal Rizvi, *Class Choreographies: Elite Schools and Globalization* (London: Palgrave, 2017).

42. Phillip Brown and Hugh Lauder, "Globalization, the Nation State and International Education," in *Globalization and Education*, edited by Fazal Rizvi and Tom Popkewitz (Chicago: National Society for the Study of Education, 2009).

43. James McDonald, "The International School Industry," *Journal of Research in International Education* 5, no. 2 (2006): 191–213.

44. Shamus Khan, *Privilege: The Making of an Adolescent Elite at St Paul's School* (Princeton, NJ: Princeton University Press).

45. Tristan Bunnell, *The Changing Landscape of International Schooling: Implications for Theory and Practice* (Abingdon, UK: Routledge, 2014). See also Alan Wechsler

"The International-School Surge," *Atlantic*, June 5, 2017, https://www.theatlantic.com/education/archive/2017/06/the-international-school-surge/528792/.

46. See Brown, "The Globalization."

47. Phillip Brown, "The Third Wave: Education and the Ideology of Parentocracy," *British Journal of Sociology of Education* 11 (1990): 65–85.

48. Kenway et al., *Class Choreographies.*

49. Xiaoxin Wu, *School Choice in China* (Abingdon, UK: Routledge 2014). While there are clear differences in China compared to the United States or the United Kingdom, it is nevertheless the case that their spectacular success in pulling many out of poverty has been bought at a cost that may exacerbate inequalities in the future.

50. See the papers in Roger King, Simon Marginson, and Rajani Naidoo, eds., *Handbook on Globalization and Higher Education* (Northampton, MA: Edward Elgar, 2011). In particular see Ellen Hazelkorn, "Measuring World Class-Excellence and the Global Obsession with Rankings."

51. Times Higher Education (THE), *Work University Rankings 2020*, https://www.timeshighereducation.com/world-university-rankings/2020/world-ranking#!/page/0/length/25/sort_by/rank/sort_order/asc/cols/stats, accessed February 22, 2020.

52. David Rothkopf, *Superclass: The Global Power Elite and the World They Are Creating* (London: Little, Brown, 2008). See also Hugh Lauder and Phillip Brown, "The Standardisation of Higher Education, Positional Competition and the Global Labour Market," in King, Marginson, and Naidoo, *Handbook.*

53. College Board, "Trends," 28.

54. Andy Green, *Education and State Formation* (London: Palgrave Macmillan, 1990).

55. UK Department of Business, Innovation and Skills, *Fulfilling Our Potential: Teaching Excellence, Social Mobility and Student Choice*, November 2015, 11. https://www.gov.uk/government/uploads/system/uploads/attachment_data/file/474227/BIS-15-623-fulfilling-our-potential-teaching-excellence-social-mobility-and-student-choice.pdf.

56. Martha Nussbaum, *Not for Profit: Why Democracy Needs the Humanities* (Princeton, NJ: Princeton University Press, 2012).

57. *The Robbins Report: Higher Education* (London: Her Majesty's Stationary Office, 1963), 6, http://www.educationengland.org.uk/documents/robbins/robbins1963.html.

58. Donald MacKenzie, "An Equation and Its Worlds: Bricolage, Exemplars, Disunity and Performativity in Financial Economics," *Social Studies of Science* 33, no. 6 (December 2003): 831–68. In this paper MacKenzie argues that economics plays a vital role in constituting and shaping economies since economies are reshaped according to the dominant theories.

59. As we will argue in the final section, Becker ignored the changing role of the labor market, reducing it to a matter of supply and demand, signaled by prices.

60. Employers vary in their estimates of the importance of soft skills. Peter Cappelli, "Skill Gaps, Skill Shortages and Skill Mismatches," NBER Working Paper No. 20382, Cambridge, MA, August 2014.

61. Hugh Lauder, Michael Young, Harry Daniels, Maria Balarin, and John Lowe, introduction, in *Educating for the Knowledge Economy: Critical Perspectives*, edited by Hugh Lauder et al. (Abingdon, UK: Routledge, 2012).

62. Peter Cappelli, *Why Good People Can't Get Jobs: The Skills Gap and What Companies Can Do About It* (Philadelphia: Wharton Digital Press, 2012).

63. Basil Bernstein, "Class and Pedagogies: Visible and Invisible," in *Education: Culture, Economy and Society*, edited by A. H. Halsey, H. Lauder, P. Brown and A. S. Wells (Oxford: Oxford University Press, 1997), 73.

64. Alvin Gouldner, *The Coming Crisis of Western Sociology* (New York: Basic Books, 1970), 73.

65. See Andrew Jackson and Ben Dyson, *Modernising Money: Why Our Monetary System Is Broken and How It Can Be Fixed* (London: Positive Money, 2012).

66. This has been misread by human capital theorists to reflect labor demand.

CHAPTER 7

1. We need new ways of describing "developing countries"; that term assumes a binary between developed and developing countries, when there are areas in wealthy countries that endure many of the conditions of developing countries and vice versa.

2. Here we refer to highly educated immigrants who live and work in developed countries, a point we will return to later in the chapter.

3. AnnaLee Saxenian, *The New Argonauts* (Boston: Harvard University Press, 2007).

4. Ha-Joon Chang, "Why Developing Countries Need Tariffs—How WTO NAMA Negotiations Could Deny Developing Countries' Right to a Future," research report, Oxfam, November 24, 2004, https://policy-practice.oxfam.org.uk/publications/why-developing-countries-need-tarifs-how-wto-nama-negotiations-could-deny-devel-112533.

5. Theodore W. Schultz, "Investment in Human Capital," *American Economic Review* 51, no. 1 (1961): 1–17.

6. Robert Lucas, "On the Mechanics of Economic Development," *Journal of Monetary Economics* 22, no. 1 (1988): 3–42.

7. Phillip W. Jones, *World Bank Financing of Education, Lending, Learning and Development*, 2nd edition (Abingdon, UK: Routledge, 2007).

8. John Williamson, "What Washington Means by Policy Reform," in *Latin American Adjustment. How Much Has Happened?*, edited by John Williamson (Washington, DC: Institute for International Economics, 1990).

9. Ha-Joon Chang, *Bad Samaritans: The Guilty Secrets of Rich Nations and the Threat to Global Prosperity* (London: Random House, 2008).

10. Chang, *Bad Samaritans*.

11. Phillip Trostel, Ian Walker, and Paul Woolley, "Estimates of the Economic Return to Schooling for 28 Countries," *Labour Economics* 9, no. 1 (2002): 1–16.

12. Eric Hanushek and Ludger Woessmann, *Education, Quality and Economic Growth* (Washington, DC: World Bank, 2007).

13. Eric Hanushek, Ludger Woessmann, and Lei Zhang, "General Education, Vocational Education, and Labour Market Outcomes over the Life Cycle," IZA Discussion Paper No. 6083, Bonn, October 2011, http://ftp.iza.org/dp6083.pdf.

14. Hanushek and Woessmann, *Education.*

15. See Chang, *Bad Samaritans,* for a detailed discussion of strong state intervention and national investment in infrastructure in promoting economic growth, especially among the Tiger economies in East Asia, which has far less to do with education expansion.

16. https://ourworldindata.org/financing-education.

17. *World Employment and Social Outlook—Trends 2017* (Geneva: International Labour Organization, 2017). https://www.ilo.org/wcmsp5/groups/public/---dgreports/---dcomm/---publ/documents/publication/wcms_541211.pdf.

18. *World Employment and Social Outlook—Trends 2017.*

19. Eric A. Hanushek and Ludger Woessmann, *The High Cost of Low Educational Performance. The long-run of economic impact of improving PISA outcomes* (OECD: Paris, 2010). https://www.oecd.org/pisa/44417824.pdf, accessed February 8, 2018.

20. Eric Hanushek and Ludger Woessmann, *The Knowledge Capital of Nations: Education and the Economics of Growth* (Cambridge, MA: MIT Press, 2015), 12, 11.

21. The "East Asian Miracle" refers to the rapid economic success of a group of East Asian countries—South Korea, Taiwan, Hong Kong, and Singapore—since the late 1980s. Despite the high educational attainment in Latin American countries, which is purported to bring economic growth, their economic performance is poor, hence "Latin American Growth Puzzle."

   Eric Hanushek and Ludger Woessmann, "Schooling, Educational Achievement, and the Latin American Growth Puzzle," *Journal of Development Economics* (2012), doi:10.1016/j.jdeveco.2012.06.004.

22. Hanushek and Woessmann, *The Knowledge Capital,* 16.

23. Hanushek and Woessmann, *The Knowledge Capital,* 28. They use the term "knowledge capital" rather than "human capital," but they share the same assumptions as orthodox theories.

24. Linsu Kim and Richard Nelson, eds., *Technology, Innovation and Learning: Experience of New Industrialized Economies* (Cambridge, UK: Cambridge University Press, 2000); Bryan Fields, "The Accidental Tiger," PhD dissertation, University of Leicester, CLMS, 2002.

25. David Ashton, Francis Green, Donna James, and Johnny Sung *Education and Training for Development in East Asia* (London: Routledge, 1999); Robert Wade, *Governing the Market: Economic Theory and the Role of Government in East Asian Industrialization* (Princeton, NJ: Princeton University Press, 1990).

26. Irmgard Nübler, "A Theory of Capabilities for Productive Transformation: Learning to Catch Up," in *Transforming Economies: Making Industrial Policy Work for Growth, Jobs and Development*, edited by José Manuel Salazar-Xirinachs, Irmgard Nübler, and Richard Kozul-Wright (Geneva: International Labour Organization, 2014); Johnny Sung, *Explaining the Economic Success of Singapore: The Developmental Worker as the Missing Link* (Northampton, MA: Edward Elgar, 2006).

27. Phillip Brown, Hugh Lauder, and David Ashton, *The Global Auction: The Broken Promises of Education, Jobs and Incomes* (Oxford: Oxford University Press, 2011); Dani Rodrik, *The Globalization Paradox: Why Global Markets, States, and Democracy Can't Coexist* (Oxford: Oxford University Press, 2011).

28. Ha-Joon Chang, *Kicking Away the Ladder: Development Strategy in Historical Perspective* (London: Anthem Press, 2002).

29. Chang, *Bad Samaritans*.

30. Expenditure on Education, Public (% GDP) %. United Nations Development Programme: Human Development Reports, 2013. http://hdr.undp.org/en/content/expenditure-education-public-gdp.

31. Henry M. Levin and Carolyn Kelley, "Can Education Do It Alone," *Economics of Education Review* 13, no. 2 (1994): 97–108.

32. See the discussion in the introduction to Hugh Lauder, Michael Young, Harry Daniels, Maria Balarin, and John Lowe, eds., *Educating for the Knowledge Economy: Critical Perspectives* (Abingdon, UK: Routledge, 2012).

33. Phillip Brown, Hugh Lauder, and Johnny Sung, "Higher Education, Corporate Talent and the Stratification of Knowledge Work in the Global Labour Market," in *World Yearbook of Education*, edited by A. van Zanten, S. Ball, and B. Darchy-Koechlin (Abingdon, UK: Routledge, 2015).

34. Hanushek and Woessmann, *Education*.

35. World Migration in Figures. OECD-UNDESA. October 2013. https://www.oecd.org/els/mig/World-Migration-in-Figures.pdf.

36. Jeanne Batalova and Michael Fix, *New Brain Gain: Rising Human Capital among Recent Immigrants to the United States* (Washington, DC: MPI, 2017), https://www.migrationpolicy.org/research/new-brain-gain-rising-human-capital-among-recent-immigrants-united-states. Figure 1.

37. Batalova and Fix, *New Brain Gain*, 9.

38. Dilip Ratha, Sanket Mohapatra, and Ani Silwal, *The Migration and Remittances Factbook* (Washington, DC: World Bank, 2011).

39. Brown, Lauder, and Ashton, *The Global Auction*.

40. AnnaLee Saxenian, "Brain Circulation and Regional Innovation: The Silicon Valley–Hsinchu-Shanghai Triangle," in *The Economic Geography of Innovation*, edited by Karen Polenske (Cambridge, UK: Cambridge University Press, 2007).

41. Ragui Assaad, "The Impact of Migration on Those Left Behind: Evidence from Egypt," Middle East Institute, April 19, 2010, http://www.mei.edu/content/impact-migration-those-left-behind-evidence-egypt; Francisca M. Antman, "The

Impact of Migration on Family Left Behind," IZA Discussion Paper No. 6374, Bonn, 2007.

42. *Education at a Glance: OECD Indicators 2007* (Paris: OECD, 2007).

43. *Global Education Digest 2010: Comparing Education Statistics across the World* (Montreal: UNESCO Institute of Statistics, 2010).

44. Jie Zong and Jeanne Batalova. *International Students in the United States. SPOTLIGHT* (Washington, DC: Migration Policy Institute, May 9, 2018). https://www.migrationpolicy.org/article/international-students-united-states.

45. US earnings estimate published in Institute of International Education, *International Students in the United States* (Washington, DC: IIE, November 2007).

46. Anthony Bohm, *Global Student Mobility 2025: Analysis of Global Competition and Market Share* (Canberra: IDP Education Australia, 2003).

47. Mario Cervantes and Dominque Guellec, "International Mobility of Highly Skilled Workers: From Statistical Analysis to Policy Formation," in *International Mobility of the Highly Skilled* (Paris: OECD, 2002).

48. Saxenian, "Brain Circulation," 190–210.

49. OECD (2017), International Migration Outlook 2017, OECD Publishing, Paris, https://doi.org/10.1787/migr_outlook-2017-en. Figure 2.6.

50. Jeanne Batalova, Michael Fix, and James D. Bachmeier, *Untapped Talent: The Costs of Brain Waste among Highly Skilled Immigrants in the United States* (Washington, DC: MPI, 2016), https://www.migrationpolicy.org/research/untapped-talent-costs-brain-waste-among-highly-skilled-immigrants-united-states. Figure 1.

51. See "This One Group Gets 70 Percent of High-Skilled Foreign Worker Visas," *Washington Post*, April 3, 2017, https://www.washingtonpost.com/news/wonk/wp/2017/04/03/this-one-group-gets-70-percent-of-high-skilled-foreign-worker-visas/?utm_term=.8810ddbc1dfa.

52. See, for example, Jayati Ghosh, "Women, Labour and Capital Accumulation in Asia," *Monthly Review Press* 63, no. 8 (2012), https://monthlyreview.org/2012/01/01/women-labor-and-capital-accumulation-in-asia/.

53. UNESCO Global Education Monitoring, Report 2013.

CHAPTER 8

1. Auguste Comte, *The Crisis of Industrial Civilization* (1877), edited and introduced by Ronald Fletcher (London: Heinemann, 1974).

2. This is overlooked by many economists who adopt a model of methodological individualism and deal primarily in abstract correlations, such as that between years of schooling (education) and income. Given this level of abstraction it's not difficult to understand how Becker and others came to confuse Comte's "happy accident" for a universal theory of educational investment.

3. See Giovanni Arrighi, *Adam Smith in Beijing* (New York: Verso, 2007), 49–50.

4. Arrighi, *Adam Smith,* 50.

5. Joseph A. Schumpeter, *Capitalism, Socialism and Democracy* (Boston: George Allen & Unwin, 1943). Human capital projected current structures into the future based on the logic of technological change rather than the logic of capitalist accumulation. Our analysis here is derived from years of interviews with companies and policy analysts around the world; both have consistently failed to anticipate change, starting in 1997. The problem of change under capitalism is not one that human capital and SBTC theorists alone encounter. Sociologists like Bourdieu, who informs some of our thinking on different forms of capital, are also confronted by capitalist change. Craig Calhoun correctly notes, "[Bourdieu's] account of the different forms of capital involved no account of capitalism as a distinctive, historically specific system of production and distribution." Craig Calhoun, "For the Social History of the Present," in *Bourdieu and Historical Analysis*, edited by Philip S. Gorski (Chapell Hill: Duke University Press, 2013), 56. Bourdieu admits that his focus is unmistakably French, which raise questions concerning his theoretical contribution to a comparative understanding of capital and capitalism. See Pierre Bourdieu, *The Social Structures of the Economy* (Cambridge, UK: Polity, 2005).

6. Gary Becker, "Investment in Human Capital: A Theoretical Analysis," *Journal of Political Economy* 70, no. 5, part 2 (1962): 9–49.

7. Gary Becker writes, "The spread of education and the increased investment in other kinds of human capital were induced in large part by technological progress . . . through the effect on the rate of return, as measured by wage differences and costs" ("Investment," 54). More recently Becker has argued, "Technology may be the driver of the modern economy, especially in the hi-tech sector, but human capital is certainly the fuel." Gary Becker, "The Age of Human Capital," in *Education in the Twenty-first Century*, edited by Edward P. Lazear (CA: Hoover Institute Press, Stanford University, 2002), 292.

8. The first statement by Becker is in his foreword to Alan Burton-Jones and J. C. Spender, eds., *The Oxford Handbook of Human Capital* (Oxford: Oxford University Press, 2011). In 1962 Becker wrote, "The spread of education and the increased investment in other kinds of human capital were induced in large part by technological progress . . . through the effect on the rate of return, as measured by wage differences and costs" ("Investment," 54).

9. For a more detailed analysis of SBTC, see Hugh Lauder, Phillip Brown, and Sin Yi Cheung, "Fractures in the Education-Economy Relationship," *Oxford Review of Economic Policy* 34, no. 2 (Summer 2018): 495–515.

10. There are two ways of explaining these anomalies within the orthodox approach. The first is to say that some four-year college graduates are not well educated; the second, that they are not being educated in the right sets of skills. Neither seems convincing.

11. Thomas Piketty, *Capital in the Twenty-First Century* (Cambridge, MA: Harvard University Press, 2014), 330–31.

12. Piketty goes on to say, "But when an individual's job functions are unique, or nearly so, then the margin of error is much greater. . . . Individual marginal productivity becomes much harder to define' (*Capital*, 331).

13. Mats Alvesson, "Knowledge Work: Ambiguity, Image and Identity," *Human Relations* 54, no. 7 (2001): 863–86.

14. Daniel Kahneman, *Thinking Fast and Slow* (London, Penguin Books, 2011), 215.

15. Piketty, *Capital*, 331.

16. Amartya Sen, "Just Deserts," *New York Review of Books*, March 4, 1982.

17. Piketty writes, "It may be excessive to accuse senior executives of having their 'hands in the till,' but the metaphor is probably more apt than Adam Smith's metaphor of the market's 'invisible hand' " (*Capital*, 332).

18. See Jerome Gautie and John Schmitt, eds., *Low-Wage Work in the Wealthy World*, Russell Sage Foundation, 2009, https://www.russellsage.org/publications/low-wage-work-wealthy-world.

19. Katrine Marcal, *Who Cooked Adam Smith's Dinner?* (London: Portobello Books, 2015), 16.

20. Marilyn Waring, "Counting for Something! Recognising Women's Contribution to the Global Economy through Alternative Accounting Systems," *Gender and Development* 11, no. 1 (2003): 35.

21. S Kuznets, with Elizabeth Epstein and Elizabeth Jenks, "National Income and Its Composition, 1919–1938," *NBER, New York* 1 (1941): 10.

22. If women's domestic labor was factored into the costs of education and training it would offer a much more realistic measure of the free human capital available to companies. See Antonia Kupfer, "The Interrelation of Twenty-First Century Education and Work from a Gender Perspective," *International Studies in Sociology of Education* 24, no. 1 (2014): 116.

23. That said, we see a direct link between inequalities in market power and the wider structures of social class, gender, and racial inequalities.

24. For example, a university professor receives a nationally agreed pay raise and can also apply for discretionary increments of relatively small sums. If judged to be doing a decent job—that is, judged to be productive—she could receive an additional increment of around $1,500. However, if approached by another university she could use her market power to bid up her salary well above her existing salary in at least two ways: by negotiating a significantly higher income by moving to the other university or by renegotiating her existing contract with her current employer, assuming that they are keen to maintain her services. In short, she can bid up her income while doing exactly the same job that she was previously doing. Her productivity hasn't changed a lot, but her salary has. There are two provisos. First, this scenario does not take into account the role of reputational capital that has an interesting, but largely unexplored, relationship to productivity. Second, it assumes a high degree of market power. Her position would be very different if

other universities were not interested in appointing her, and likewise if her existing employer would be more than happy to see her leave. Hence it is possible to see bureaucracy as a way of trying to reduce this exploitation of the use of market power through the establishment of internal labor markets based on incremental progression and job security.

Stiglitz defines rent-seeking as "using political and economic power to get a larger share of the national pie, rather than to grow the national pie." And he argues that America has become a rent-seeking society. See Joseph E. Stiglitz and Linda J. Bilmes, "The 1 Percent's Problem," *Vanity Fair*, May 30, 2012, http://www.vanityfair.com/news/2012/05/joseph-stiglitz-the-price-on-inequality.

25. See especially Joseph E. Stiglitz, *The Price of Inequality* (London: Penguin, 2012).

26. Similar arguments were used to explain why market capitalism would become less important as knowledge and expert systems would take over from the market. See Daniel Bell, *The Coming of Post-Industrial Society* (New York: Penguin Books, 1973).

27. See Census Atlas of the United States: Census 2000 Special Reports, Chapter 10, 2007. https://www.census.gov/population/www/cen2000/censusatlas/pdf/10_Education.pdf.

28. See Andrew Shonfield, *Modern Capitalism* (Oxford: Oxford University Press, 1965).

29. See Werner Holzl and Andreas Reinstaller, *The Babbage Principle after Evolutionary Economics*, MERIT-Infonomics Research Memorandum Series, Maastricht, Netherlands, 2003.

30. Technological innovation in the form of digital Taylorism and the creation of a global auction for high-skilled and low-skilled jobs have shifted power decisively in the direction of business, as we will explain in the final section of the book.

31. Holzl and Reinstaller, *The Babbage Principle*, 2003, 14.

32. Paradoxically, human capital ideas were used to achieve this by asserting that a knowledge economy offered such good employment prospects that people no longer needed welfare support, etc. The market could be left to deliver freedom, prosperity, and justice.

33. See Norton Garfinkle, *The American Dream vs. the Gospel of Wealth: The Fight for a Productive Middle-Class Economy* (New Haven, CT: Yale University Press, 2006), 156.

34. Hence the revisionist view that the redefinition of human capital and how to rebuild a productive economy has to consider the politics of redistribution head-on because it can't be resolved through supply-side or labor market solutions. This is addressed in the chapter on rethinking returns.

35. David Cooper and Lawrence Mishel, *The Erosion of Collective Bargaining Has Widened the Gap between Productivity and Pay* (Washington, DC: Economic Policy Institute, 2015).

36. See Karl Polanyi, *The Great Transformation: The Political and Economic Origins of Our Time* (Boston, Mass.: Beacon Press, 1944), with introduction by Fred Block, (2001), xxxiv.

CHAPTER 9

1. See David Autor, "Why Are There Still So Many Jobs? The History and Future of Workplace Automation," *Journal of Economic Perspectives* 29, no. 3 (2015): 28.

2. For further discussion of this point, see Hugh Lauder, Phillip Brown, and Sin Yi Cheung, "Fractures in the Education-Economy Relationship," *Oxford Review of Economic Policy* 34, no. 2 (Summer 2018): 495–515

3. See Overview and Chapter 1 but esp. 36–37 in World Bank, *World Development Report 2013: Jobs* (Washington, DC: World Bank, 2012). http://documents. worldbank.org/curated/en/263351468330025810/World-development-report-2013-jobs.

4. They continue, "Strategies should identify which types of jobs would have the highest development pay-offs, given a country's circumstances." World Bank, *World Development Report, 2013*, 3.

5. This absolute dimension includes issues around skills and the ability to do the job (the traditional focus of orthodox theory). What counts as having the ability to do the job obviously depends on job complexity and whether there are formal training requirements. We've seen more of a focus on noncognitive soft skills along with the technical requirements of job performance. But many employers are also putting a greater emphasis on "job readiness" rather than "trainability" in what it means to be a suitable candidate.

6. This is a serious blind spot in neoliberalism: its model of methodological individualism fails to grasp the social character of economic life that structures individual actions in groups, crowds, or wider communities, which may increasingly be virtual.

7. In an excellent article Lester C. Thurow, "Education and Economic Equality," *Public Interest* 28 (1972): 66–81, outlines the idea of a "job competition" in contrast to the neoliberal theory of "wage competition." Thurow defines the labor market in terms of job competition in the following way: "Instead of people looking for jobs, there are jobs looking for people—'suitable' people. In a labor market based on job competition, the function of education is not to confer skill and therefore increased productivity and higher wages on the worker; it is rather to certify his 'trainability' and to confer upon him a certain status by virtue of this certification. Jobs and higher incomes are then distributed on the basis of this certified status." Here the labor market is not a technical "matching device" of supply and demand, as presented in orthodox capital theory, where market signals directed at both job seekers and employers serve to create equilibrium between skills and wages (supply and demand), but a labor market in which jobs are allocated on the basis of certified trainability. Along with other "signaling" theories, Thurow's job competition model offers a crucial insight into the complex relationship between skills and

wages. In an age of mass higher education and impatient capitalism, we've seen a shift away from trainability to an emphasis on experience and being job-ready. In many professional and managerial jobs, performance is more important than potential (trainability). Moreover, what it means to be a suitable candidate has been extended to include a range of behavioral competences that reflect a new technology of exclusion (legitimation of recruitment decisions) as many more potential recruits have gained access to the credentials that were the preserve of a bygone elite. As certified knowledge or expertise has given way to a greater emphasis on performance, trainability has been replaced with an emphasis on organizational talent and an increasing emphasis on a talented few rather than the meritocratic hierarchy of talent, incrementally rewarded, rather than that based on winner-takes-all markets.

8. James Bernard Murphy, *The Moral Economy of Labor: Aristotelian Themes in Economic Theory* (New Haven, CT: Yale University Press, 1993), 228.

9. This comes close to Irving Fisher's classic definition of capital as any form of assets that gives rise to an income stream, as it remains central to individual life chances. This way of thinking about human capital is interesting in relation to Alfred Marshall. Blaug notes that the standard answer to why Smith's idea of humans as expensive machines was not developed by economists until the 1960s "is that Alfred Marshall's Principles of Economics (1890) killed off such interest in the problem. . . . Marshall rejected the notion of 'human capital' as unrealistic and his magisterial authority is said to have been responsible for its demise. As a matter of fact, however, what Marshall rejected was the idea of including the acquired skills of a population in the measurement of the 'wealth' or 'capital' of an economy, but he accepted Adam Smith's suggestion that an educated man may be usefully likened to an expensive machine" (Mark Blaug, *An Introduction to the Economics of Education* (London: Allen Lane, 1970), 2.) While we reject the idea of treating educated people like expensive machines, our redefinition of humans as capitalizing also rejects the stock theory of education and skills as a measure of national wealth or capital, which concurs with Marshall.

10. Lester Thurow, *Generating Inequality: Mechanisms of Distribution in the U.S. Economy* (New York: Basic Books, 1975), 17. The scale of forced labor, modern slavery, and human trafficking is difficult to measure, but the International Labor Organization gives a global figure of 21 million people, with estimated annual profits of $150 billion, much of which is attributed to Asia Pacific countries, followed closely by Western developed economies. For a definition, see the work of the International Labor Organization, "What Is Forced Labour, Modern Slavery and Human Trafficking," 2019, http://www.ilo.org/global/topics/forced-labour/definition/lang--en/index.htm. These figures can be found at International Labour Organization, "Statistics on Forced Labour, Modern Slavery and Human Trafficking," 2017, http://www.ilo.org/global/topics/forced-labour/statistics/lang--en/index.htm.

An investigation into modern slavery in the United Kingdom found evidence in "every town and city" of the treatment of humans as capital. BBC News, "Modern Slavery and Trafficking 'in Every UK Town and City,'" August 10, 2017, http://www.bbc.co.uk/news/uk-40885353.

11. The orthodox theorists were well aware that humans are considered capital only under conditions of slavery, which they found abhorrent but of little contemporary relevance in the mid-twentieth century, when they were outlining the theory's basic tenets. At a time when modern slavery appears to be on the rise, the realities of humans as capital cannot be ignored. However, although orthodox theorists do not treat humans as capital, they treat them like capital by virtue of educational and training investments being viewed as capital investment in individuals.

12. The OECD, for example, defines human capital as a catch-all, although it is primarily focused on economic returns from educational investment. Becker economizes the whole of the social field which is antithetical to the liberation of the self, which he sees as merely a calculating pleasure machine.

13. Thurow makes the related point that human capital is embodied and therefore limited in significant ways. You still get rent from property or investments if you're ill, but if you miss work due to illness you will not get paid for long, if at all.

It can be argued that human labor is not a form of capital because its accumulation does not rest on the labor of others. This was key to Marx's classic definition of capital. Capital in the form of rent or equity investments invariably involves the labor of others, whereas human capital focuses on individual knowledge, skills, effort, and activities as the source of income. We do not use this narrower definition of capital but argue that the translation of skills, etc. into the wider returns of a more liberated life is central to our definition of a new human capital.

14. Thurow, "Education," 18.

15. Michel Foucault. *The Birth of Biopolitics*: Lectures at the College De France 1978–1979, translated by Graham Burchill (London: Palgrave, 2008), 252.

16. Martha C. Nussbaum, *Creating Capabilities: The Human Development Approach* (Cambridge, MA: Harvard University Press, 2011), 18. We agree with Nussbaum's view that the most important elements of a person's quality of life incorporate a range of capabilities, including health, bodily integrity (including freedom from sexual harassment), education, and other aspects of individual lives that "cannot be reduced to a single metric without distortion." But the absence of any account of the division of labor under capitalism and the centrality of work—whether paid or unpaid, formal or informal, etc.—represents a serious limitation. In defining what are capabilities in terms of what each person is able to do and to be, it is difficult to answer this question without reference to waged and unwaged work given that much of what we are able to do and to be has been defined in occupational terms.

17. See Daniel Kahneman, *Thinking Fast and Slow* (London: Penguin, 2011); Mark Pagel *Wired for Culture: The Natural History of Human Cooperation* (New York: Penguin Books, 2012).

18. See John Guiggin, *Zombie Economics: How Dead Ideas Still Walk among Us* (Princeton, NJ: Princeton University Press, 2010).

19. Dewey, *Democracy and Education*, 408.

20. If people have different reasons for what they value then, this also reveals that people can be culturally or institutionally encouraged to behave in ways that lead to a greater recognition of neighborly or community-spirited behavior, or to act in self-interested ways that celebrate market freedom. The key point is that these are not hardwired in human nature but represent political and cultural choices.

21. Margaret Archer distinguishes between personal and social identity, which may be in conflict. She argues, "The 'I' may be distressed to learn that its 'me' is considered to speak with the wrong accent, to be of a disfavoured colour or gender, and that nothing that 'I' can immediately do will change matters. . . . As a reflexive monitor, the 'I' may squirm inwardly to distance itself from the disfavoured 'me': whether it can eventually do so will depend upon intra-personal, inter-personal and societal factors." Margaret Archer, *Being Human: The Problem of Agency* (Cambridge, UK: Cambridge University Press, 2000), 264.

22. Richard Bronk, *The Romantic Economist* (Cambridge, UK: Cambridge University Press, 2009).

23. While rejecting the "mechanical" view of human action often found in neoclassical economics, practical strategies of action cannot be explained by dispositions of the habitus. An Achilles's heel in Bourdieu's theoretical framework is the use of the concept of habitus to explain how entrenched social inequalities lead to the creation of enduring individual dispositions that contribute to the reproduction of social inequalities, and yet to claim that the concept can cope with changes in habitus, for example, resulting in social mobility. The more the concept of habitus is presented as offering a theory of change, the more it undermines its starting premise of representing durable dispositions that shape practical strategies of action. Mastafa Emirbayer and Erik Schneiderhan (2013) Dewey and Bourdieu on Democracy, in Philip S. Gorski (ed.), 2013.

24. Karl Marx writes, "Men make their own history, but they do not make it as they please; they do not make it under self-selected circumstances, but under circumstances existing already, given and transmitted from the past. The tradition of all dead generations weighs like a nightmare on the brains of the living." *18th Brumaire of Louis Bonaparte*, 1852.

25. Pierre Bourdieu, *The Logic of Practice* (Stanford: Stanford University Press, 1980) 55. This may be thought of as "habitus lite," as Bourdieu's concept was not developed to explore the changing conception of self.

26. In short, it is not determined by investments in education and skills alone but includes self-development and identity work, which impact the way people approach the job market. Here social background matters through primary and secondary socialization. They can be encouraged or discouraged. It depends on the structure of opportunities and permissions. This will take different forms that will

be structured by background characteristics (not reducible to habitus), including educational biography.

27. See Amartya Sen, *Development as Freedom* (Oxford: Oxford University Press, 1999), 18.

28. Sen, "Editorial," 1959.

29. Sen, "Editorial," 1959.

30. It is this wider recognition of human capabilities and educational purpose that distinguishes it from approaches that treat humans as or like capital.

31. We have noted that Becker is happy to embrace measures of intelligence based on IQ, but orthodox economists continue to do so. In the United States the Armed Forces Qualification Test (AFQT) is often used like IQ tests, to identify what is assumed to be intelligence. See, for example, Elizabeth U. Cascio and Ethan G. Lewis, "Schooling and the AFQT Evidence from School Entry Laws," NBER, Working Paper 11113, Cambridge, MA, February 2005, http://www.nber.org/papers/w11113. This paper references a range of other papers that use this measure.

32. See Phillip Brown and Hugh Lauder, *Capitalism and Social Progress* (London: Palgrave, 2001), 67.

33. Plato's *Republic* (London: Heinemann, 1937), vol. 1, book III, p. 125. There is a lively debate in which psychologists and geneticists are making a concerted effort to turn this "royal lie" into a "scientific truth." See, for example, Robert Plomin, *Blueprint: How DNA Makes Us Who We Are* (London: Allen Lane, Penguin, 2018); Charles Murray and Richard Herrnstein, *The Bell Curve: Intelligence and Class Structure in American Life* (New York: The Free Press, 1994). The decisive refutation on the work of Herrnstein and Murray is Claude Fischer, Michael Hout, Martin Sanchez Jankowski, Samuel Lucas, Anne Swidler, and Kim Voss, *Inequality of Design: Cracking the Bell Curve Myth* (Princeton, NJ: Princeton University Press, 1996).The initial work on intelligence that influenced educational policy was that by Sir Cyril Burt. See, for example, "The Experimental Study of General Intelligence," *Child Study* 4, nos. 43–45 (1909): 78–100. The view of intelligence advanced by Burt was not limited to judgments about "whom should be educated"; it also offered a powerful justification for the segregation of students and curriculum within the classroom and labor market. "Intelligent" people, it was believed, should be encouraged to follow a different curriculum from the masses, who were thought incapable of benefiting from an academic education. It was assumed that brighter students would take subjects such as physical science, mathematics, and foreign languages, deemed to be more difficult and demanding. Less intelligent people would take the less demanding subjects, such as home economics, office practice, or woodwork. It was further assumed that proficiency in the difficult subjects reflected a more general ability to engage successfully in professional and managerial work, so that restricting entry to the prestigious and highly paid jobs to those with high credentials was a rational process. An outstanding example of how this notion of intelligence influenced what children learned was the introduction

of selective secondary education in England and Wales in 1944. Under the influence of Burt's findings that it was possible to scientifically measure the potential of a child at the age of eleven, children were examined for selection to three kinds of school: academic (grammar), technical, and practical (secondary modern).

34. See the discussion of Becker's views on intelligence and sociobiology in chapter 2.

35. Nussbaum, *Creating Capabilities*, 23–24.

36. Dewey, *Democracy and Education*, 58.

37. This applies to individuals within Western economies and also exposes the full extent of cognitive imperialism—the idea that Westerners are smarter than the rest. The middle classes in affluent Western societies have typically assumed a cultural and technological, if not innate, superiority over non-Westerners, with a few notable exceptions, such as the Japanese economic miracle in the 1970s and 1980s. This cognitive imperialism is again challenged by the rise of China and India, along with a number of other emerging economies. It is proving difficult for the developed economies to cling to the idea of a world divided between "head" and "body" nations, the former being Western and the latter the rest of the world. See Phillip Brown, Hugh Lauder, and David Ashton, *The Global Auction: The Broken Promises of Education, Jobs and Incomes* (Oxford: Oxford University Press, 2011).

38. This is often associated with a pathological view of social disadvantage, which assumes that many lack the incentives or moral character to make the most of the opportunities presented to them. On the other side of the coin it is associated with exaggerated claims about the innate talents of a few, recognized by the size of their paychecks.

39. Erzsebet Bukodi and John Goldthorpe, *Social Mobility and Education in Modern Britain* (Cambridge, UK: Cambridge University Press, 2019).

40. Although having to make this statement testifies to the power of the neoliberal narrative. We need to make clear that in the next chapter we will challenge Becker's view of *Homo economicus*.

41. Karl Polanyi, *The Great Transformation* (New York, Beacon Press, 2001), 74, 2nd paperback edition. For Marx, the creation of labor markets was not an expression of economic freedom but a requirement for capital accumulation as it only becomes capital when it's in a position to buy other people's labor in order to make a surplus profit. Labor markets are required for this to happen, which involves forcing people to forfeit the means of production or rights of bondage under the feudal system, therefore forcing people to sell their capacity for labor to an employer, without which they confront destitution, if not starvation. (See Polanyi's discussion of the English Poor Laws and policies of enclosure.) Today the foodbank has replaced the workhouse.

42. At the same time that this offered them political freedoms it was practically meaningless in the social and economic conditions of the age.

43. Karl Polanyi, *The Great Transformation* (New York: Beacon Press, 1944), 74.

44. Foucault describes this as the "economization of the entire social field." Michel Foucault, *The Birth of Biopolitics: Lectures at the College de France 1978–1979* (London: Palgrave, 2008), 242.

45. By sleight of hand much of human behavior was reinterpreted as economic behavior, which can be studied as part of a wider model of neoliberalism involving next to no account of social, cultural, or political context.

46. Polanyi, *The Great Transformation*, 75. John Gray points out that the theme of disembedding the economy from society was also found in major sociological works such as Max Weber's. He argues, "Like Japanese economic culture, though in sharply different ways, Chinese businesses challenge the standard account of the growth of capitalism advanced by Max Weber and other western sociologists. In the conventional western account, capitalism develops by displacing family and personal relationships from centrality in economic life. It makes the economy a separate, autonomous domain, ruled by an impersonal calculus of profit and loss, and held together not by relationships of trust but contractual-legal obligations. In this conventional narrative, capitalism develops by disembedding itself from its parent society." John Gray, *False Dawn: The Delusions of Global Capitalism* (London: Granta, 1998), 184. A related point is that markets have a vital role to play in social and economic organization, but they are the means to achieving goals, such as sustaining living standards, rather than treated as a utopian ideal from which everything else, including human freedom, will follow.

47. Fred Block, *Postindustrial Possibilities* (Berkeley: University of California Press, 1990), 152.

48. Isaiah Berlin wrote, "If free creation, spontaneous development along one's native lines, not inhibited or suppressed by the dogmatic pronouncements of an elite of self-appointed arbiters, insensitive to history, is to be accorded supreme value; if authenticity and variety are not to be sacrificed to authority, organization, centralization, which inexorably tend to uniformity and the destruction of what men [and women] hold dearest—their language, their institutions, their habits, their form of life, all that has made them what they are—then the establishment of one world, organized on universally accepted rational principles—the ideal society—is not acceptable." Isaiah Berlin, *The Crooked Timber of Humanity—Chapters in the History of Ideas*, edited by Henry Hardy and John Murray (1990), 224, in Richard Bronk, *The Romantic Economist*, 150.

49. This mirrors a long-standing debate about the essence of capitalism and its relationship to democracy. There is no political, social, or cultural convergence harbored in "the belief that prosperity drags liberal democracy in its wake." As John Gray says, this "is an article of faith, not a result of disciplined inquiry". For an interesting discussion of capitalism, societies and globalization see, Giovanni Arrighi, *Adam Smith in Beijing* (New York: Verso, 2007).

50. Gray, *False Dawn*, 191.

51. Robert K. Merton, *Social Theory and Social Structure* (New York: Free Press, 1957), 5, 6.

52. This is at the heart of Becker's economic approach, founded on universal laws of market competition and a static model that assumes economic life can be reduced to statistical modeling and quantitative measurements of scholastic attainment and rates of return.

CHAPTER 10

1. A banking model of education was presented by Paulo Freire, *Pedagogy of the Oppressed* (New York: Continuum, 2000).

2. While we need to tackle the exploitative nature of some of these working relationships, there is little doubt that how we understand labor demand is being transformed, as we will discuss in the next chapter. But there is also a significant change in the way education has come to be defined solely as a preparation for employment.

3. The future may include dancing with robots, but many educated people will be in jobs for which they are overqualified and clearly capable of doing more technically complex work. They may also be paid well below what their labor is worth. They may spend less of their lives in wage work, and they are unlikely to have the freedom to consume the world's resources as Westerners have done over the twentieth century.

4. This challenges the front-loading view of education, of getting as much in the bank as early as possible for the life journey ahead. Although this may include additional investment in training to remain occupationally relevant, there is little sense of a broader notion of lifelong learning linked to human capital development.

5. E. P. Thompson, "Time, Work-Discipline and Industrial Capitalism," *Past and Present* 38 (1967): 96. The full phrase is this: "re-learn some of the arts of living lost in the industrial revolution: how to fill the interstices of their days with enriched, more leisurely, personal and social relations, how to break down once more the barriers between work and life."

6. See Freire, *Pedagogy of the Oppressed*. It was first published in 1968. See also Paulo Freire, *The Pedagogy of Hope* (New York: Bloomsbury, 2014).

7. It encourages *having* over *being* and *memory* over *experience*. See the reference to the work of Erich Fromm in Freire, 1968.

8. Rifkin use the term *factory model*, which has a number of common features. He observes, "The 'why' of things was less discussed than the 'how' of things." Jeremy Rifkin, *The Zero Marginal Cost Society* (Basingstoke: Palgrave Macmillan, 2014), 109.

9. Tomas Lemke, *Foucault, Governmentality and Critique* (Boulder, CO: Paradigm, 2012), 49. He continues, "Fear fulfils an important moral function in neo-liberal governance. The constant threat of unemployment and poverty, and anxiety about

the future . . . stimulates a consciousness of economic risks and uncertainties that accompany the . . . expected entrepreneurship" (49).

10. In the past the teacher was an authority and typically in authority, but both forms of authority have been mediated by the test or exam, which becomes the ultimate authority, the arbiter of a student's future.

11. See chapter 3.

12. Earlier chapters describe how orthodox approaches discovered it was almost impossible to justify the distinction between education for investment and for consumption, opting to focus on "rates of return."

13. Theodore W. Schultz, "Investment in Human Capital," *American Economic Review* 51, no. 1 (1961):12n15. This is the published version of Schultz's presidential address to the American Economics Association, which we highlighted at the beginning of the book. This quotation is a forgotten endnote where he reflects on the role of education and its relationship to human capital, in a context remarkably similar to the current age of mass higher education.

14. Charity work may make people feel good, a source of "psychic consumption," in Becker's terms, but this is ontological cynicism in the extreme. Learning within most educational contexts is not zero-sum; it is not consumed by one person at the expense of another. This positive-sum dimension of education is also an increasingly important part of today's economy. See Rifkin's *The Zero Marginal Cost Society*. However, there is a positional dimension to education that does have zero-sum consequences, which also need to be considered.

15. We are indebted to Harry Torrance for this reference and the insight concerning the changing nature of assessment. See his "Blaming the Victim: Assessment, Examinations, and the Responsibilisation of Students and Teachers in Neoliberal Governance," *Discourse: Studies in the Cultural Politics of Education* 38, no. 1 (2017): 83–96. The specific reference to the RAND Corporation report is L. Hamilton, B. Stecher, J. Marsh, J. McCombs, A. Robyn, J. Russell, S. Naftel, and H. Barney, Standards-Based Accountability under No Child Left Behind (Santa Monica, CA: RAND Education, 2007).

16. Sam Carr, *Motivation, Educational Policy and Achievement* (Abingdon, UK: Routledge, 2015), 93).

17. Simon Head, *Mindless: How Smarter Machines Are Making Dumber Humans* (New York, Basic Books, 2014), 185. John Dewey writes, "We lose rather than gain in change from serfdom to free citizenship if the most prized result of the change is simply an increase in the mechanical efficiency of the human tools of production." John Dewey, *Democracy and Education* (New York: Macmillan, 2016), 300.

18. Dewey, *Democracy*, chapter 23.

19. Frank Levy and Richard Murnane, *Dancing with Robots: Human Skills for Computerized Work*, Third Way, Next Series. 16, 2013. http://content.thirdway. org/publications/714/Dancing-With-Robots.pdf.

20. In a recent, well publicized book, Bryan Caplan, *The Case against Education* (Princeton, NJ: Princeton University Press, 2018), has argued that formal education is for the most part irrelevant to the demands of the labor market. This section can be seen as a response to his argument as to why an education for individual growth is central to rethinking the education-economy relationship.

21. UNESCO, "Education 2030: Incheon Declaration and Framework for Action," 2015, ITEM 9, page IV. This new vision for education to 2030 was agreed by UNESCO together with the World Bank, UNICEF, and other transnational organizations.

22. It is problematic both in the sense that we cannot assume that the future employment of the workforce will lead to high levels of individual satisfaction and opportunities for personal growth, and in the sense that economic life has become increasingly demanding, requiring continuously solving the problem of making a living and leading a fulfilled life at a time of great economic and social uncertainty.

23. Where this social potential for education is harnessed, it holds out the prospect of becoming a new "empire of energy." Alfred Marshall, "Features of American Industry," quoted in Sylvia Nasar, *Grand Pursuit: The Story of the People Who Made Modern Economics* (London: Fourth Estate, 2011), 78.

24. Dewey, *Democracy*, 372–73. He also suggests that this extended view of character building "might even be dangerous to the interests of the controlling class, arousing discontent or ambitions 'beyond the station' of those working under the direction of others" (115).

25. The four pillars were originally outlined in UNESCO's "Learning: The Treasure Within," also known as the Delors Report (1996), and continues to inform UNESCO's approach to educational reform: http://www.unesco.org/new/fileadmin/MULTIMEDIA/HQ/ED/ED/pdf/FFA_Complet_Web-ENG.pdf.

26. See Jacques Delors, "The Treasure Within: Learning to Know, Learning to Do, Learning to Live Together and Learning to Be. What Is the Value of That Treasure 15 Years after Its Publication?," *International Review of Education* 59 (2013): 321.

27. Jean-François Lyotard, *The Postmodern Condition: A Report on Knowledge* (Manchester, UK: Manchester University Press, 1984), 3.

28. What it means to enable an understanding of the world in a context of the new human capital is not without contention, as are many debates about educational reform.

29. See Michael Young, *Bringing Knowledge Back In: From Social Constructivism to Social Realism in the Sociology of Education* (London: Routledge, 2008). These quotations are taken from Michael Young "The Curriculum—'An Entitlement to Powerful Knowledge': A Response to John White," New Visions for Education Group, May 3, 2012. https://www.newvisionsforeducation.org.uk/about-the-group/home/2012/05/14/powerful-knowledge-too-weak-a-prop-for-the-traditional-curriculum/.

30. Learning to know is not only about what it is worth knowing but also how people come to know it. The International Baccalaureate is consistent with education for

lifelong learning. It offers a broad curriculum aimed at students sixteen to nineteen years old who are encouraged to take a central role in the learning process. This includes the study of a theory of knowledge, where students are expected to reflect on the nature of knowledge and on "how we know what we claim to know." Students also take courses in language and literature, do an independent self-directed project in the form of an extended essay, learn a second language, and study the relationship between the individual and wider society through a choice of subjects, such as history, psychology, economics, geography, and information technology in a global society, which closely relate to issues of learning to be. "Example Subject Choices," International Baccalaureate, 2019, http://www.ibo.org/programmes/diploma-programme/curriculum/example-subject-choices/.

31. Marilyn Binkley, Ola Erstad, Joan Herman, Senta Raisen, Martin Ripley, with Mike Rumble, "Draft White Paper 1: Defining 21st Century Skills. Assessment and Teaching of 21st Century Skills," University of Melbourne in collaboration with Cisco, Intel, and Microsoft, 2009. They do not include tools for thinking, which is a bit surprising given that without them twenty-first-century skills are content-free. For a comparison of approaches, see Irenka Suto, "21st Century Skills: Ancient, Ubiquitous, Enigmatic?," Cambridge Assessment, University of Cambridge, 2013, http://www.cambridgeassessment.org.uk/images/130437-21st-century-skills-ancient-ubiquitous-enigmatic-.pdf. Related approaches are "P21 Partnership for 21st Century Learning," http://www.p21.org/about-us/p21-framework and Tony Wagner's seven survival skills in *The Global Achievement Gap* (New York: Basic Books, 2008).

32. We will solve the fundamental problems of living only through interdisciplinary inquiry. Most universities are only starting to develop curricula that address the issues we now confront. The more orthodox economists and policymakers focus on the narrow subjects and courses that will bring the greatest returns in the labor market, the greater the disservice they do to the next generation.

33. David Brookes, "Schools for Wisdom," *New York Times*, Opinion Pages, October 16, 2015, 2. http://68.77.48.18/RandD/Other/Schools%20for%20Wisdom%20-%20NYT.pdf.

34. This returns us to the questions raised in W. Lloyd Warner, Robert J. Havighurst, and Martin B. Loeb, *Who Shall Be Educated? The Challenge of Unequal Opportunities* (London: Routledge, 1946).

35. Richard Sennett, *The Craftsman* (London, Allen Lane, The Penguin Press, 2009), 9. This relates to what Thorsten Veblen called "the instinct of workmanship." See Thorsten Veblen, *The Instinct of Workmanship and the State of the Industrial Arts*, e-artnow, 2015, info@e-artnow.org.

36. Henry Marsh, *Do No Harm* (London: Weidenfeld & Nicolson, 2014), 52–53.

37. Dewey, *Democracy*, 309.

38. Dewey, *Democracy*, 372–73.

39. See Derrick Bell, *Ethical Ambition: Living a Life of Meaning and Worth* (London: Bloomsbury, 2002). Jefferson also distinguished the "natural aristocracy," which he regarded as the "most precious gift of nature," from what he called "artificial aristocracy" that lacked both virtue and talent. Although we would reject his assertion of a "natural" elite, given the widespread distribution of human capability, it is interesting to observe how issues around talent management lost their relationship to virtue. See "Equality," Thomas Jefferson to John Adams, October 28, 1813, http://press-pubs.uchicago.edu/founders/documents/v1ch15s61.html.

40. See Bell, *Ethical Ambition*.

41. Clarence Karier, "Humanizing the Humanities: Some Reflections on George Steiner's 'Brutal Paradox,'" *Journal of Aesthetic Education* 24, no. 2 (1909): 49–50.

42. Richard Sennett, *The Corrosion of Character* (New York: Norton, 1998), 10. This idea of character as involving personal connections to the wider world makes it more encompassing than the modern concept of personality (see 10).

43. We are grateful to Ian Jones, a former doctoral student of Phil Brown's, for contributing to our understanding of projectivity, which is different from the idea of career.

44. Arlie Hochschild, *The Managed Heart: Commercialization of Human Feeling* (Berkeley: University of California Press, 1983). A major part of economic activity is less about shaping, moving, or building things and more about servicing, advising, treating, teaching, caring for, or persuading other people. More of the self is involved in doing a good job. This exposes competing pressures on time management in fulfilling social roles such as mother, partner, wage earner, caregiver (for aging parents), etc.

45. Head, *Mindless*, 126-27. He also says, "Equality has an economic and social dimension, providing employees with the dignity, confidence, and skill to provide good service for all, irrespective of income and rank. The economic preconditions for this are generous pay and benefits and an equitable distribution of workplace power between managers and labor, provided in turn by high rates of unionization."

46. See Delors, "The Treasure."

47. B Ansell and J. Gingrich, "The End of Human Capital Solidarity," paper prepared for the Anxieties of Democracy Program, November 2018, Oxford.

48. Data on recruitment should be publicly available in much the same way that companies are now having to provide evidence on employee gender and income.

49. Dewey, *Democracy*, 104.

50. An immediate problem here is that companies do not hire for social justice. They take account of price as well as capabilities even if they want to be fair to job applicants. Their hiring decisions may also be arbitrary not because they are indifferent but because of market crowding that makes it more difficult to make fair, even if rational, decisions. However, the degrading of human resources functions in many firms does not bode well.

51. If we focus only on "methodological individualism" we are led to the conclusion that inequalities can be overcome by increasing access to good quality education, giving those from disadvantaged backgrounds the same qualifications and skills as those typically achieved by students from more privileged backgrounds. This is the pathological view of social mobility.

52. See Fred Hirsch, *The Social Limits to Growth* (London: Routledge, 1976). It often resembles a jousting tournament on an escalator where students are competing closely for superiority as more people are going into higher education. In the competition for educational credentials and jobs, people do not act alone, one at a time, as in a game of chess, because we are all in play at the same time. This is why a distinction needs to be drawn between what it takes to do a particular job from what it takes to get such a job. Here economic theory is socially blind, given its foundations on methodological individualism. For the purity of their modeling they pretend that there is no such thing as society, although institutional economics has gone a long way to overcome the weaknesses of methodological individualism.

53. This exposes an "adding up" problem at the heart of orthodox supply-side accounts, which is surprising given a penchant for mathematical equations. It results from their focus on individuals rather than their social relations, which shape the way people act and influence their life chances.

54. While this part of our account draws on the work of Pierre Bourdieu, there are significant limitations to his approach that lead us to outline a different interpretation of humans as capitalizing.

55. "Equality," Jefferson to Adams.

56. Dewey, *Democracy*, 58. Finland invests in teacher education rather than testing, and students are in their late adolescence before they take a public exam. It is noticeable that in countries where there is high trust in teachers, testing regimes have not been the major focus of education. Like Finland, New Zealand does not have a central role for testing. Rather it has a light-touch form of sampling where national progress on achievement is judged by a nationally representative sample, which provides an indication of progress. Where there are examinations they are practitioner-set and -marked.

57. See Martha C. Nussbaum, *Creating Capabilities: The Human Development Approach* (Cambridge, MA: Belknap Press of Harvard University Press, 2011).

58. Nussbaum, *Creating Capabilities*, 24.

59. Dewey, *Democracy*, 62.

CHAPTER 11

1. Gary S. Becker, foreword to Alan Burton-Jones and J. C. Spender, eds., *The Oxford Handbook of Human Capital* (Oxford: Oxford University Press, 2011), xiii.

2. David H. Autor, "Why Are There Still So Many Jobs? The History and Future of Workplace Automation," *Journal of Economic Perspectives* 29, no. 3 (2015): 27.

3. Francis Green and Golo Henseke, "Should Governments of the OECD Countries Worry about Graduate Over-Education?" Working Paper No. 3, Centre for Global Higher Education, London, June 2016.

4. This leads us to a different way of thinking about the labor market, not as a skills competition, as presented in orthodox theory, but as a jobs competition. But rethinking labor demand cannot be limited to the formal labor market because all countries have a significant shadow economy, because there are significant numbers who are designated as formally self-employed, and because new technologies are transforming the social foundations of innovation, which is likely to impact the future of work and therefore labor demand.

5. World Development Report 2013, "The Jobs Challenge," team estimates, http://siteresources.worldbank.org/EXTNWDR2013/Resources/8258024-1320950747192/8260293-1322665883147/Chapter-1.pdf.

6. This has implications for our understanding of both learning and earning as people capitalize within both formal and informal models of employment.

7. OECD, *In It Together, Why Less Inequality Benefits All* (Paris, 2015), chapter 4, "Non Standard Work and Inequality."

8. International Labor Organization, "Non-Standard Forms of Work," Geneva, 2015, http://www.ilo.org/wcmsp5/groups/public/@ed_protect/@protrav/@travail/documents/meetingdocument/wcms_336934.pdf.

9. All figures are from the US Bureau of Labor Statistics, "Employment Situation Summary," May 2016 http://www.bls.gov/news.release/empsit.nr0.htm. See Table A-1, http://www.bls.gov/news.release/empsit.t01.htm.

10. "Industrial revolutions are revolutions in standardization," Jay Tate, "National Varieties of Standardization," in *Varieties of Capitalism: The Institutional Foundations of Comparative Advantage,* edited by Peter A. Hall and David Soskice (New York: Oxford University Press, 2001), 442.

11. Klaus Schwab, *The Fourth Industrial Revolution* (Geneva: World Economic Forum, 2016); *Foreign Affairs, The Fourth Industrial Revolution*, December 12, 2016. https://www.foreignaffairs.com/articles/2015-12-12/fourth-industrial-revolution.

12. Schwab, *The Fourth*, 45.

13. Daniel Bell, *The Coming of Post-Industrial Society: A Venture in Social Forecasting* (New York: Penguin, 1973), 191.

14. Bell, *The Coming*, 191. He points out that these are incommensurate, which also poses a problem of measurement: "How do we combine all these different things under one rubric and seek a measurement?"

15. Frank Levy and Richard J. Murnane, *Dancing with Robots: Human Skills for Computerized Work*, June 1, 2013, https://dusp.mit.edu/uis/publication/dancing-robots-human-skills-computerized-work; Eric Brynjolfsson and Andrew McAfee,

The Second Machine Age: Work, Progress and Prosperity in a Time of Brilliant Technologies (New York: Norton, 2014).

16. Brynjolfsson and McAfee, *The Second.*
17. Levy and Murnane, *Dancing*; Paul Beaudry, *et al.*, "The Great Reversal in the Demand for Skill and Cognitive Tasks," 2013.
18. Tate, "National Varieties," 442.
19. Ha-Joon Chang, *Bad Samaritans: The Myth of Free Trade and the Secret History of Capitalism* (New York, Bloomsbury Press, 2007).
20. Bell, *The Coming,* 343–44.
21. The idea of a double movement but of a rather different kind from what is described here was outlined in Karl Polanyi, *The Great Transformation* (New York: Beacon Press, 1944).
22. Phillip Brown, Hugh Lauder, and David Ashton, *The Global Auction: The Broken Promises of Education, Jobs and Incomes* (Oxford: Oxford University Press, 2011).
23. See Brown, Lauder, and Ashton, *The Global Auction,* chapter 5.
24. Accenture, "The Point: Automation for the People," 2007, http://www.accenture. com/Global/Services/By_Industry/Financial_Services/Insurance/The_Point/ Y2007/fsi_thepoint47a.htm.
25. He is talking about drones as radio-controlled aircraft, not human beings!
26. Simon Head, *Mindless: How Smarter Machines Are Making Dumber Humans* (New York, Basic Books, 2014). See also Brown, Lauder, and Ashton, *The Global Auction*; Richard Susskind and Daniel Susskind, *The Future of the Professions: How Technology Will Transform the Work of Human Experts* (Oxford: Oxford University Press, 2015).
27. When Fredrick Winslow Taylor outlined the principles of scientific management the idea was not simply to capture and mechanically mimic what craft workers were doing but to transform the entire process, making it conducive to hire low-skilled workers.
28. Caroline Hanley, "Putting the Bias in Skill-Biased Technological Change: A Relational Perspective on White-Collar Automation at General Electric," *American Behavioral Scientist* 58, no. 3 (2014): 413.
29. Brown, Lauder and Ashton, 2011, 81.
30. The societal level of analysis retains descriptive and analytical value even in the context of globalization.
31. In part this is because new technologies are at the heart of the global auction for jobs. This includes aspects of digital Talyorism but also automation and the global integration of supply chains. This makes it difficult to assess what proportion of jobs is subject to the forces of the global auction for jobs, but it is a growing proportion, as it includes job migration both directly, in terms of individuals in labor markets, and indirectly, when companies make decisions to relocate operations. Although not strictly part of the global auction for jobs, we could also include many activities in the public sector as the ability of nation-states to provide services

depends on how much can be borrowed from global markets; hence the global auction shapes the capacity of the nation-state to buy jobs. This is far removed from the idea of human capital as an investment in education and training.

32. The distinction between jobs that are digitally nomadic through wireless connections and those that are dependent on context, this "unconventional divide," as Blinder calls it, does not correspond to traditional distinctions between jobs that require high skills and those that don't. See Alan Blinder, "How Many U.S. Jobs Might Be Offshorable?," CEPS Working Paper No. 142, Princeton, March 2007.

33. To our knowledge, Robert Reich, *The Work of Nations* (New York: Knopf, 1991), was the first to identify this process,

34. Jenny Chan, Ngai Pun, and Mark Selden, "The Politics of Global Production: Apple, Foxconn and China's New Working Class," *New Technology, Work and Employment* 28, no. 2 (2013): 100–115.

35. Gerald F. Davis, *The Vanishing American Corporation: Navigating the Hazards of the New Economy* (Oakland, CA: Berrett-Koehler). On the superstar firms and their part in inequality in the labor market, see J. Song, D.Price, F. Guvenen, N. Bloom, and T. von Wachter, "Firming Up Inequality," Working Paper 750, Research Division, Federal Reserve Bank of Minneapolis, Oakland, CA, April 2018; David Autor, David Dorn, Lawrence F. Katz, Christina Patterson, and John Van Reenen, "The Fall of the Labor Share and the Rise of Superstar Firms," NBER Working Paper No. 23396, Cambridge, MA, May 2017, nber.org/papers/w23396.

36. See also Brown, Lauder, and Ashton, *The Global Auction*.

37. A global auction for cut-price knowledge and skills does not contradict orthodox theories of human capital that fully recognize that the value of skills in the labor market can go down as well as up. However, it is widely assumed to apply to less rather that more qualified workers given that new technologies would increase the demand for highly skilled workers captured in the idea of a race between education and technology.

38. The traditional workplace—which continues to structure the working lives of millions of Americans—is more than a physical location requiring people to commute to join with coworkers. It also defines a social relationship beyond what Marx described as the "cash nexus." To have a job is to have a degree of job security, a regular paycheck, holiday entitlement, promotion prospects, and even entitlement to retirement pay and/or a pension when the contract of employment is broken, etc. Within orthodox human capital, labor demand remains premised on this standard model of full-time regular employment.

39. Guy Standing, *The Precariat: The New Dangerous Class* (New York: Bloomsbury, 2011).

40. Schwab, *The Fourth*, 20. Much is made of freelance professions selling their services on a global basis no longer requiring them to conform to traditional models of employment. Apple app developers are an example,

41. Jeremy Rifkin, *The Zero Marginal Cost Society* (New York: Palgrave Macmillan, 2014), 2–3. Rifkin's view may be considered overly optimistic. See Shoshana Zuboff, *The Age of Surveillance Capitalism* (London: Profile Books, 2019).

42. Rifkin, *The Zero*, 4. "What if the marginal cost of human labor in the production and distribution of goods and services were to plummet to near zero as intelligent technology substitutes for workers across every industry and professional and technical field, allowing businesses to conduct much of the commercial activity of civilization more intelligently, efficiently, and cheaply than with conventional workforces? That too is occurring as tens of millions of workers have already been replaced by intelligent technologies in industries and professional bodies around the world. What would the human race do, and more importantly, how would it define its future on Earth, if mass and professional labor were to disappear from economic life over the course of the next two generations? That question is now being seriously raised for the first time in intellectual circles and public policy debates" (70).

43. Rifkin, *The Zero*, 121.

44. Rifkin, *The Zero*, 132. Here Rifkin identifies a key element in that consumers also become producers but in doing so they are open to exploitation from the superstar tech giants.

45. All figures are taken from BLS, "Occupational Employment Projections to 2022," *Monthly Labor Review*, December 2013. See Table 25, https://www.bls.gov/opub/mlr/2013/article/occupational-employment-projections-to-2022.htm.

46. See William Baumol, *The Cost Disease: Why Computers Get Cheaper and Health Care Doesn't* (New Haven, CT: Yale University Press, 2012). Baumol has made a major contribution to the economics of the service sector through his notion of the cost disease, arguing that slow productivity growth is endemic to the service sector.

47. However, in Japan robot baristas are being developed. See Lila Gross, "Barista Robot Now Remembers Order Based on Facial Recognition," New Channel 8, July 19, 2017, http://wfla.com/2017/07/19/barista-robot-now-remembers-order-based-on-facial-recognition/.

48. The cultural factors that lead to the employment of baristas rather than Nespresso machines is not taken into account by the typical estimates that calculate the impact of robots on jobs. There are now global awards for baristas and league tables of barista performance. Yet, although a good barista exhibits considerable skills, wages are typically low, although profits from coffee chains remain high.

49. These jobs have an annual median wage of $27,670, approximately $7,000 below the median wage for all occupations. Median salaries are for 2012.

50. Employment Projections 2018-2028 Bureau of Labor Statistics. US Department of Labor. September, 2019. https://www.bls.gov/news.release/pdf/ecopro.pdf.

51. See European Centre for the Development of Vocational Training CEDEFOP Briefing Note, *Road to Recovery: Three Skill and Labour Market Scenarios for*

2025," 2013) Figure 2, 2. Taking CEDEFOP data for EU as a whole is fraught with difficulties; it is based on a faithful commitment to the idea that the demand for high-skilled workers will continue to increase following past trends. It seems extraordinary to most people living in Europe that CEDEFOP revised its figures in 2013 to suggest that there would be greater demand for high-skilled workers than previous projects in 2010. See CEDEFOP (2010) Skills Supply and Demand in Europe: Medium Term Forecast Up to 2020.

52. There is little evidence to support the idea of a polarization of jobs, although incomes have been stretched at both the top and bottom of occupational earnings. Much of the evidence used to support the hollowing-out thesis is an artifact of methodology that is highly questionable. Autor seems to have become less sanguine in his article on automation and jobs. See also Craig Holmes and Ken Mayhew, "Overqualification and Skills Mismatch in the Graduate Labour Market," CIPD Report, London, August 2015.

53. Terence Hogarth and Rob Wilson, "The Outlook for Skills Demand and Supply in Europe," in *Technology, Globalisation and the Future of Work in Europe*, edited by Tony Dolphin (London: Institute of Public Policy Research, 2015), 23.

54. Peter Evans, *Embedded Autonomy: States and Industrial Transformation* (Princeton, NJ: Princeton University Press, 1995), 10. The classic study of the scale of state involvement in the creation of a market society is Polanyi, *The Great Transformation*.

55. Ken Warwick, "Beyond Industrial Policy: Emerging Issues and New Trends," *OECD Science, Technology and Industrial Policy Papers*, no. 2 (2013): 47. http://www.oecd-ilibrary.org/science-and-technology/beyond-industrial-policy_5k4869clwoxp-en.

56. Phillip Brown, Sin Yi Cheung, and Hugh Lauder "Beyond a Human Capital Approach to Education and the Labour Market: The Case for Industrial Policy," in *New Perspectives on Industrial Policy for a Modern Britain*, edited by David Bailey, Keith Cowling, and Philip R. Tomlinson (Oxford: Oxford University Press, 2015), 217.

57. Jerome De Henau, Susan Himmelweit, Zofia Łapniewska, and Diana Perrons, "Investing in the Care Economy: A Gender Analysis of Employment Stimulus in Seven OECD Countries," International Trade Union Confederation, March 2016, https://www.ituc-csi.org/IMG/pdf/care_economy_en.pdf.

58. For an interesting account of the comparative differences in the organization of employment in the service sector, see Caroline Lloyd and Jonathan Payne, *Skills in an Age of Over-Qualification: Comparing Service Sector Work in Europe* (Oxford: Oxford University, 2016).

59. Jose Salazar-Xrinches, Irmgard Nubler, and Richard Kozul-Wright, *Transforming Economies: Making Industrial Policy Work for Growth, Jobs and Development* (Geneva, International Labor Organization, 2014).

60. What gives industrial policy a bad name is when it seeks to bail out sunset industries because of the unemployment that is caused by failing industries.

61. Job quality needs to be broadly defined and consistent with the International Labor Organization's campaign on decent jobs, and the World Bank's *World Development Report 2013*. The middle classes are more highly educated, but the rationalization of high-skilled occupational roles may lead to a decline in the attractiveness of some technical, managerial, and professional jobs given declining job discretion, job complexity, or stagnant, if not declining, incomes. Some occupations' labels fail to capture the realities of changing working conditions and income prospects. See Holmes and Mayhew, "Overqualification."

62. Helen Bound, Sahara Sadik, Karen Evans and Annie Karmel, *How Non-Permanent Workers Learn and Develop: Challenges and Opportunities* (London: Routledge, 2018).

CHAPTER 12

1. David Autor, "Why Are There Still So Many Jobs? The History and Future of Workplace Automation," *Journal of Economic Perspectives* 29, no. 3 (2015): 28.

2. Over time it may well be that when the combination of technologies that are available are deployed, jobs may be lost, despite the protestations of economic historians who have noted that new industrial revolutions have always created a Luddite response provoked by the fear of job loss. So far these fears have been misplaced, but we cannot rely on the past to guide our future. While the estimates vary considerably, there is little doubt that in some economic sectors robots will replace skilled workers. As we have seen, the remedy for SBTC theorists is that workers need to be more highly educated. Yet despite the assumption of orthodox economists that workers who lose their jobs can always upskill, low-paid service jobs are the typical destination for those who have previously had higher-paid manufacturing jobs.

3. Emile Durkheim explains in *The Division of Labor* that a forced division of labor is the opposite of a spontaneous division. John Dewey talks about an ideal state of work "based upon its congeniality to [the worker's] own aptitudes." John Dewey, *Democracy and Education* (New York: Macmillan, 2016), 370.

4. Joseph Stiglitz, Amartya Sen, and Jean-Paul Fitoussi, *Mis-Measuring Our Lives: Why GDP Doesn't Add Up. The Report by the Commission on the Measurement of Economic Performance and Social Progress* (New York: New Press, 2010), 2.

5. Amartya Sen, *Development as Freedom* (Oxford: Oxford University Press, 2001), 295.

6. Stiglitz, Sen, and Fitoussi, *Mis-Measuring,* 10.

7. Stiglitz, Sen, and Fitoussi, *Mis-Measuring,* 11.

8. Lester C. Thurow, *Building Wealth: The New Rules for Individuals, Companies and Nations in a Knowledge-Based Economy* (New York: HarperCollins, 1993), 130.

9. F. List, *The National System of Political Economy*, English edition (London: Longman, 1904), 113.

10. Adam Smith, *The Wealth of Nations* (Chicago: University of Chicago Press, 1976), 19–20. On the scarcity of talent Smith wrote, "The difference in natural talents in different men is, in reality, much less than we are aware of; and the very different genius which appears to distinguish men of different professions, when grown up to maturity, is not upon many occasions so much the cause, as the effect of the division of labour. The difference between the most dissimilar characters, between a philosopher and a common street porter, for example, seems to arise not so much from nature, as from habit, custom, and education. When they came into the world, and for the first six or eight years of their existence, they were perhaps, very much alike, and neither their parents nor playfellows could perceive any remarkable difference. About that age, or soon after, they come to be employed in very different occupations. The difference of talents comes then to be taken notice of, and widens by degrees, till at last the vanity of the philosopher is willing to acknowledge scarce any resemblance. But without the disposition to truck, barter, and exchange, every man must have procured to himself every necessary and conveniency of life which he wanted. All must have had the same duties to perform, and the same work to do, and there could have been no such difference of employment as could alone give occasion to any great difference of talents."

11. John Kenneth Galbraith, *The Affluent Society* (London: Hamish Hamilton, 1962), 273–74, quoted in in Alan Fox, *Beyond Contract* (London: Faber and Faber, 1974), 16.

12. Philippe Van Parijs, *Real Freedom for All: What (If Anything) Can Justify Capitalism?* (Oxford: Oxford University Press, 1997). See especially his chapter "Jobs as Assets."

13. "The social internal rate of return refers to the costs and benefits to society of investment in education, which includes the opportunity cost of having people not participating in the production of output and the full cost of the provision of education rather than only the cost borne by the individual. The social benefit includes the increased productivity associated with the investment in education and a host of possible non-economic benefits." OECD, "Social Internal Rate of Return," *Glossary of Statistical Terms*, January 30, 2003, https://stats.oecd.org/glossary/detail.asp?ID=5426.

14. Here the problem with the orthodox approach is not the familiar one of putting the horse before the cart but of taking the horse and forgetting the cart exists!

15. As Heilbroner observes, "Our continuing existence as a rich nation hinges on the tacit precondition that the mechanism of social organisation will continue to function effectively. We are rich, not as individuals, but as members of a rich society, and our easy assumption of material sufficiency is actually only as reliable as the bonds that forge us into a social whole." Robert Heilbroner, *Behind the Veil of Economics* (London: Penguin, 1989), 4.

16. This again highlights the fact that occupational performance is ultimately a social achievement by technical means. The quality of the workplace as a social environment is every bit as important as skills training for determining the competitiveness of firms, regions, and nations.

17. Canadian Council on Learning, *The 2010 Composite Learning Index: Five Years of Measuring Canada's Progress in Lifelong Learning* (Ottawa: Canadian Council on Learning, 2010), http://communityindicators.net/indicator-projects/canadian-composite-learning-index/.

18. Michaela Saisana, "ELLI-Index: A Sound Measure for Lifelong Learning in the EU," Joint Research Committee publication, 2010, http://publications.jrc.ec.europa.eu/repository/bitstream/JRC60268/reqno_jrc60268_saisana_jrcvalidation_elli.pdf%5B1%5D.pdf.

19. Johnny Sung and Simon Freebody, "Lifelong Learning in Singapore: Where Are We?," *Asia Pacific Journal of Education* 37, no. 4 (2017): 615–28.

20. See the MySkillsFuture website, https://www.myskillsfuture.sg/content/portal/en/index.html.

21. The original quotation is from James Truslow Adams, *The Epic of America* (New York: Blue Ribbon Books, 1931), 214–15. "In 1931, the writer James Truslow Adams coined the term 'The American Dream.' His definition holds up well today. The dream, he said, is of a land in which: life should be better and richer and fuller for everyone, with opportunity for each according to ability or achievement. It is a difficult dream for the European upper classes to interpret adequately, and too many of us ourselves have grown weary and mistrustful of it. It is not a dream of motor cars and high wages merely, but a dream of social order in which each man and each woman shall be able to attain to the fullest stature of which they are . . . capable, and be recognized by others for what they are, regardless of the fortuitous circumstances of birth or position." Quoted in Brookings, "Opportunity, Responsibility, and Security: A Consensus Plan for Reducing Poverty and Restoring the American Dream," December 3, 2015, http://www.brookings.edu/research/reports2/2015/12/aei-brookings-poverty-and-opportunity, 7.

    In this report the word "innately" has been removed because it now has more biological connotations than it did in Adam's time (see their footnote 1).

22. R. H. Tawney, *Equality* (London: George Allen and Unwin, 1931), 108.

23. 2014. Thomas Piketty, *Capital in the Twenty-First Century* (Cambridge, MA: Harvard University Press, 2014).

24. Jacob R. Holm, Edward Lorenz, Bengt-Ake Lundvall, and Antoine Valeyre, "Organizational Learning and Systems of Labor Market Regulation in Europe," *Industrial and Corporate Change* 19, no. 4 (2010): 1143.

25. Aditya Chakrabortty, "A Basic Income for Everyone? Yes, Finland Shows It Really Can Work," *Guardian*, October 31, 2017, https://www.theguardian.com/commentisfree/2017/oct/31/finland-universal-basic-income.

26. For a fuller discussion, see Verena Drabing and Moira Nelson, "Addressing Human Capital Risks and the Role of Institutional Complementarities," in *The Use of Social Investment*, edited by Anton Hemerijck (Oxford: Oxford University Press, 2017).

27. Thomas Paine, "The Agrarian Justice" (1797), Blackmask Online, 2001, http://public-library.uk/ebooks/10/51.pdf.

28. Erik Olin Wright discusses this as part of a "social economy." See Erik Olin Wright, "The Social Economy: A Niche in Capitalism or a Pathway Beyond?," May 2010, https://www.ssc.wisc.edu/~wright/Social%20Economy%20PDFs/EOW--Social%20economy.pdf.

29. Libby Brooks, "Scotland United in Curiosity as Councils Trail Universal Basic Income," *Guardian*, December 25, 2017, https://www.theguardian.com/uk-news/2017/dec/25/scotland-universal-basic-income-councils-pilot-scheme.

30. Hillary Clinton, *What Happened* (New York: Simon & Schuster, 2017), 238–39.

31. Michalis Nikiforos, Marshall Steinbaum, and Gennaro Zezza, *Modeling the Macroeconomic Effects of a Universal Basic Income* (New York: Roosevelt Institute, August, 2017).

32. Anthony B. Atkinson, *Inequality: What Can Be Done?* (Cambridge, MA: Harvard University Press, 2015). Atkinson argues for a universal child benefit (allowance) to be paid for all children at a substantial rate and taxed as income (216–18).

33. Estimates in Britain suggest that a universal basic income to cover social security would also need a top-up in terms of housing benefit. Overall the major concern is that various scenarios related to a universal basic income would have adverse distributional consequences and would cost too much. See Luke Martinelli, "The Fiscal and Distributional Implications of Alternative Universal Basic Income Schemes," Working Paper, Institute for Policy Research, University of Bath, March, 2017. However, the scenarios analyzed do not take the approach we are indicating. The key is to take first steps in applying the principle of a universal basic income.

34. See Piketty, *Capital*, 481. Recent evidence also tells us that progressive reforms are never won but constantly need to be fought over and rewon in different political and economic contexts.

35. Katherine Newman, *Chutes and Ladders, Navigating the Low Wage Economy* (New York: Russell Sage, 2008).

36. John Preston and Andy Green, "Benefits of Education, Training and Skills in Comparative Perspective," Wider Benefits of Learning Research Report No. 92001, London, Centre for Research on the Wider Benefits of Learning, 2003.

37. It has been addressed by human capital theorists, although not under the present labor market conditions. See Joop Hartog and Maria Bajdechi, "Human Capital and Risk," in *Human Capital: Theory and Evidence*, edited by Joop Hartog and Henriette Massen van den Brink (Cambridge, UK: Cambridge University Press, 2009). Orthodox theorists assumed that a clear distinction could be made between the returns to education that accrued to individuals and that which benefited

the wider society. From this it was a short step to charging students for post–compulsory education because when the average wages of graduates were compared to the average wages of nongraduates there was a clear graduate premium. The evidence seemed to support Milton Friedman's ideological vision of a market society in which, if students were charged for their education, they would pay attention to market signals as to which degree programs would yield optimum results. It was not only that they would act according to market disciplines, but they would become "entrepreneurs of themselves." It is for this reason that at the end of Schultz's 1960 address to the American Economic Association, Friedman quizzed him about who should pay for education. Because he saw the value of education as a public good, Schultz was uncertain of the answer; however, Friedman believed that human capital ideas would be used to create a society of human capitalists.

Putting aside ethical and theoretical issues, the empirical evidence for a user-pays model falls apart when the data on graduate and nongraduate returns are disaggregated. Where it is assumed that the advantages to graduates over nongraduates are unequivocal, that is not the case for the large majority of graduates. The only graduates that can be certain about their futures are those that attend elite universities. For a report on the discussion between Schultz and Friedman see, Peter Fleming, *The Death of Homo Economicus*, (London, Pluto Press, 2017, p181–2

38. Piketty, *Capital,* 493.
39. OECD, Table 1.7, "Top Statutory Personal Income Tax Rate and Top Marginal Tax Rates for Employees," accessed March 18, 2018, http://stats.oecd.org/index.aspx?DataSetCode=TABLE_I7.
40. Oxfam America, "Broken at the Top: How America's Dysfunctional Tax System Costs Billions in Corporate Tax Dodging," April 14, 2016, 1, https://www.oxfamamerica.org/static/media/files/Broken_at_the_Top_FINAL_EMBARGOED_4.12.2016.pdf.
41. Mariana Mazzucato, *The Entrepreneurial State: Debunking Public vs. Private Sector Myths* (New York: Anthem Press, 2013), 87.
42. Mazzucato, *The Entrepreneurial State,* 87; Oxfam America, "Against the $1.4 Trillion in Offshore Accounts the GDP of Canada Stood at $1.46 Trillion, Russia $1.13 Trillion and Mexico $1.08," accessed August 21, 2016, http://statisticstimes.com/economy/countries-by-projected-gdp.php.
43. Oxfam, "US Corporations have stashed Trillion Offshore."
44. Lester Thurow used the idea of a "random walk" to highlight these unpredictable fluctuations in the price structure. This is a good term to refer both to the instability of stocks and the fortunes that are made (and sometimes lost, although rarely due to public protection reflected in the largest renationalization in history, perhaps since the abolition of the British slave trade). See Lester Thurow, *Generating Inequality* (New York: Basic Books, 1975), 142–54: "Those who are lucky and end up owning the stocks that are capitalized at high multiples win large fortunes in

the random walk. Once passed on, not because of 'homo economicus' desires to store up future consumption but because of desires for power within the family, economy, and society" (154).

45. "US House Prices Are Rising Twice as Fast as Wages," *New York Post*, May 30, 2017, https://nypost.com/2017/05/30/us-housing-prices-are-rising-twice-as-fast-as-wages/. See also the changing distribution of property ownership in Britain: Laura Gardiner "Homes Sweet Homes—The Rise of Multiple Property Ownership in Britain," Resolution Foundation, August 19, 2017, http://www.resolutionfoundation.org/media/blog/homes-sweet-homes-the-rise-of-multiple-property-ownership-in-britain/.

46. Thomas Piketty, "Capital and Wealth Taxation in the 21st Century," *National Tax Journal* 68, no. 2 (2015): 455. Piketty writes, "One of the main conclusions of my research is . . . that there is substantial uncertainty about how far income and wealth inequality might rise in the twenty-first century, and that we need more financial transparency and better information about income and wealth dynamics, so that we can adapt our policies and institutions to a changing environment, and experiment with different levels of wealth tax progressivity. This might require better international scale coordination, which is difficult, but by no means impossible."

47. This follows Thurow's discussion of how the economic game is played. He puts the two fundamental problems this way: "What are the rules of a fair economic game and what is the optimum structure of economic prizes? These questions are key to the future of human capital theory. Depending upon the initial distribution of income and demand, markets can be adjusted to yield very different distributions of prizes" (*Generating Inequality*, 27–28).

CHAPTER 13

1. The epigraph is taken from Lorenzo Pecchi and Gustavo Piga, *Revisiting Keynes: Economic Possibilities for Our Grandchildren* (Cambridge, MA: MIT Press, 2008), 25. All unattributed quotations in this chapter are from Keynes.

2. See the discussion of these issues in the introduction to Herbert Marcuse's *One Dimensional Man: The Ideology of Industrial Society* (London: Routledge and Kegan Paul, 1964).

3. The influence of orthodox theory was not limited to changing the role of education or the imposition of market competition; it also encouraged people to redefine human behavior as economic behavior. It is this view of capitalism that has dominated discussions about human capital, with its focus on individual prosperity being extended though investment in education rather than from the wholesale redistribution of income and wealth. Bell assumed that as economies became more dependent on technical administration and scientific endeavor, individual utility and profit maximization would become subordinated to broader conceptions of social welfare and community interest. History has shown that along with many others, he underestimated the enduring appeal of neoliberal ideals.

4. If anyone is in any doubt about the importance of this, think only of the direction of technological change. And its implications for education. Productivity capture is closely linked to knowledge capture, which perpetuates the banking model of education. It requires a social revolution in our understanding of human purpose. The sense of human purpose has become corrupted, and economic means (such as the accumulation of wealth) have become ends rather than the means to a better life in a better society.

5. Pecchi and Piga, *Revisiting Keynes*, 20–21.

6. The new human capital offers a different way of thinking about the fundamental economic problem based on efficiency, security, and justice.

7. While more can be done at the workplace and in the design of labor contracts, these issues cannot be solved through the labor market or at the level of the individual given the unique character of human capital when compared to other forms of capital.

8. See Karl Polanyi, *Great Transformation*, with an introduction by Fred Block (Boston: Beacon Press, 2001). Block writes, "The more fundamental point learned from Polanyi is that market liberalism makes demands on ordinary people that are simply not sustainable. Workers, farmers, and small business people will not tolerate for any length of time a pattern of economic organization in which they are subject to periodic dramatic fluctuations in their daily economic circumstances. In short, the neoliberal utopia of a borderless and peaceful globe requires that millions of ordinary people throughout the world have the flexibility to tolerate—perhaps as often as every five to ten years—a prolonged spell in which they must survive on half or less of what they previously earned. Polanyi believes that to expect that kind of flexibility is both morally wrong and deeply unrealistic. To him it is inevitable that people will mobilize to protect themselves from these economic shocks," (xxxiv).

9. We've described this as a crisis in the currency of credentials resulting from the failed promise of what credentials could buy in the labor market. Many younger Americans, Europeans, and East Asians, including those from middle-class backgrounds, feel the promised returns from investments in education have not been honored. The current economic system is failing to recognize the skills, talents, and contribution of the majority, at the same time that it totally ignores the plight of those excluded from the labor market altogether. The result is both a deep sense of unfairness and social wastage on a huge scale.

10. Sylvia Nasar, *Grand Pursuit: The Story of the People Who Made Modern Economics* (London: Fourth Estate, 2011), 62.

11. Nasar, *Grand Pursuit*, 52.

12. E. F. Schumacher, *Small Is Beautiful: A Study of Economics as if People Matter* (New York: Harper Collins/Blond and Briggs, 1973), 92.

13. This will be central to delivering a new human capital because the deepest problems of our age cannot be solved by education alone.

14. Bryan Caplan, *The Case against Education: Why the Education System Is a Waste of Time and Money* (Princeton, NJ: Princeton University Press, 2018).

15. R. H. Tawney, *Equality* (London: George, Allen and Unwin, 1931).

16. Joseph Stiglitz, *The Price of Inequality* (New York: Norton, 2012), introduction, offers a useful model.

17. See Phillip Brown, "Education, Opportunity and the Prospects for Social Mobility," *British Journal of Sociology of Education*, 34, nos. 5–6 (2013): 678–700.

18. See C. Wright Mills, *The Sociological Imagination* (New York: Oxford University Press, 1959).

19. Simon Head, *Mindless: How Smarter Machines Are Making Dumber Humans* (New York, Basic Books, 2014), 185. We have not reached the technological limits beyond which existing social relations become "fetters" to future capitalist accumulation, even if there are increasing contradictions between the technological possibilities and social realities. Still, we must avoid repeating the mistake of treating technology as destiny, as though it were a race between education and technology, rather than assessing its potential to do things differently. The new human capital points to the possibilities of technology to reorder economic activities undermining existing accounts of the market and labor scarcity, but as Harry Braverman has argued, the development of technologies and the application of scientific discovery to work organization may increase the "average" scientific, technical, and skill content of the labor process, but this is largely meaningless unless we know "whether the scientific and 'educated' content of labor tends towards *averaging*, or on the contrary, towards *polarization*." If it leads to polarization, " 'to then say that the 'average' skill has been raised is to adopt the logic of the statistician who, with one foot in the fire and the other in ice water, will tell you that 'on the average,' he is perfectly comfortable." Harry Braverman, *Labor and Monopoly Capitalism: The Degradation of Work in the Twentieth Century* (New York: Monthly Review Press, 1974).

20. Pecchi and Piga, *Revisiting Keynes*, 23.

21. Fox, *Beyond Contract*, 46–48.

22. Robert Solow, "Whose Grandchildren?," in Pecchi and Piga, *Revisiting Keynes*, 92–93.

Index

Tables and figures are indicated by *t* and *f* following the page number

For the benefit of digital users, indexed terms that span two pages (e.g., 52–53) may, on occasion, appear on only one of those pages.